Border Contraband

INTER-AMERICA SERIES / EDITED BY HOWARD CAMPBELL, DUNCAN EARLE, AND JOHN PETERSON

In the new "Inter-American" epoch to come, our borderland zones may expand well past the confines of geopolitical lines. Social knowledge of these dynamic interfaces offers rich insights into the pressing and complex issues that affect both the borderlands and beyond. The Inter-America Series comprises a wide interdisciplinary range of cutting-edge books that explicitly or implicitly enlist border issues to discuss larger concepts, perspectives, and theories from the "borderland" vantage and will be appropriate for the classroom, the library, and the wider reading public.

: : GEORGE T. DÍAZ : :

Border Contraband

A HISTORY OF SMUGGLING ACROSS THE RIO GRANDE

University of Texas Press AUSTIN

First edition, 2015
First paperback printing, 2015

Requests for permission to reproduce material from this work should
be sent to:
    Permissions
    University of Texas Press
    P.O. Box 7819
    Austin, TX 78713-7819
    http://utpress.utexas.edu/index.php/rp-form

♾ The paper used in this book meets the minimum requirements of
ANSI/NISO Z39.48-1992 (R1997) (Permanence of Paper).

LIBRARY OF CONGRESS CATALOGING-IN-PUBLICATION DATA

Díaz, George T., 1980–
Border contraband : a history of smuggling across the Rio Grande /
by George T. Díaz. — First edition.
pages cm. — (Inter-America series)
Includes bibliographical references and index.
ISBN 978-0-292-76106-3 (cloth : alk. paper)
1. Smuggling—Mexican-American Border Region—History. 2. Rio Grande
(Colo.-Mexico and Tex.)—History. 3. Mexican-American Border Region—
History. I. Title.
HJ6690.D53 2015
364.1′33609721—dc23

                                                                2014011403

ISBN 978-1-4773-1013-7 (pbk. : alk. paper)

doi:10.7560/761063

For my mother and father

Contents

Acknowledgments

After ten years of working on this topic I have a great many people to thank. My time at Southern Methodist University was the happiest time of my life, and the wonderful people I met there nurtured me greatly. Sincere thanks to my mentor, Ben Johnson, who provided endless guidance and challenging questions that prompted me to make connections where I once saw none. John Chávez offered innumerable insights and served as a source of encouragement throughout the writing process. Octavio Herrera Pérez contributed valuable knowledge on the economic and borderland history of Mexico, and his comments helped refine the book you are reading. I greatly appreciate the assistance of the William P. Clements Center for Southwest Studies, particularly Andrea Boardman and Ruth Ann Elmore for their tireless support, logistical and otherwise. The anonymous donors of the Bill Clements Dissertation Fellowship gave me the resources and time I needed to complete my doctoral work, and their support helped immensely. My education at SMU would have been entirely impossible without the vision of David Weber, who established its doctoral program in history. Professor Weber read one of my early papers on contrabandistas, and his enthusiasm convinced me to stick with my topic. The viceroy is greatly missed.

Additionally, I am thankful for the excellent education provided by Texas A&M International University in Laredo. As an undergraduate and graduate student at TAMIU, I benefited tremendously from the mentorships of Jerry Thompson, Stanley Green, Carlos Cuéllar, and Deborah Blackwell, and I am happy to say that these collegial relationships did not end when I left my alma mater, but continue to this day.

Many scholars also assisted me along the way. I would like to especially thank Arnoldo De León, Elaine Carey, and Andrae Marak for their interest in my work and for their general care about my professional development. Oscar J. Martínez, Miguel Ángel González Quiroga, Stephen Haber, Brian DeLay, Kelly Lytle Hernández, Andrew Graybill, James Sandos, Andres Reséndez, Tom Miller, and Robert Utley were kind enough to answer questions that came up in my investigations, and I am very thankful for their expertise. Howard Campbell's and Josiah McC. Heyman's interest and encouragement in my work came at a critical time in my career and helped me believe in myself when few others did.

During my time at South Texas College, I had the good fortune of working with a talented and dedicated group of people who welcomed me and made being in the office a joy. Special thanks to Jeff Zents, Moraima Cardenas, and Ana Riojas for their friendship and for showing me what is best about teaching. The dedication of Jenny Clark, Tammy Slippy, and María Esther Rodríguez to women's studies showed me what is best about service, and I am grateful to have worked beside them. The efforts of Trinidad Gonzales, Esther García, and Victor Gómez in Mexican American studies impressed upon me the value of engagement with the community in which you work. I credit Victor in particular for motivating me to work harder and to not settle for less.

You cannot make a house without bricks, and you cannot write a history without sources. I would like to extend my deepest gratitude to Barbara Rust and the staff of the National Archives and Records Administration in Fort Worth; Joan Gosnell, the Good Fairy of the DeGolyer Library; Jeanette M. Hatcher and her staff at the special collections at the Killam Library at Texas A&M International University; Joe Moreno of the special collections at the Laredo Public Library; George Gause (recently retired) from the University of Texas–Pan American; and Adán Benavides at the Benson Latin American Collection at the University of Texas at Austin for their generous assistance. Manuel Ramos Medina of the Centro de Estudios de Historia de México CARSO in Mexico City and Yolia Tortolero Cervantes and Enrique Melgarejo Awezcua at the Archivo General de la Nación went out of their way to help me locate and access critical files for which *estoy muy agradecido.*

Tatcho Mindiola and the Center for Mexican American Studies at the University of Houston provided a year to write and revise my book through the Visiting Scholar Program and helped my work immeasurably. Aside from thanking Lorenzo Cano and the rest of the faculty and staff at CMAS Houston and the History Department, I would like to thank the students who attended my class in illicit trade and undocumented migration in the U.S.-Mexico borderlands. Their great interest in the course and their excellent questions reminded me of the excitement I first felt when I came upon my topic, and that energy helped me finish this book.

The History Department at Sam Houston State University provided me the opportunity to teach a graduate course on smuggling in the U.S.-Mexico borderlands, and this class, along with the generous support of the department, let me give the project its finishing touches. Special thanks to Brian F. Domitrovic, Juana Sánchez Jiménez, Bernadette Pruitt, Steve Rapp, Jeremiah Dancy, and Lila Rakoczy for making the fourth floor what it is.

I would also like to acknowledge the friends and peers who helped make the journey a joy, especially Jeff Crane, Suzanne and Andrew Orr, Erik Torres, Tony Díaz (El Librotraficante), Patrick J. Johnson, David Rex Galindo, Clive Siegle, José Ramírez, Francis Galán, James Garza, Patricia Portales, Paul Nelson, Houston Faust Mount, Aaron Sánchez, Eduardo Morález, Alicia Dewey, Carla Mendiola, Luis García, Ruben Arellano, Anna Banhegyi, Albert González, Gilberto López, Richard Ferry, Jessica Pence, and Antonio Medellín.

Shepherding of the book came through the careful attention of Theresa May, Nancy Bryan, Leslie Tingle, and Abby Webber, and I thank them and staff of the University of Texas Press for their excellent work.

My understanding of life on the border was shaped by growing up in Laredo, Texas. It is my hope that the people of my hometown find this history familiar. Finally, I would like to thank my tía Adelita; my sister, Dolores Judith; and my parents, Dolores Virginia and George Hinojosa Díaz, for loving me and supporting me through my many travails.

Border Contraband

Introduction

I On April 25, 1890, U.S. consul Warner P. Sutton wrote his superiors in Washington about the prevalence of smuggling along the Rio Grande. The alarm went up after a seemingly innocent dinner with friends in Piedras Negras, Coahuila, when Sutton discovered that the majority of the items that made up his meal had been introduced illicitly. He was literally consuming contraband. Indeed, prices for necessities in Mexico compelled the household's servant to cross into Texas and smuggle food daily under her clothes. Stunned, Sutton warned Washington that if Mexico enforced its full import duties, its border population would either have to leave, "smuggle, or take very short rations."[1] Like many borderlanders before and since, the woman who provided Sutton his supper chose to disregard the law rather than let it interfere with her needs and desires.

This book is about how governments regulated and prohibited trade on their borders and how border people subverted state and federal laws through smuggling, particularly along the Rio Grande, which divides Texas and northeastern Mexico. States' creation and enforcement of borders directly led to smuggling by making a market for contraband goods. People became smugglers when they sought something that states wished to regulate or deny them. Whether borderlanders smuggled out of ignorance of the law, to save or make money, or to avoid the inconvenience of finding a customs post, states viewed unregulated trade across the border as illegal. However, many border people had a more nuanced view of illicit trade. Government interference in free trade caused local resentment, and rather than acquiesce to what they regarded as arbitrary trade regulations, borderlanders on both sides of the river developed a moral economy of illicit trade, a contrabandista community, which accepted some forms of smuggling as just.[2]

When people today think of the U.S.-Mexico borderlands, they often imagine a dangerous and violent place. This image stems largely from the media and popular culture. Nightly news programs and series such as *Border Wars* regularly remind us that violent smugglers routinely violate national laws along the U.S.-Mexico divide. Constant exposure to these images ties an inseparable bind between smuggling and violence and creates the perception of the border as a criminal space. Yet smuggling, the root phenomenon behind these impressions, remains underresearched and poorly understood. As Consul Sutton's story illustrates, much of the smuggling on the border was neither violent nor related to drugs. For much of the border's history, contraband trade across the international line consisted of tariff evasion on consumer goods, not the smuggling of prohibited items. Rather than being romantic outlaws or violent offenders, contrabandistas acted more as opportunists who exploited state weakness to save money and as entrepreneurs who filled a niche created by national trade restrictions.[3]

One of the principal aims of this book is to provide a social history of smugglers by humanizing them as consumers as well as drug traffickers. Additionally, this book seeks to historicize smuggling, an enduring borderlands issue. For all of the attention of historians to borders, none have studied smuggling along the U.S.-Mexico border in depth, though it is the most iconic thing that occurs there. *Border Contraband* sheds light on the rise of smuggling as a popular response to states' border-building efforts and provides a context for understanding current debates about the drug war.

II Smuggling is an elusive subject for historical scrutiny. Historians love documents, and illicit trade is by its very nature a clandestine activity difficult to research. It is therefore not surprising that some of the best work on smuggling comes from political scientists, anthropologists, and sociologists. Building on the work of James C. Scott in *Seeing Like a State: How Certain Schemes to Improve the Human Condition Have Failed*, social scientists have made significant strides in understanding the multifaceted nature of contraband trade. For instance, in *Illicit Flows and Criminal Things: States, Borders, and the Other Side of Globalization*, Willem van Schendel and Itty Abraham rightfully assert that the dominant imagery of nation-states fighting valiantly against global criminal networks is far too simplistic[.] . . . Many transnational movements of people, commodities, and ideas are illegal because they defy the norms and rules of formal political authority, but they are quite acceptable, "licit," in the eyes of participants in these transactions and flows.[4]

Indeed, what governments define as illegal and what people consider wrong can differ widely. In his book *Illicit: How Smugglers, Traffickers, and Copycats are Hijacking the Global Economy*, Moisés Naím expands on the concept of the relativistic nature of illicit trade, arguing that "there is an enormous gray area between legal and illegal transactions, a gray area that illicit traders have turned to their advantage."[5] This gray area between illegal and licit is most felt in the borderlands. Although Naím does not focus on the border, his comment that "the more states seek to raise barriers against the flow of illicit goods . . . the more traffickers stand to profit from their trade" keenly applies to the spaces where different states meet.[6] States may seek to create obstacles to illicit trade, but borders inadvertently up the ante by making unauthorized flows more dangerous, lucrative, and professional.

Howard Campbell examines present-day illicit flows across the U.S.-Mexico border directly. Using ethnographic techniques, Campbell's *Drug War Zone: Frontline Dispatches from the Streets of El Paso and Juárez* provides an unparalleled look into the lives of those directly involved in the drug war. Oral histories allow Campbell to open a window to the "cultural world of drug trafficking," which he refers to as a "drug war zone," where the lives of those touched by the narcotics trade intersect and "transcend international boundaries, moral categories," class, and ethnicity.[7] I argue that this cultural world of drug trafficking exists as an extension of an older and broader world of border people's common practice of smuggling. Drugs, although the most conspicuous items smuggled across the border today, are but a part of a wide milieu of illicit flows that border people, and even states, view with varying degrees of criminality.

Using varying methodologies, a handful of historians have reached back to trace the development of smuggling over time. Eric Tagliacozzo's *Secret Trades, Porous Borders: Smuggling and States Along a Southeast Asian Frontier, 1865–1915* does an excellent job examining how states' boundary enforcement programs were linked intimately with border people's boundary transgressions, but no similar work exists on the U.S.-Mexico divide.[8] Despite smuggling's ubiquitous connection to the U.S.-Mexico border, with the exception of notable works by James Sandos, Gabriela Recio, and Peter Andreas, very little scholarship considers its history there.[9] Rachel St. John's rightfully acclaimed *Line in the Sand: A History of the Western U.S.-Mexico Border*, although not focused on smuggling, is similar to Tagliacozzo's work in that it examines how state efforts transformed a poorly defined boundary into a patrolled and fenced, flexible barrier that states could see. On illicit trade St. John writes, "Smugglers created an underground economy that allowed them to profit by evading state regulations."[10] I develop this concept further, arguing that customs enforcement directly led to commercial trafficking because greater policing made the circumvention of state authority profitable. Moreover, I argue that border people did not regard smugglers' trades as something altogether underground, but in many cases as a licit practice.

Throughout history, entrepreneurs have sought to profit from dodging state law. Robert Chao Romero's *The Chinese in Mexico, 1882–1940* richly illustrates how merchants in the Pacific Rim capitalized on U.S. Chinese exclusion laws to create sophisticated transnational human trafficking rings and provides great detail on the many ruses that smugglers of migrants used to cross borders and evade authority.[11] *Border Contraband* tackles a scholarly gap by considering the movement of goods in equal detail. Elaine Carey and Andrae Marak's edited collection, *Smugglers, Brothels, and Twine: Historical Perspectives on Contraband and Vice in North America's Borderlands*, to which Robert Romero and I both contribute chapters, offers a fascinating series of examinations about the many ways border people sought to exploit North America's emerging boundaries and points to new avenues for scholars to follow.[12] This book follows one of these avenues by directly examining the history of smuggling across the U.S.-Mexico border. Aside from providing a transnational model of a persisting and prevalent borderland phenomenon, my work provides a theoretical framework with which to understand it.

Smuggling occurs across both sides of the U.S.-Mexico border and it must be considered transnationally. Historians have made great strides in revealing states' relationships with their borderlands, but it is important to point out that the U.S.-Mexico border is a place where *two* states meet. Historically, border communities crossed borders. As Kelly Lytle Hernández's *Migra! A History of the U.S. Border Patrol* strikingly shows, sporadic collaboration between Mexico and the United States allowed the "boundary to function as a bridge" between state systems of migration control.[13] Mexico, like the United States, had concerns about its national security at the border. Like U.S. efforts, however, the Mexican government's best efforts to regulate its territory were frustrated by border people's desire to trade freely.

Indeed, states' peripheral people showed remarkable persistence in trading freely despite federal dictates. By the 1880s the lower Rio Grande borderlands had passed to the "bordered lands" phase of state control that Jeremy Adelman and Stephen Aron discuss in their highly influential article "From Borderlands to Borders: Empires, Nation-States, and the Peoples in Between in North American History." [14] Nevertheless, border people on both sides of the river continued to routinely subvert state authority through smuggling. The hardening of borders did not prevent smuggling as much as make illicit trade more lucrative. Models of state consolidation of borders in the late nineteenth and early twentieth centuries proposed by Elliott Young, Friedrich Katz, and Eric Tagliacozzo argue that state authorities ultimately prevailed in imposing order at their nation's edge.[15] While it is not debatable that states greatly increased the policing of their boundaries, smuggling endured and in many cases flourished due to Mexico's and the United States' efforts to enforce laws on their borders.

Examining the persistence of smuggling both advances and complicates the image of the U.S.-Mexico border as a "fugitive landscape," or a place of marginal state control.[16] Although smugglers' success could be seen as an example of states' failures, government attempts to regulate borders made smuggling a viable trade. Thus smuggling, specifically the profits that smuggling brought, demonstrates how border people at times used international boundaries to their own benefit.[17] National laws pushed illicit activities to borders, and the creation and enforcement of an international boundary made many aspects of everyday border commerce illegal. Shopping for bargains on one side of the border was often rendered pointless unless transborder shoppers evaded national tariffs by smuggling their goods across, and this social reality made many acts of smuggling popularly accepted.

In his classic 1978 essay "The Problem of Identity in a Changing Culture: Popular Expressions of Culture Conflict along the Lower Rio Grande Border," noted ethnographer and pioneering ethnomusicologist Américo Paredes wrote that border people engaged in smuggling as a "libertarian practice" against excessive customs laws.[18] Paredes elaborated that border people "paid little attention to the requirements of the law" when crossing regulated goods and casually smuggled as part of their common practice.[19] I expand on Paredes's concepts by arguing that illicit trade was a nuanced process where smugglers negotiated their needs and desires with

U.S. and Mexican laws. Those that chose to violate these laws, whether to save money on a few cans of tomatoes or to make money transporting large amounts of tequila across the Rio Grande into Texas, became smugglers in the eyes of the state but not necessarily their community.

For the purpose of this book I divide smuggling into two forms: low-level contraband trade for personal consumption (petty smuggling) and professional smuggling for profit (trafficking). It is important to point out that not everything smuggled was inherently illegal. Borderlanders routinely smuggled perfectly licit items such as food and clothing to avoid paying tariff duties. Other items such as narcotics and arms, however, were largely prohibited by states, and merely possessing them was illegal by U.S. and Mexican law. The interplay between border people's need and desire to acquire goods regulated or prohibited by U.S. and Mexican law and states' efforts to enforce sovereignty and law on their borderlands shaped a moral economy of smuggling on the international divide. To borrow from E. P. Thompson and Karl Jacoby, I argue that rather than accept state laws at face value, border people negotiated state laws with their own conceptions of what was and was not acceptable transnational trade.[20] Like Jacoby, I write a "bottom up" history of a secret trade. I argue that local views on smuggling often contrasted sharply with those of states. Whereas the Mexican and U.S. governments considered smugglers as criminals and threats, border people regarded many of these same individuals as simple consumers, merchants, or folk heroes. I often use the metaphor of speeding to illustrate the moral economy of smuggling. Individuals driving forty-five miles per hour on a stretch of road with forty miles per hour posted as the limit break the law but are generally accepted by society. Drivers traveling sixty miles per hour in a school zone while parents are picking up their children violate both laws and social mores. Smuggling is like that. For instance, border people generally accepted the smuggling of rationed sugar or wool for personal consumption during the First World War but not the trafficking of opium through their community. Smuggling, like speeding, had its limits of social acceptance.

State law saw smuggling in black and white terms, but the social reality of life on the ground came in various shades of gray. Deborah Kang, Rachel St. John, and Samuel Truett in particular have had success revealing the hidden history of informal relations between state agents and the community they policed.[21] For example, Truett provides a story of two amicable U.S. and Mexican federal agents in 1890 who agreed to forego state-mandated tariffs on cattle that "Crossed the Imaginary Line" between Arizona and Sonora.[22] Finding when and what Customs agents of both the United States and Mexico conceded to, and why, helps reveal the inner workings of the moral economy of illicit trade on the border.

Unraveling the history of smuggling across the Rio Grande offers a host of challenges. Smugglers themselves sought to avoid detection, and we mostly know of them for the occasions on which they were caught. The best smugglers, however, were never apprehended. Given the fragmented nature of sources on illicit trade, I have decided to forgo what could only be conjectural statistical analysis of smuggling. Still, U.S. and Mexican government attempts to police their borderlands did leave a window into smugglers' secret trades. Oral histories also inform my work, particularly ethnic Mexican folk ballads, or *corridos*, which recount smugglers' exploits. Whereas court cases, customs records, and newspapers were primarily controlled by elites and the state, oral histories provide insight into popular perceptions and offer a fascinating counternarrative to that of those in power. By examining when locals reported smugglers, when juries decided to find suspects guilty or innocent, and why border people celebrated certain smugglers in song, we can see how borderlanders expressed their own views of acceptable and unacceptable trade as part of a moral economy of smuggling.

Rather than focus on exceptional cases of large contraband seizures or violent confrontations with state law enforcement, this book examines trafficking and violence within a larger process of common smuggling. Unauthorized activity across the U.S.-Mexico border was typical, not atypical. Aside from being a study of smuggling, this book is also a social history of border people, particularly in regard to how they conducted business and consumption across international lines, how they resisted state efforts to impose restrictions on their free trade, how they formed their own values about breaking laws, and how they exploited state laws for self-gain.[23] Few of the people or groups of people examined in this book would have called themselves smugglers or even conceived of themselves in such a way at all. I use the term "smuggler" when describing someone who attempted to cross regulated or prohibited goods from one side of the border to the other. Those who smuggled professionally or in commercial amounts I refer to as "traffickers." The Spanish word for smuggler is *contrabandista*. For the purposes of this book, I use contrabandista to describe the community of petty smugglers and traffickers. The interplay between states, petty smugglers, and traffickers forms the contrabandista community whose story follows.

III Part I examines the period between 1848 and 1910 when the United States' and Mexico's trade concerns focused on tariff collection. In the late nineteenth century Mexico and the United States relied heavily on tariffs for their national revenue. Tariffs not only protected domestic industries, tariff proceeds served as the principal source of income for the U.S. government prior to the institution of the federal income tax in 1913.[24] Similarly, import duties provided the majority of Mexico's revenue until internal taxes overtook them in the first decade of the twentieth century.[25] With federal revenue dependent on tariff collection, both governments levied duties on the commercial and noncommercial crossing of goods and livestock. Border people on both sides of the river in turn resented what they considered the arbitrary taxation of what was once local commerce and formed a moral economy that accepted some forms of illicit trade.

Part II examines the period between 1910 and 1945 when national customs and other security forces in the region shifted their emphasis from tariff collection to the interdiction of prohibited items that threatened the state. Beginning roughly with the onset of the Mexican Revolution in 1910 and lasting until the end of the Second World War in 1945, a succession of national and international crises and new drug and alcohol prohibitions altered the way states guarded against the illegal movement of goods across their borders. While the years preceding the revolution had also been contentious, new national security concerns after 1910 coupled with Mexico's and the United States' move away from tariff revenues as their primary source of income made prohibiting the entry of national threats—particularly arms and controlled substances—states' primary objective on the border. With the ethical and structural basis for modern trafficking in place by the end of the Second World War, 1945 serves as a fitting moment to end an initial history of smuggling on the U.S.-Mexico border. The moral economy's endurance and place within the twenty-first-century drug war is considered in the book's epilogue.

IV Laredo and Nuevo Laredo provide an excellent locale in which to examine the formation of borderlands and borders through the practice of smuggling. Unlike many of the border cities between Brownsville and San Diego, Laredo predates the formation of the U.S.-Mexico divide. Over time, state laws and borders came down upon these communities, upsetting local practices and creating new ones. Founded in 1755, Laredo evolved from what

Adelman and Aron describe as a borderland to a bordered land.[26] The advantageous location near a ford of the Rio Grande made the two Laredos a hub of commerce and international trade. With the arrival of the railroad in the 1880s the twin communities grew immensely in population and importance, and by 1893 los dos Laredos had each become the greatest inland ports of their respective countries, earning them their titles as "gateway" cities.[27]

Los dos Laredos based their existence on international trade, yet much of this commerce was illicit. Indeed, the sheer volume of commercial traffic made customs inspection cursory. On February 23, 1895, Frank B. Earnest, U.S. customs collector for Laredo, complained that "petty smuggling is constantly carried on . . . and it is almost impossible to prevent." [28] These cases happened every day along the border. Laredo and Nuevo Laredo can be called contrabandista communities. Members of the contrabandista community regarded petty smuggling as a common right. What borderlands historiography lacks, and what my study provides, is an in-depth examination of the common violation of state laws on the U.S.-Mexico divide. Border people routinely violated Mexican and U.S. law by smuggling, but with certain exceptions this practice did not seriously threaten either government. That contrabandistas continued to smuggle in spite of the state not only shows the limits of state power on the border, but also demonstrates border people's ability to bring the state into accommodation with local values. Although both the United States and Mexico significantly improved their border enforcement efforts by the mid-1940s, borderlanders on both sides of the river continued to subvert state authority through smuggling. Despite what federal laws dictated, this moral economy of illicit trade persisted through war, revolution, and the best efforts of the U.S. and Mexican governments.

PART I

Taxing Trade

ONE

Creating a Contrabandista Community, 1848–1881

On the afternoon of January 17, 1856, a group of riders crossed the Rio Grande into Texas near Paso del Águila, or as the Americans called it, Eagle Pass. Although the U.S.-Mexican War (1846–1848) had made the Rio Grande an international boundary, the men crossed it as they would any river, at a place that seemed convenient and without informing authorities. Still, crossing the river was not as easy as it had been before the war. Upon learning of their crossing, the U.S. deputy customs collector for Eagle Pass ordered two agents to pursue the riders. When the agents returned with the men, the deputy collector discovered the crossers had failed to declare "nine Spanish horses, eight saddles, eight blankets, seven bridles, and two ropes."[1] The deputy collector promptly seized the goods because they had been smuggled into the United States.

The establishment of the Rio Grande as an international boundary at the end of the U.S.-Mexican War made many aspects of everyday trade illicit by placing international regulations and tariffs on local commerce. Rather than accept these seemingly arbitrary restrictions, border people sought to continue carrying goods freely across the Rio Grande. State agents' taxation and seizure of borderlanders' property, especially their personal belongings, interfered with common practices and created resentment. As this chapter shows, border people responded to state-imposed trade restrictions by creating their own values about what was and was not illicit trade within a moral economy of smuggling.[2]

CONTRA BANDO COMMUNITY

Contraband activity in Laredo is as old as the town itself. The *Oxford English Dictionary* defines contraband as "illegal or prohibited traffic: smuggling."[3] The Spanish word for smuggling is *contrabando*, an amalgamation of *contra* (against) and *bando* (proclamation or decree). Two shallow crossings, or *pasos*, across the Rio Grande drew Spaniards to establish the settlement of San Agustín de Laredo along the north bank of the river in 1755.[4] Tomás Sánchez, Laredo's founder, had orders to settle on the Nueces River, but received permission to establish a community on the Rio Grande after claiming he could not find a suitable site on the Nueces.[5] In truth, few Spaniards wished to live so far from their compatriots, and Sánchez opted to settle farther south, where his people felt safer. Although crown policies dictated that colonists live together for defense against Indian raids, less than twenty years after the town's founding a number of Laredoans lived in *contra bando* settlements south of the river. Despite Mayor Sánchez's repeated *bandos* ordering Laredoans living on the south bank of the river to return under penalty of fine, many people continued to live where they saw fit, inadvertently beginning the community practice of evading unpopular laws.[6]

Aside from the turmoil that often troubled the lower Rio Grande borderlands, los dos Laredos remained sleepy hamlets at the time of U.S. entry. During his 1846 voyage upriver, U.S. Army Lieutenant Bryant J. Tilden commented that most buildings north of the river were made of stone; however, his view from the boat did not let him see the numerous *jacales* and ranches where some 1,500 Laredoans lived and worked.[7] The community was less developed south of the river, where only about 500 persons resided. For the most part, buildings there were cruder than those on the north bank and composed mostly of cane, wood, and mud.[8] Soldiers also noted the heat. Summers began earlier and lasted longer, with the thermometer reaching 107 degrees in the shade.[9] Los dos Laredos may have been small ranching villages, but Tilden saw the potential of a community that existed along a direct route from San Antonio to Monterrey. Snags and other obstacles along the river north of Laredo defeated Tilden's hopes of commercial shipping, but his observations would prove accurate. By the mid-1850s San Juan Bautista, near modern-day Eagle Pass, was no longer on the principal route from Mexico to Texas. Although San Juan Bautista's population outnumbered Laredo's by almost 500 people, its use as a trade route community faded as San Antonio's,

Monterrey's, and other cities' development came to push the east-west traffic across the Rio Grande into the north-south axis that exists today.[10]

THE UNITED STATES AND LAREDOANS

Captain Mirabeau B. Lamar had his work cut out for him. The former president of the Republic of Texas (1838–1841) and orchestrator of the failed Santa Fe Expedition arrived at Laredo on November 8, 1846, with orders to command the local garrison and bring the hamlet under government control by the United States. Although the town changed hands peacefully, with most locals being friendly or simply curious of Americans, other problems abounded.[11] Indian raids around Laredo depopulated outlying ranches and left the town's citizens fearing for their lives. Moreover, Mexican and U.S. negotiations in the Treaty of Guadalupe Hidalgo created an international boundary within a community that had always straddled the river.[12]

With a daunting task ahead of him, Lamar prioritized physical security and protecting U.S. possessions on the borderlands. The immediacy of Lamar's orders was warranted. Indian raids in the wake of the Texas Revolution and U.S-Mexican War had left Laredo and the outlying area, in Lamar's words, as "little more than a heap of ruins."[13] Between 1810 and 1846 regional conflicts and wars for independence in Texas and Mexico sapped Mexico's northern frontier of much of its strength, allowing Lipan Apache and Comanche Indians to make significant inroads at Anglo and Mexican borderlanders' expense.[14] Lamar exaggerated when he stated that Indians had killed seven hundred Laredoans in the last twenty years, but the community had definitely suffered greatly.[15] In 1836, for example, Comanche raiders captured over 1,000 horses and 184 mules around Laredo.[16] U.S. forces began securing the region immediately. Not long after Lamar arrived, he and his men retrieved a local boy abducted by Comanche raiders. The garrison's presence in Laredo as well as soldiers' escort of local travelers and cattle drivers deterred Indian assaults for the moment, but sporadic Indian attacks would plague the community for decades.[17]

Lamar's orders to protect Laredo from Indian depredations reflected U.S. efforts to gain Laredoans' goodwill and trust. Upon his arrival, Lamar concentrated on protecting the community from Indian attacks and took no "steps towards extending the laws of the State over this portion of its

FIGURE 1.1. Mirabeau Lamar *by John Sartain, Philadelphia. Prints &*
Photographs 2005/1-24-1. Texas State Library and Archives Commission.

territory."[18] Rather than alienating Laredoans by attempting to vigorously
regulate the new international boundary dividing the town, Lamar chose
to focus his resources on serving the community. Lamar's forces guarded
the area from Indian intrusions and made medicine available in times of
sickness, thereby gaining local trust.[19] Border people responded favorably
to the new security and found the Americans' presence unobtrusive, regarding them with an amiable interest rather than fear. The U.S. sailors
who steamed up the Rio Grande aboard the *Major Brown* in 1846 reported
being "literally thronged" with curious guests anxious to see their equip-

ment.[20] Citizens of Santa Rosa, in what was to become Cameron County, went so far as to invite Lamar and his officers to a dance hosted by a local don.[21] Logistical constraints in supplying the garrison by steamboat required Lamar to purchase foodstuffs and other necessary items from local markets. The boost to the local economy and these daily interactions between the garrison and Laredoans served to lessen ethnoracial tensions between the groups and would, in time, lead to community building based on common interests.[22]

REGIONAL IDENTITY

Local ambivalence over the loss of Mexican citizenship was one of the principal reasons for the lack of conflict between the groups. Like many communities on Mexico's northern frontier, Laredo had only lightly felt the presence of a national government. Far from the power centers in Mexico City, *fronterizos* (borderlanders) relied on themselves and evinced more devotion to their regional community than their national government.[23] Except for the change in flag and currency, it is doubtful that many *fronterizos* felt a loss of Mexican national identity. Lower Rio Grande borderlanders' concern over their welfare and sense of regional identity over a Mexican national identity is apparent in their declaration of independence from Mexico. On January 17, 1840, border people frustrated with power struggles in Mexico but unwilling to join the Republic of Texas met in Laredo and formed the Republic of the Rio Grande. For 283 days the fledgling republic survived attacks and counterattacks from Mexican centralist forces, internal strife, and all the burdens of creating a new government.[24] Laredo served as capital of the republic for a time, but the town's lack of a printing press prompted the government to move to Guerrero, Tamaulipas.[25] By November 1840 Mexican centralist forces succeeded in putting down the rebellion but failed to reincorporate the region. In truth, the area had never been fully integrated. Centralist forces withdrew at the end of the uprising and left locals to fend off Indian and filibuster incursions alone. Border people's strong sense of regional identity, coupled with the Mexican government's inability to provide for the community's welfare, made the prospect of a more effective, albeit foreign, U.S. government acceptable.[26]

Although Laredoans lacked a Mexican national identity, the community maintained a strong ethnic Mexican or Tejano identity. The changing of flags did not change the community's culture or traditions. Lamar maintained a garrison over a distinctly Tejano town, and he made little effort to change that. Despite his power as an agent of the United States, he and his men were minorities in a town that was Mexican in everything but government. This reality led Lamar to accord Laredoans certain concessions that other Mexican communities did not receive.[27] Demographics coupled with locals' ability to maintain power forced Lamar and his garrison to respect local practices. U.S. soldiers needed to deal with Laredoans to purchase supplies, and Anglos and Tejanos learned some of each other's language and culture in these exchanges. Still, the sheer weight of the Mexican borderlands forced this middle ground of mutual adaptation in *fronterizos'* favor. Garrison soldiers' amorous pursuit of local women led to marriages. Some soldiers returned home with their wives after their terms of service, but many others stayed, becoming Laredoans, and eventually border people. Over time the pull of the borderlands would continually work to erode the power of the state but never fully overcome it.[28]

The U.S. government's acceptance of local practices and desires had its limits. While the casual violation of the new international boundary did not raise Lamar's eyebrows, he did not tolerate challenges to U.S. sovereignty. Shortly after the ratification of the Treaty of Guadalupe Hidalgo in 1848, a group of prominent Laredoans penned a letter to Lamar's superior officer requesting a return of their rights as "Mexicans." [29] Claiming that Lamar had failed to protect the community from Indians and had carried off cattle and other local goods to supply the garrison, the citizens asked permission to administer their own affairs. The request by the "Commission of the People" for the return of Mexican "liberty" should not be seen as an indication of their wish for Mexican rule so much as a sign of local leaders' desire for a return to the status quo.[30] Basilio Benavides, one of the signers of the complaint, had fought against Mexico's central government under the banner of the Republic of the Rio Grande, and he and others like him felt that U.S. rule posed a threat to local elites' authority. Lamar's response to the commission that "Mexico had lost Laredo forever" did not put an end to the power struggle between locals and the federal government; instead, contestation between local authority and that of the state would continue throughout the community's long history.[31]

TRADE

Mexico's and the United States' inability to administer their borderlands led to great discrepancies between the letter of the law and the social reality of life on the ground. Lamar and other Anglos believed that Laredo and all the lands south of the Nueces River had belonged to Texas since Santa Anna's defeat at the Battle of San Jacinto in April of 1836. After the battle the victorious rebels forced the captured Mexican president to sign the Treaties of Velasco recognizing Texan independence and placing the border at the Rio Grande. Lamar, a veteran of the battle, very likely witnessed Santa Anna's decision to give away Mexican land and skulk away with his life. Mexico's congress, with good reason, never recognized the treaties, and the territory was left in dispute. Texan and U.S. forces' failure to occupy this contested territory meant that towns along the north bank of the Rio Grande effectively lived beyond Anglo law. Lamar's arrival in 1846 should have meant that U.S. federal trade codes would finally be uniformly enforced in the community, but this was not the case.[32] Although garrison forces engaged in some tariff collection, Lamar prioritized safeguarding against Mexican clashes and the Indian threat, not regulating trade.[33] The most Lamar did in regard to regulating trade was forbid the sale of liquor, and that decision came more out of the desire to keep his men sober and the community pacified.[34] Lamar did not have the ability or perhaps even an interest in regulating everyday trade across the river; moreover, his orders to "conciliate" locals to U.S. rule led him to overlook casual illicit commerce.[35] Above all, Lamar showed pragmatism in regulating trade, going so far as to loosen restrictions where he thought wise. On October 10, 1847, Lamar suggested that Nuevo Laredo's mayor discontinue the wheel tax on trade carts because the tax was no longer collected in other "parts of the country," and it seemed unjust to enforce it.[36] Although his logic appeared reasonable, a repeal of the tax would also ease trade across the river and increase American goodwill. Moreover, because Lamar's duties obligated him to collect Mexican tariffs, an end of the tax freed his men to perform other tasks.

The U.S.-Mexican War, although a tragedy for Mexico, exposed many Mexican citizens along the new northern border to the benefits of American trade.[37] American forces repeated Lamar's relaxation of trade regulations as they advanced across Mexico. U.S. forces were supposed to administer Mexican customs regulations, but for the most part free trade followed the American flag.[38] Inexpensive American manufactured goods began to inundate northern Mexico with the capture of the port of Matamoros in 1846. U.S.-made calico and gingham cloth became affordable commodities for many Mexicans and whetted their appetite for other American goods. American merchants following the invading U.S. Army brought with them scores of dutiable supplies like tobacco and dry goods, commodities they sold to Mexican citizens. Mexican tariffs returned at the conclusion of the war, but the ties of trade that developed during U.S. occupation continued as *fronterizos* still wanted to buy American goods, and Anglo merchants north of the river still wished to sell to them. With business booming, towns along the north bank of the Rio Grande developed to accommodate the large warehouses being built for goods fated to be smuggled into Mexico.[39]

U.S. CUSTOMS

The mission of enforcing U.S. trade regulations fell to the Customs Service. Established on July 31, 1789, the Customs Service was essentially a revenue-collecting agency, providing the nation nearly 95 percent of its total federal proceeds until the mid-nineteenth century.[40] Customs agents were effectively tax men with guns, or a federal police force that collected tariffs for the Department of the Treasury. Although customs collection provided substantial national revenue, the burden fell acutely on border people, who faced tariffs on what until U.S. occupation had been local commerce. Imports from Mexico consisted mainly of foodstuffs and animal products, which had a 20 percent duty. For instance, on October 18, 1851, Basilio Benavides, a local don, paid U.S. Customs officers in Laredo $10.40 in import duties on 156 bushels of corn valued at $52.[41] Hamilton P. Bee, one of Lamar's lieutenants, paid $56 on fourteen mules valued at $280 that he crossed from Mexico on December 20 of that same year.[42] Benavides and Bee could afford the 20 percent duty on imports, but many locals could not find the money for the charge or simply preferred not to pay it and chose to smuggle instead.[43]

The Customs Service, although one of the oldest federal agencies, had little experience with border trade. Whereas U.S. Customs traditionally concentrated its forces at coastal ports, federal agents soon realized that customs operations needed to adapt to effectively regulate the new international boundary. Beginning in 1853 the U.S. Customs Service employed mounted inspectors to collect duties on animals crossed into the United States.[44] Despite this adaptation, huge gaps existed in Customs' vigilance. Between 1853 and 1856 only sixteen mounted U.S. Customs inspectors patrolled the border between the Gulf of Mexico and Laredo.[45] Given that Laredo and Eagle Pass recorded over $500,000 in trade annually during the 1850s, one can only speculate how much illicit commerce went unrecorded.[46]

In addition to being shorthanded, early U.S. customs enforcement on the border suffered from a lack of professionalism and organization.[47] Indeed, many customs agents lacked knowledge of the tariff codes they were charged to administer. On January 9, 1855, mounted U.S. Customs inspectors who set out in search of a "party of Mexicans" that had taken animals across the Rio Grande found more than they anticipated.[48] In searching one of the saddlebags agents discovered over one hundred dollars in gold coins and two hundred dollars in silver bullion. Deputy Collector Edmund Wallace was so flabbergasted at the discovery he did not know how to proceed. Wallace wrote his supervisor in Eagle Pass that "not knowing I was correct in considering the specie confiscated, I have not entered it in my return, preferring to wait your decision."[49]

Aside from not knowing the law, U.S. Customs agents encountered difficulties collecting tariffs at inland ports. Although borderland commerce was an everyday affair, significant gaps appear in import ledgers of the era. For instance, Laredo's import entries for August 1852 begin on the third of the month, but no entries are recorded for the fourth, sixth, seventh, or eighth.[50] The last two weeks of August have no recorded entries at all, suggesting negligence.[51] Noticeable gaps in U.S. Customs ledgers would continue until the end of the nineteenth century.[52] An example of the kind of commerce that fell through the gap came on February 1, 1855, when U.S. soldiers acting under a request by the regional customs collector intercepted José Herrera outside of Eagle Pass with a load of red chiles he failed to declare.[53] In his defense, Herrera simply responded that he tried three times to find the collector before deciding to continue his journey and pay the officer upon his return as he had done in the past.[54]

The anarchic condition of customs enforcement became manifest on April 16, 1856, at Fort Bliss outside El Paso when Major James Longstreet ordered his men to draw their rifles and "shoot down" the U.S. customs collector if he attempted to seize the 1,320 *fanegas* of corn the fort's quartermaster failed to pay import duties for.[55] The company quartermaster pled ignorance to any violation of the revenue laws and the matter was settled peacefully.[56] Still, Major Longstreet's refusal to surrender his supplies on the basis of a law he felt trivial is evocative of the general disregard for tariff duties, and Collector Sherman concluded that it was "useless to attempt to have the [revenue] laws enforced" when "almost the entire population are with the military and contractors in [their] suppression."[57]

Borderlanders' collusion with military contractors provides a window on the workings of a moral economy that accepted tariff evasion. Locals simply refused to cooperate with laws they felt unjust and found ways to subvert them. Caleb Sherman, the customs collector for El Paso, admitted as much to the secretary of the treasury when he informed him that it was "impossible to convict any one for smuggling before a Mexican [American] jury," and that "ninety-nine out of every hundred persons . . . think it legitimate to cheat the government when they can."[58] Worse still, Collector Sherman complained that in his district there existed a "desperate gang of men both Mexicans and Americans who live by smuggling."[59] With Anglos, ethnic Mexicans, and even elements of the U.S. state enjoying the benefits of illicit trade, tariff evasion became virtually licit. William Emory, who helped survey the U.S.-Mexico boundary, noted seeing large warehouses for goods destined to be smuggled into Mexico being built in the new communities of Eagle Pass, Edinburgh, Rio Grande City, and Roma. Emory went so far as to claim that these settlements owed their "existence chiefly to the contraband trade with Mexico."[60] After having one of his evenings interrupted by a contraband-laden caravan, Emory captured locals' growing acceptance of illicit trade when he observed, "Where the duties on foreign goods amount almost to prohibition, smuggling ceases to be a crime, but is identified with the best part of the population, and connects itself with the romance and legends of the frontier."[61]

RUSTLING

Border people's emerging moral economy of smuggling did not bring with it an amoral acceptance of all illicit trade; certain types of smuggling remained criminal in local eyes. The first decades of the U.S.-Mexico border's existence were marked with conflict and cross-border raiding. Many incoming Anglos seeking land and cattle preyed on ethnic Mexicans for both. Although the United States (and Mexico) depended on tariff revenue, in times of crisis state forces on both sides of the border focused on preserving their territorial integrity and imposing order. Therefore, it is not surprising that some of the earliest suspects prosecuted for smuggling were those whom authorities believed had rustled livestock. In the winter of 1855–1856 mounted U.S. Customs inspectors apprehended several parties of rustlers along the Rio Grande border smuggling horses and mules into the United States. Although the suspects claimed to have taken the ten horses and three mules in "mustang chases," or roundups of stray or feral animals, north of the Rio Grande, inspectors discovered Mexican brands on the animals.[62] U.S. Customs agents did not believe the men's stories and seized the animals.

Given most Anglos' negative impression of ethnic Mexicans at the time, it is surprising that customs agents did not look the other way. What did they care about a Mexican rancher's loss? The Customs inspectors themselves may have felt this way, but the U.S. government did not. The U.S. government took great care in maintaining order across the border-lands and collector James Durst, the area supervisor, ordered his men to seize all suspected rustled animals in the future for investigation.[63]

Rustling fell outside the moral economy of illicit trade on the border-lands. Unlike other forms of smuggling, rustling not only denied national governments' tariff revenues, it also robbed individuals of their personal property. Therefore rustling was not a tolerated victimless crime.[64] There were of course exceptions. Mexican Customs agents in Nuevo Laredo quickly sold the twenty-eight assorted horses and mules they impounded bearing the brand of cattle baron Richard King rather than return the rustled stock to the gringo land-grabber.[65] Late in November 1875 U.S. commercial agent James Haynes reported that Mexican Customs agents and citizens had known the animals belonged to King before the sale, but Haynes said he would assist King in recovering his stock if he wished.[66]

Contrabandistas' ethics and the parameters of the moral economy are illustrated by informants' selective denunciations. For instance, locals re-ported rustlers but not smugglers of consumer goods. *Fronterizo* ranches were more than simple sites for raising animals; they were communities of extensive familial and fictive kinships with many ties of obligation, particularly for reasons of defense.[67] Self-interest also prompted locals to report suspects. The informants who told Deputy Customs Collector Edmund Wallace of the suspected Mexican rustlers in the winter of 1855 applied for a share of the seizure.[68] Although Wallace did not grant the request, individuals stood to gain from reporting suspected smugglers to authorities. Aside from the reward money or portion of the seizure, in-formants could purchase seized items at government auction. Moreover, personal grudges prompted smugglers to report rivals and neighbors to denounce their enemies.

MEXICO'S STRUGGLE FOR FINANCES

Mexico's independence in 1821 came at a heavy price. Along with the loss of life and property, the country's mines, which had produced upward of 3 million pesos of revenue at the end of the colonial era, lay devastated. Fighting and lack of maintenance damaged Mexico's mines so badly that by 1816 national mining proceeds amounted to less than 300,000 pesos.[69] The wreckage would take decades to repair. With the government's most lucrative source of funds crippled, republican Mexico placed much of its financial hopes on tariff collection. These hopes, however, faced serious constraints. Mexico inherited an archaic colonial fiscal structure that placed little emphasis on port taxes. At the end of the Spanish period, such taxes amounted to only 650,000 pesos of the 14-million-peso yearly tax revenue.[70] Only three functional Mexican customs ports existed in the 1820s, none of which was located near the future border with Texas.[71] The Mexican government's new port taxes conflicted with a long-standing tradition of low international tariffs and caused resentment among domestic merchants. High tariff rates and poor administration made corruption and smuggling rampant. Moreover, for many Mexicans the newly independent government lacked the authority of the old colonial regime with its ties to the Spanish king, and this perception likely contributed to citizens' reluctance to pay their taxes. Sadly, severe governmental instabilities in these years proved many of these views correct. With the exception of nine brief months, Mexico's economy ran a consistent deficit between 1821 and 1856.[72] Mexico's economic difficulties in this period became so acute that lending money to the government became a profession.[73]

Government efforts to collect tariffs led to outright revolt in Mexico's northern territories. In an attempt to colonize its distant northern claims, Mexico granted tariff exemptions as an incentive to its settlers in Coahuila y Texas in the 1820s. Although historians have often pointed to the reforms of April 6, 1830, which prohibited immigration from the United States and cancelled *empresario* contracts, as among the principal causes of the Texas Revolution, few have considered the new customs duties imposed on the Mexican state at that time.[74] Squabbles over tariffs prompted colonist attacks on Mexican forces at Anáhuac on Galveston Bay and eventually forced the garrison soldiers to withdraw in 1832. Mexican forces returned and reestablished the customs post in 1835 only to encounter near shameless smuggling that tested the law and challenged government authority. After the Mexican government's arrest of one of these suspected smugglers, Anglo colonist William Barret Travis led a company of twenty-five to fifty armed volunteers on Anáhuac, forcing the abandonment of the outpost once again. Travis went on to command Texan forces at the Alamo the following year. Anglo settlers' confrontations with Mexico of course went beyond anger over tariffs, but like the rebels of the American Revolution, the patriots of Texan independence fought for the right to trade freely.[75]

Mexico's economic problems continued after the Texas Revolution (1835–1836) and the U.S. invasion that followed it ten years later. U.S. indemnity payments for the conquest of Mexican territory did not satisfy Mexico's national debts. Although the United States paid Mexico 15 million pesos for the loss of 55 percent of its territory after the war ended in 1848, payments to private and international debt holders quickly consumed the money.[76] Internal strife contributed to problems collecting taxes and left customs duties as Mexico's only reliable source of revenue. Between 1848 and 1850 tariff revenues provided over 60 percent of the Mexican budget.[77] Mexico relied primarily on tariff proceeds from 1846 to 1856 because internal taxes produced almost nothing at all.[78] Moreover, state and local governments depended on regional tariffs, or *alcabalas*, due every time goods were transported from one place to another.[79] Mexico's plan to gain more revenue through tariff increases had the unintended effect of prompting more smuggling and less international trade.[80]

Aside from financial problems, Mexico suffered severe political instability after independence. Between 1821 and 1855 power changed hands over twenty-six times as Mexico struggled to find itself as first an empire and then as either a federalist or centralist republic. Wars plagued the era. Various conflicts between federalist and centralist forces occurred perennially. To worsen this chaos, Mexico endured repeated invasions at the hands of European powers, the United States, filibusters, and hostile Indian peoples. Massive foreign claims against Mexico led to incursions to reclaim owed money. In 1838 France dispatched a fleet of warships to blockade the port of Veracruz as punishment for Mexico's failure to pay $600,000 in damages to French citizens for property destroyed during the tumultuous years after independence. The so-called Pastry War ended with the French being driven back, Santa Anna losing his leg, and Mexico paying the French $600,000 it could ill afford. Beginning in 1858 Liberals and Conservatives clashed during the War of Reform. When Liberals under Benito Juárez emerged victorious in 1861, Mexico faced economic ruin. With the national deficit reaching $400,000 monthly, Juárez declared a two-year moratorium on the payment of foreign debts. Mexico's inability to cover its foreign loans prompted France to invade the country again in 1861.[81]

ADUANA

The job of collecting tariffs and rescuing the country from its deep financial difficulties fell to the Aduana (Mexican Customs Service). Anglo-backed revolution in Texas and the U.S. invasion pushed the Mexican Customs Service to the country's new northern border. In order to stop the "scandalous contraband" being smuggled into the northeastern frontier and curb capital flight, the Ministerio de Hacienda (Mexican Department of Treasury) established the Contraresguardo de Gendarmería Fiscal in November 1850.[82] The fiscal police force consisted mainly of agents responsible for economic security and acted as a special customs guard. Aside from patrolling the border, Contraresguardo monitored the numerous paths, trails, roads, and mountain passes where articles could be introduced clandestinely. Contraresguardo agents remained especially vigilant on fair days, when merchant-smugglers gathered to sell American finished goods.[83]

Guidelines for the special customs guard set high standards of professionalism and dictated that agents be educated men of integrity, health, and valor. Officials preferred retired military personnel and former federal employees who fit the criteria. Contraresguardo protocols stipulated that agents deal "moderately" with all merchants without offending them in either "word or deed," and dictates held that such professionalism also extend to the agency's treatment of apprehended smugglers.[84] Regulations called for a force of fifty Contraresguardo agents to patrol Nuevo León's and Tamaulipas's borders with Texas. The Ministerio de Hacienda mandated that the force be well paid to curb the temptation of bribery, with Contraresguardo's commanders entitled to a yearly salary of 4,000 pesos, lieutenants 1,000 pesos, and guards 600 pesos. In addition, the Mexican government ordered that Contraresguardo forces be provided 1,000 pesos a year for expenses such as mounts and firearms.

Regulations did not necessarily mirror practice, however. Despite the Ministerio de Hacienda's hopes for Contraresguardo, the department did not put much faith in its ability to collect revenue. Unlike other customs units that were self-sustaining, financing for the special customs guard originated from revenue collected at the gulf port of Tampico, not from the proceeds gained from their mounted patrols. For the Mexican government, collecting tariffs at a single coastal port proved an easier task than taxing commerce along the porous Rio Grande borderlands.[85]

Contraresguardo's mission to collect national tariff revenues went against the economic best interests of powerful regional leaders, in particular corrupt merchants who profited greatly from evading government tariffs. Though corrupt, merchants smuggling goods enriched themselves while providing less expensive household items like clothing and foodstuffs that border people enjoyed. Regulations demanded that Contraresguardo agents maintain every courtesy with other government agencies; however, this regard was rarely returned.[86] Decorum required local leaders to agree to assist Contraresguardo agents, but locals' best interests dictated resistance. For instance, in the fall of 1851 a Contraresguardo agent on a secret mission in Nuevo León failed in his assignment due to municipal authorities' refusal to force suspects to submit to inspection.[87] Even regional leaders who agreed to help did not always cooperate. Late in 1851 the governor of Nuevo León, Agapito García, suggested that Contraresguardo agents present themselves before local officials in order to prevent customs forces from being confused for bandits or rebel bands. This request, though practical, had the effect of alerting some of the very suspects that Contraresguardo agents were trying to apprehend.[88]

Contraresguardo seized goods for a number of offenses. Traders misrepresenting their merchandise risked having their goods taken from them. Persons who lied about the number of articles they carried or falsified customs receipts in order to evade national and state taxes risked the confiscation of their goods, as did individuals who simply failed to transport their items to appointed customs stations for declaration. Transporting goods to points other than the designated place also transformed licit products into contraband.[89] Other than the fraudulent exportation of precious metals, few items were prohibited from entering or leaving Mexico.[90]

Aside from enforcing tariffs, Mexican Customs faced the additional challenge of keeping the country's liquid capital from fleeing the country. Late in December of 1853 Mexican Customs agents reported silver specie being smuggled out of the country along the Villas del Norte, "particularly in Monterey [Nuevo] Laredo."[91] Mexico's struggle to collect revenue on its precious metals went back as far as the colonial period, when producers routinely lied about the quality and quantity of silver they produced.[92] After independence, Mexico exchanged a great deal of silver specie for American manufactured goods. Between 1824 and 1884 silver constituted 50 percent or more of all legal U.S. imports from Mexico.[93] Onerous Mexican export tariffs assured that even more Mexican silver left the country illicitly.[94] What most troubled Mexican Customs agents about the smuggling of silver out through Nuevo Laredo was that it was done through permits given by regional alcaldes and justices of the peace.[95]

Area alcaldes and judges wrote passes for the exportation of money in false amounts thereby cheating the federal government of its export tariff. Borderlanders seeking to evade Mexican tariffs often negotiated prices with Mexican agents, going so far as to try several outposts before settling on the one that offered the best terms. Although federal authorities considered this to be corruption at the local level, contrabandistas simply regarded it as a way to save money and lower the price of doing business.

It was simply more affordable for smugglers to bribe officials than to pay duties. In relating this common practice on the border an American resident wrote a friend late in 1849, stating:

> It is not contemplated by any merchant exporting from the American to the Mexican side, or by any merchant residing in Mexico, and importing goods into that country to pay the duties imposed by law. No one pretends to do this. Arrangements are made with the officers of the Mexican Customs Houses on the most advantageous terms possible for a permit to enter the country, and where the duties by the Mexican tariff would amount to [$10,000] to $12,000 in almost every instance some [$1,200] or $1,500 will accomplish the object, [and] the guards stationed on the river are bribed and the goods enter the country.[96]

THE MERCHANTS' WAR

The most dramatic confrontation between smugglers and the state came in 1851 with the onset of the Merchants' War. In September 1851 a group of *norteños* exasperated with the central government's failure to look after their best interests and sick of the onerous trade restrictions placed on them gathered near Guerrero, Tamaulipas, and issued the Plan de la Loba. The rebels' plan called for the withdrawal of the federal army, a reduction of customs duties, the abolition of trade prohibitions, an end to heavy fines for smuggling, and the allowance of certain goods to enter the region duty-free for five years.[97] As the uprising developed, however, the movement to free the region from prohibitive tariffs gained the support of numerous Anglo merchants in South Texas and became a revolution to create the Republic of the Sierra Madre in northern Mexico.[98]

José María de Jesús Carvajal, the rebellion's commander, embodied the complexities of this transnational uprising. Carvajal was a Tejano Protestant educated in the U.S South. Upon his return to Mexican Texas, Carvajal befriended *empresarios* Stephen F. Austin and Martín de León and joined the Texas Revolution because he saw it as an extension of Mexico's federalist wars. Carvajal championed regionalism throughout his life. In 1839 he lost the use of an arm following an injury he received leading American volunteers in a battle against Mexican centralists outside Mier, Tamaulipas. Carvajal's wounds, however, did not prevent the borderland patriot from leading a division of the Mexican Army against the U.S. invasion in 1846. After the U.S.-Mexican War Carvajal, like many borderlanders, felt frustrated by national tariffs on what he considered local commerce. Given his distinguished military record and deep devotion to his *patria chica* (modern-day San Antonio, Texas), revolutionaries chose Carvajal to lead a rebellion to create a state that served border people's economic best interests.[99]

Fronterizos did not so much object to tariffs as much as to the way governments spent them. Carvajal and his merchant-revolutionaries did not wish to end tariffs entirely.[100] Instead of customs duties going to the national government, their plan proposed that customs revenues serve the regional community by going toward defense against the Indian threat, or as the Plan de la Loba's signers put it, "the exclusive and sacred purpose of making war upon the savages."[101] Although people of the borderlands smuggled as a common right, when illicit trade hurt the community it fell outside the moral economy. The plan called for a loosening of customs regulations, not deregulation. It even called for the addition of a customs house for the town of Reynosa, Tamaulipas. Smuggling remained a crime under the plan, and given the proposed benefits of tariff enforcement, it would have been a crime much less tolerated by the community.[102]

The Republic of the Sierra Madre's war for independence (or what came to be known as the Merchants' War) would be fought on both sides of the Rio Grande for the next four years. Financed by Anglo merchants and reinforced by some three hundred American adventurers and soldiers of fortune, the forces of the Republic of the Sierra Madre captured the city of Camargo in September 1851. Carvajal's forces entered Reynosa two weeks later and might have gone on to take the port of Matamoros had Carvajal not blundered in instituting his tariff reforms. Although he declared that all necessities "be admitted duty free, and every other article of commerce at a fair proportionate rate," borderland merchants proved unwilling to accept even this impediment to their trade.[103] The Mexican government pounced on the revolution's misstep by removing the tariff restrictions that Carvajal and his men had fought against, and the movement's financiers abandoned Carvajal when his forces entered Matamoros. Facing federal resistance and without hope of succor, Carvajal withdrew.

Luis de la Rosa, Mexico's minister to the United States, dismissed the uprising as "nothing more than [the] result of a scheme, on the part of certain smugglers," but he was wrong.[104] Prohibitive tariffs coupled with Mexico's failure to provide for the best interests of its peripheral peoples led Mexican *fronterizos* to form a transnational coalition with Anglo merchants capable of threatening Mexico's territorial integrity. Mexican law viewed the participants as smugglers and traitors, but border people viewed these same fighters as merchants and patriots. Only after Carvajal's ranks became too "agringado" with Americans and the Mexican government instituted its own tariff reforms did his uprising sputter to an end.[105] Carvajal may have been defeated, but he raised small armies and threatened the Mexican state for several more years. Although Carvajal captured small Mexican borderland communities, his forces were never strong enough to hold them against the power of the state. Still, border people's desire for a freer economy prompted the Mexican government to grant them a major concession.[106]

THE ZONA LIBRE

Heavy tariffs caused Mexican towns along the border to wither after the end of the U.S.-Mexican War in 1848. Mexico's high national tariffs and restrictive local *alcabalas* pushed the price of imports up by 30 percent to 40 percent, while U.S. duties averaged only 15 percent.[107] In fact, some scholars estimate that customs duties composed 50 percent of the total value of Mexico's imports between 1825 and 1870.[108] Unable to compete economically with their American neighbors or to afford Mexico's tariffs on consumer goods, many Mexicans moved north across the border. With U.S. border cities growing at Mexico's expense, Mexican leaders took action. On March 17, 1858, Ramón Guerra, the governor of Tamaulipas, responded to this flight by decreeing a federal tariff exemption for the towns and outlying ranches along the southern bank of the Rio Grande.[109] Beginning just west of Nuevo Laredo and extending to Matamoros on the coast, the Zona Libre was a six-to-eight-mile-wide strip along the entirety of Tamaulipas's border with Texas that promised to create a more favorable economic relationship with the United States and end the depopulation of Mexico's northern cities. What Guerra's decree created, however, was a bonanza for contraband American goods.[110]

Guerra did not define the parameters of the Zona Libre; he only stated that the Mexican cities that bordered Texas along with these communities' outlying ranches resided within the free-trade zone. Truth be told, it is doubtful that any state-mandated limitation could have prevented determined borderlanders from taking advantage of the chance to get imported goods tariff-free, as the Zona Libre allowed. Within the Zona Libre, goods formerly subject to Mexican national tariffs could be introduced duty-free.[111] Rather than curbing illicit trade, the Zona Libre added to the widespread smuggling in the region. Many borderlanders took goods legally into the Zona Libre with the purpose of smuggling them to markets in the interior of Mexico later. Entire warehouses, both privately and government owned, sprang up in Tamaulipas's border cities to service the new trade. Unlike imports on the U.S. side, which could only be warehoused for two years, imports in Mexican warehouses could remain indefinitely. Patient opportunists smuggled their warehoused goods the moment *fiscal* agents lost their vigilance. Smuggling along the Zona Libre occurred to such an extent that in his 1868 report on the condition of the Mexican Treasury, Matías Romero attributed Mexico's lack of national funds to the "large contraband trade carried through the Free Zone and enjoyed by the frontier towns of Tamaulipas."[112]

THE FRENCH INTERVENTION

Deficient tariff revenues contributed to Mexico's decision to place a moratorium on its debt payments to its principal foreign creditors. Unwilling to let the debt go, representatives of Great Britain, Spain, and France agreed on October 31, 1861, to occupy the Mexican customs house at Veracruz until the tariffs they collected there equaled the money they were owed. France, however, wanted more. Driven by hopes of resurrecting France's empire in the New World, Napoleon III decided to conquer Mexico. U.S. arms supplied Mexican republican forces, but until 1865 these weapons were trafficked contrary to American law. France's invasion of Mexico violated the Monroe Doctrine, and Union forces feared that a French regime in Mexico might side with the Confederacy. Still, the United States did not wish to provoke France by directly selling arms to Mexican patriots, and American law prohibited arms sales to Mexico. Despite these constraints, demand, potential profits, and public sympathy led invariably to arms trafficking. Confederate war needs prevented the South from serving as a source for Mexican arms, but U.S.-made arms found their way illicitly to Mexico through California and over the Pacific. The U.S. customs collector for San Francisco seized three thousand rifles destined for Mexico in April of 1864. How many more weapons shipments passed unmentioned under the eyes of agents of a government sympathetic to the Mexican cause may never be known.[113]

THE U.S. CIVIL WAR

The American Civil War (1861–1865) spurred borderlands smuggling and the moral economy that accepted it to new heights. Union efforts to strangle Confederate trade through a naval blockade had the unintended effect of making the border the greatest outlet and entry point for the South. The Union flotilla that made the body of the "Anaconda Plan" stretched from Virginia in the East around the Florida peninsula and into the Gulf of Mexico, but ended on the border offshore of Brownsville. There, at the tail of the snake, smuggling reached its apogee. Prior to the development of railroad linkages between the United States and Mexico, the majority of South Texas trade came through the ports of Brownsville and Matamoros, with mule trains, ox teams, and carts laden with cotton from throughout Texas meeting there. The long, seemingly unending wagon trains of Mexico-bound cotton were equaled by Texas-destined caravans carrying goods and Confederate materiel north from Mexico. As the only accessible ports for the South, the Zona Libre town of Matamoros and its neighbor Bagdad became major centers of international trade, attracting speculators and businessmen from Europe, the Union, and the Confederacy. By 1866 Matamoros's population had reached sixty thousand inhabitants, twenty thousand more than before the "Cotton Times." [114]

Smuggling, a violation against the state, became not a crime at all when borderlanders rebelled against their national governments. Union forces considered the exportation of Confederate cotton unlawful, but Southerners did not. Similarly, although Benito Juárez's government considered U.S. arms sales licit, French imperial forces didn't. Matías Romero, Mexico's minister to the United States and a constant critic of the Zona Libre for the smuggling it fostered, directed arms shipments to Mexico contrary to U.S. law.[115] Although some might have smuggled out of patriotism, self-gain cannot be discounted. Despite Confederate commander Colonel Santos Benavides's exhortations that the cotton piled high in Laredo's plaza "belonged to the Confederacy," it also represented a major investment by local elites such as himself.[116] Coinciding notions of patriotism, profitability, and self-interest contributed to border people's general disregard for tariffs and helped make smuggling a mundane practice.

THE LEGITIMACY OF ILLICIT TRADE

The ease of conducting illicit trade, coupled with the seeming arbitrariness of government tariffs, granted contraband trade a certain legitimacy on the border. For example, elites such as Richard King, Charles Stillman, and Mifflin Kenedy made their fortunes trading contraband Confederate cotton.[117] Santiago Vidaurri, governor of Nuevo León y Coahuila (1855–1864), secured his northern fiefdom for a time on revenues generated from illicit trade with the Confederacy.[118] Vidaurri's son-in-law, Irishman Patrick Mullins, immigrated to Monterrey in the mid-nineteenth century and changed his name to Patricio Milmo. Milmo used the money he made managing contraband to establish successful brokerage and forwarding agencies across the Rio Grande borderlands. In Laredo, Milmo invested his money in a number of community-building measures such as his establishment of the town's first bank in 1883.[119]

The case of the Benavides brothers exemplifies how local elites' illicit trades could be popularly accepted. Locals Santos and Cristóbal Benavides served as Confederate officers during the Civil War and personally defended Laredo from Union attack.[120] The brothers went on to form a thriving mercantile business after the war and figured prominently in local politics.[121] Although Santos and Cristóbal paid their import tariffs on numerous occasions, their business involved smuggling as well.[122] On February 22, 1872, Mexican Customs agents in Nuevo Laredo refused to allow Santos and Cristóbal to export seventy-six rawhides into Laredo because "they were openly engaged in contraband."[123] Worse still, the Mexican customs collector accused the Benavides brothers of trying to bribe port agents.[124]

Closer examination of the Benavides brothers' case reveals how merchants could easily become smugglers. Santos and Cristóbal claimed they had every right to conduct their business across the border and that they had all the proper permissions to do so, but with such political turmoil in Mexico, they were ignorant of their commercial rights under the legitimate Mexican authorities.[125] Indeed, the Mexican Customs officers charging the brothers acted under the dubious authority of the revolutionary party then in arms against the government of Benito Juárez, Mexico's president.[126] With the Mexican customs collector's precarious claim to authority, it is no wonder that Santos and Cristóbal chose to conduct their business as usual. Moreover, revolutions and counterrevolutions across Mexico forced the port of Nuevo Laredo to close throughout most of the spring and summer of 1872.[127] These closures upset commerce on the border, transforming all Mexican trade into smuggling. Seen in this light, the Mexican collector's bribery accusations against the Benavides brothers seem less like the brothers trying to corrupt authority and more like the cost of doing business on the border.[128]

Despite their involvement in illicit trade, the names of Patricio Milmo as well as Santos and Cristóbal Benavides came to be respected. In downtown Laredo's central plaza, a historical plaque devoted to the Benavides brothers describes them as "members of a prominent family" who "distinguished themselves as political, commercial, and social leaders." [129] Locals later named an elementary school after Santos Benavides.[130] Such elite participation in contraband trade prompted boundary surveyor William Emory's remark that border residents considered smuggling a meritorious occupation "identified with the best part of the population." [131] Border people viewed Milmo and the Benavides brothers not as criminal smugglers but as businessmen conducting commerce. As long as smugglers limited their activity to the evasion of unreasonable government trade restrictions and did not adversely affect individuals through theft or physical harm, contrabandistas fell within the moral economy of illicit trade.[132]

MERCHANT-SMUGGLERS

After the American Civil War, the U.S. government felt itself strong enough to enforce its customs policy in the region, and locals began to feel the hardening of the border. As the United States asserted its authority, locals on both sides of the Rio Grande adapted to new barriers to interstate commerce by smuggling. Violence rarely surrounded smuggling, with successful contrabandistas preferring ruses. For example, in the late 1860s women used specially made skirts to smuggle cigars into the United States under the noses of inspectors at Brownsville.[133] Many smugglers were merely consumers or merchants.[134] Throughout the late nineteenth century borderlanders carried their goods across the river as they had done for the past hundred years only to find themselves in violation of federal customs laws. The creation of the international border upset the customary course of regional trade. Local vendors seeking to sell their wares across the river in the United States were required to pay a tariff on their imports. Unwilling to waste their earnings on a seemingly arbitrary tax, many local traders subverted the law and smuggled their goods across the river into the United States. The items these merchants traded were basic consumer goods and staples that fit well within the moral economy of smuggling on the border.[135]

The goods smuggled from Mexico into the United States included produce such as corn and beans, *piloncillo* (brown sugar cones), livestock horses and sheep, and mescal used for local consumption.[136] An examination of Safarino Pérez's seized goods is evocative of the contraband trade of the time. Pérez took five crates of grapes and assorted produce along with seventy pounds of *piloncillo* across the ferry from Nuevo Laredo into the United States only to have U.S. Customs agents confiscate his merchandise.[137] Pérez showed wisdom taking the ferry. Merchants caught fording the river not only had their merchandise seized, but also had their wagons and draft animals impounded. For example, John Collins's contraband cargo of three pounds of potatoes and six and a half gallons of mescal cost him his "old wagon" and "two old plug horses." [138] Although the description of the seized articles indicates that Collins was nothing more than a modest merchant, he somehow managed to come up with the thirty-eight dollars for the assessed value of his forfeited goods.[139]

Smuggling saved border people money while accumulated tariff evasion denied Mexico and the United States significant revenues. In 1878 the Mexican Treasury Ministry estimated the volume of contraband trade at 3 to 4 million pesos, one-fifth of the total value of imports for that year.[140] The United States faced similar losses. On December 31, 1878, Henry Stille, the U.S. consul for Guerrero, begged his superiors for more Customs agents, stating that tariff revenues on only a "few articles which are daily passed contraband into the United States would pay the salary of the collectors from Brownsville to Laredo." [141] Stille cited the thirty thousand to forty thousand pounds of wool smuggled into his district as "one case in many." [142] Merchants used many methods to evade tariffs. For instance, merchants often divided their purchases into increments of less than one hundred dollars to avoid paying consular processing fees, while at other times traders consolidated their shipments into the United States to save additional charges.[143]

Many borderlanders smuggled for personal consumption while others trafficked as part of their business. Most consumers of contraband bought their goods from merchants, who themselves often smuggled or evaded tariffs in one form or another. Borderlanders' general unwillingness to pay what they considered arbitrary tariffs and local juries' reluctance to convict illicit traders prompted the state to grudgingly concede to local values.[144] Then, as today, tired border guards looked the other way rather than take the time to charge petty smugglers.[145] Moreover, with agents and officially designated ports so few, there is something to be said for just how easy it was to smuggle. Borderlanders living in the country-side had to go out of their way to cross items lawfully, not that govern-ment tariffs provided any incentive to declare items at all.[146] Smuggling not only saved money, it offered locals a way to subvert state authority by violating the border that the United States and Mexico had created through their homeland. Still, it is important to point out that during this time of intense contestation, many smugglers preferred discreet methods to violent confrontations; moreover, many people inadvertently smuggled out of ignorance of tariff laws.

A VOICE IN THE WILDERNESS

On October 2, 1881, Charles Winslow, the acting U.S. consul in Gue-rrero, Tamaulipas, wrote the secretary of state about the low value of docu-mented imports into the United States. In the third quarter of 1881 de-clared livestock and hides entering the United States at Guerrero totaled $1,968.69 in value. Consul Winslow speculated, however, that "fully two thirds of the goods exported to the United States, pay no duty."[147] Winslow explained that the government's 20 percent duty on live ani-mals "almost compel the owner to pass them as contraband, and there is little or no hindrance to do so if he wishes."[148] The Customs Service, the largest federal employer after the Postal Service, proved ineffective.[149] "From Laredo to Mier, a distance of 110 miles, there is only one U.S. Cus-toms House," and it was at Carrizo, Texas, six miles from the river.[150] Mes-quite and cactus thickets covered the area. The twelve mounted Customs guards who patrolled the region did not know the land, whereas "Ran-cheros, and the Contrabandistas" knew the only passageways through the chaparral jungle.[151] Canoes and skiffs abounded along the river, and in many places the Rio Grande could be forded on horseback. Conditions were such that locals passed contraband "even in daytime without knowl-edge of the guards," and once across, smugglers easily cached their cargo in the thicket or in their homes.[152] Contrabandistas also used bonfires and messengers to signal the approach of Customs agents. Winslow concluded that the "collection of duties is almost a farce . . . only the most honorable merchants ever think of paying duties," and "there are numbers of men in Guerrero whose sole business it is to pass contraband."[153]

CONCLUSION

In the wake of the U.S.-Mexican War, both the United States and Mexico focused on enforcing the territorial integrity of their new shared border. Although tariffs served as a vital source of U.S. and Mexican national revenue, state forces prioritized sovereignty over enforcing national tariff laws in the region. By the 1870s, however, the situation had changed. The end of the U.S. Civil War followed by the arrival of occupation forces during Reconstruction led to a greater state presence on the U.S. side of the border. Similarly, Mexico's overthrow of French rule and the rise of Porfirio Díaz strengthened the Mexican government's ability to enforce its trade laws. Despite the United States' and Mexico's increasing vigilance against untaxed international commerce, borderlanders for the most part circumvented states' best efforts to stop free trade through their homeland. Moreover, border people's popular evasion of tariff duties led to common values about smuggling and the formation of a moral economy of illicit trade.

Widespread smuggling persisted throughout the first three decades of the border's creation, but the arrival of the railroad in 1881 transformed it. Whereas smuggling was previously situational, increased trade and customs enforcement caused smuggling's professionalization. Although casual smuggling for personal consumption endures to today, commercial smuggling or trafficking came more and more to define illicit trade in the Mexican and U.S. governments' national mindsets.

TWO

Rails, Trade, and Traffickers, 1881–1910

On April 26, 1887, Mexico's foreign minister to the United States, Matías Romero, sat down to write a very difficult letter to the American secretary of state in Washington. Romero wrote that north of the Rio Grande between the villas of Camargo and Laredo resided the known smuggler Mariano Reséndez, leader of an armed band of contrabandistas that had left members of the Mexican Customs force dead and wounded.[1] Using the border to his advantage, Reséndez organized parties from his refuge in the United States capable of resisting Mexican authorities in force. Reséndez posed a particular threat to Mexico; Romero stressed that "simply calling his band smugglers was insufficient," and "wrongdoers" would be more apt.[2] Unable to root out the threat on the border, Romero pleaded that the American secretary stop Reséndez from readying "smuggling expeditions" that "invade" Mexico from U.S. soil.[3]

How did a man who smuggled textiles for a living pose a threat to the Mexican state? In the late nineteenth century Mexico and the United States continued to struggle to regulate border trade. Although few cases were as dramatic or violent as that of Mariano Reséndez, smugglers from both sides of the border routinely violated Mexican and U.S. authority by evading tariffs. Contrabandistas smuggled Mexican mescal, foodstuffs, and trade goods across the border illegally into the United States and carried consumer goods illicitly into Mexico. Mexican and U.S. national forces, however, attempted to enforce tariff collection evenly despite local perceptions of tolerable and intolerable illicit trade. The arrival of the railroad to los dos Laredos led to a greater state presence in the borderlands as both the United States and Mexico sought to regulate increasing international commerce. Greater state presence, however, did not end smuggling on the border or locals' moral economy of illicit trade. Rather, increased government vigilance served to make smuggling a profession.

RAILHEADS

Railroads and the capital that followed the lines linked Laredo and Nuevo Laredo to trade networks across North America. The Texas-Mexican railroad reached Laredo in November 1881, connecting it to Corpus Christi and the Texas Gulf Coast, and the International and Great Northern linked Laredo to San Antonio later that year. In 1882 the Rio Grande and Pecos, later renamed the Rio Grande and Eagle Pass, arrived at Laredo. The Mexican National Railway connected los dos Laredos with Mexico City in 1888.[4] Matías Romero noted that prior to the arrival of the railroad, the value of goods introduced through Laredo never exceeded $180,000 a year, but in 1882 the duties reached $1.2 million.[5] By 1893 U.S. exports through Laredo exceeded the total exports through all other Texas towns along the border, and Nuevo Laredo ranked as Mexico's principal port on the border.[6] Los dos Laredos' designation as the principal inland ports for both their nations would continue to modern times.[7]

Despite increased trade along the railroad, documented cases of traffickers hauling contraband by train are rare.[8] Though smugglers were known for their discretion, their silence regarding railways bears explanation. U.S. Customs' concern for enforcing the integrity of the border by riding in mounted patrols caused negligence in inspections of railroad cargos and proper landing certificates. For large cargos, Customs depended on shipment manifests (provided by the conductor) that detailed the quantity and quality of the goods. Given the scale of shipments through the port, and that U.S. Customs dictates designated inspection of only one package of every invoice, many opportunities for smuggling through tariff fraud existed. Aside from lax inspection, corruption among officials monitoring the railroad cannot be discounted either. For example, the U.S. consul for Nuevo Laredo, R. B. Mahone, complained in 1899 that the customs collector for Laredo, a local customs broker, and consignment agent J. Archibald had the "insane idea that this office belongs to Laredo, Texas; that Laredo is the United States and that this office represents them only. They also think they own Mexico."[9] With political cronyism and corruption endemic to South Texas politics of the time, it is likely that some federal employees compromised their duty by making informal arrangements with the community they were charged to police.[10]

J. Archibald's habits serve as an example of the unscrupulous activities of the era. Archibald worked as a customs agent for the Mexican National Railroad, but unlike other customs officers who served the national government exclusively, Archibald also doubled as a consignment agent. As a consignment agent, Archibald facilitated the shipping of goods across the border. This basically meant that Archibald cosigned for the ultimate recipient of the goods, worked to ensure his employer's goods got through whatever red tape inevitably came up, and tried to save his employer money wherever he could. Archibald executed many of his duties by smuggling. On June 27, 1898, Consul Mahone informed his superiors in Washington of Archibald's illicit practices. Rather than paying the American consulate office its $2.50 due for each of two separate shipments Archibald cosigned for Loeb Huos's business in Mexico City, Archibald consolidated the shipments into one landing certificate.[11] While Archibald's evasion of $2.50 seems inconsequential, U.S. consular offices functioned on handling fees.[12] Archibald routinely defrauded the government. On January 11, 1899, Consul Mahone complained that Archibald cheated the government of $12.50 by consolidating eight separate shipments into three landing certificates.[13] Moreover, because Archibald often failed to report crossings, or did so a "day or two" after the shipping, the depths of his fraud probably went much deeper.[14]

Whatever revenues Archibald denied the U.S. government pale in comparison to what he sought to deny the Mexican state. In December 1899 alone Archibald defrauded the Mexican government of over $106 in import revenues.[15] Instead of introducing items clandestinely, Archibald used subterfuge by lying about the quantity, quality, and nature of the goods for which he cosigned. Late in November 1899 Mexican Customs agents in Nuevo Laredo discovered that Archibald's declared shipment of 1,404 kilos of plaster was instead 988 kilos of colored cement.[16] While this discrepancy may seem trivial, Mexican Customs did not see the $69.16 difference in tariff duties as something to overlook.[17] Another time Archibald falsely declared aluminum stoves as steel stoves in an attempt to cheat the Mexican government of $27.13 in tariffs.[18] Pedro Argüelles, administrator for the Nuevo Laredo customs house, became so frustrated he informed his superiors, "Archibald laughs off infractions with each pass." [19]

Archibald worked as a broker for businesses far away from the border, like the Florsheim Shoe Company of Chicago. In fact, Archibald was so important to Florsheim's operations in Mexico that on October 8, 1899, the company wrote U.S. consul R. B. Mahone in reference to the landing certificate issue. After consulting U.S. Customs agents in Chicago, Flor-

FIGURE 2.1. *Customs house, Nuevo Laredo, early twentieth century. Photographer unknown. Special Collections, Laredo Public Library.*

sheim told Consul Mahone the company believed that landing certificates could be combined so long as exports went through the same port of entry and were signed by the same consignee. Florsheim argued that its operations in Mexico were small and that "if there is no relief from these charges . . . it will naturally prohibit the exportation of this class of goods." [20] Simply put, Florsheim claimed it could not do business in Mexico without Archibald's tariff evasions.

Archibald was not so much a professional smuggler as a professional who smuggled. He did not traffic in prohibited items for personal gain; rather he acted as a middleman for merchants seeking to maintain a low overhead by evading U.S. and Mexican trade fees. The articles Archibald helped smuggle were consumer goods like American-made leather shoes, decorated earthenware, and cooking stoves.[21] Unlike Mariano Reséndez, whose conflicts with mounted guards won him respect and local esteem, Archibald corresponded with businessmen and government agents. While Reséndez was a rogue, Archibald was a scoundrel. Rather than carry a rifle, Archibald, we can imagine, wore a suit. Because he grossly cheated governments as a profession, not to get by, and did not prove his manhood physically like mounted smugglers, Archibald's illicit trades did not inspire ballads of praise like those of his contemporary Reséndez. Still, Archibald and other traffickers like him were products of the increased trade that followed the railroad and of the U.S. and Mexican tariff laws that sought to regulate and profit from such commerce.

THE TWO LAREDOS

The creation of the Zona Libre and the arrival of the railroad spurred the rapid development of los dos Laredos. Laredo was a sleepy hamlet of 3,811 people when the railroad arrived in 1881, but ten years later the community had grown into a bustling town of 11,319 inhabitants.[22] By 1900 the community claimed some 13,400 citizens, with Nuevo Laredo's population reaching 6,500 that same year.[23] Although Anglo and European immigrants accounted for much of the population growth, Laredo remained a predominately Mexican American town. Laredo's ethnic Mexican community largely escaped the social and economic subordination that followed Anglo entry into the U.S. Southwest for a number of reasons. Unlike communities in the Lower Rio Grande Valley such as Brownsville, which Anglos created after 1848, Laredo had existed as a Hispanic settlement prior to the establishment of the international border. "White" immigrants settling the Lower Rio Grande Valley displaced much of the region's ethnic Mexican population, but in Laredo wealthy and middling Anglo and, more importantly, predominantly Catholic French and Italian immigrants, commonly intermarried with Tejano elites and created a less racially dichotomous class considered *gente decente* (literally translated as decent people).[24] Although local elites were considered more "white" than the working-class Mexican American majority, their interethnic makeup, with its shared culture and common goals, dissuaded the violent racism that characterized Anglo/ethnic Mexican relations at the time.[25] Mexican Americans controlled most of the city's public offices. Of the thirty men to hold the office of mayor of Laredo between 1848 and 1900, only seven had non-Spanish surnames.[26] Demographics and power relations in the community were such that the Anglos and Europeans who did immigrate to Laredo "appeared more Mexicanized than *mexicanos* appeared Americanized."[27] Still, the *gente decente* steered the community along conservative, Progressive, pro-American lines.[28]

The origins of Laredo's most popular, and perhaps peculiar, local festival began as an attempt to impress an American identity on a Mexican town. Laredoans continued to celebrate Cinco de Mayo and Diez y Seis de Septiembre as holidays after the Treaty of Guadalupe Hidalgo, but during Reconstruction U.S. occupation forces attempted to give Laredo a more American image. In February 1870 Mayor Samuel Jarvis ordered flyers distributed announcing a celebration in honor of the first president of the United States' birthday. Although city hall discontinued the celebration after Jarvis stepped down in 1872, George Washington's Birthday would not be forgotten. As more and more Anglos immigrated to Laredo after the arrival of the railroad in 1881, they sought ways to make the community more amenable to them, and the first president's birthday proved useful in that regard. Along with other Progressive initiatives like closing "noxious" food stands and arresting mescal peddlers, city fathers embraced George Washington's Birthday in order to promote a "modern" American image for Laredo.[29]

Although Anglo elites created the celebration, the sheer number of ethnic Mexicans in all classes of Laredo society made interactions inclusive rather than exclusive, with cooperation, not conflict, characterizing ethnoracial relations in town. For instance, Anglo and European immigrants to the community learned Spanish by necessity and the city published ordinances in both English and Spanish.[30] Racial barriers came down as "white" immigrants intermarried with Tejano elites, but the demographics of the area (not to mention the proximity of Mexico itself) ensured that Anglo and European immigrants became Mexicanized. Poor-, working-, and middle-class ethnic Mexicans also participated in the celebration to a great extent. Class divisions ensured that only the well-to-do attended the Washington's ball culminating the festivities, but Laredoans of all walks of life attended the parade. Even borders could be disregarded, as was the case in 1905 when Laredoans used the Rio Grande to reenact Washington's crossing of the Delaware River.[31] In time Laredo's ethnic Mexican majority would co-opt the celebration implemented to Americanize them. By 1909 Mexican and U.S. flags adorned the festivities, and during the 1920s a *noche mexicana* became a regular part of the expanding celebration.[32]

Illicit trade played a large part in los dos Laredos' development, with one U.S. vice consul going so far as to attribute the communities' growth to their "excellent facilities for smuggling."[33] Petty smuggling continued as a common practice, but U.S. border towns' proximity to the Zona Libre prompted trafficking by merchants specializing in illicit commerce.[34] Indeed, storefronts provided a veneer of legitimacy for illegal trade. Because nothing is smuggled until it crosses a border, and there was nothing inherently illegal about muslins, American prints, and other consumer articles commonly traded at the time, U.S. officials could only look on as individuals carried off loads and loads of goods from businesses at night.[35] Smug-

FIGURE 2.2. *"Smuggling on the Rio Grande,"* Harper's Weekly, *September 4, 1886. Library of Congress.*

glers took these packages to ranches near the river where they wrapped them in canvas bundles weighing up to 150 pounds and strapped them to the backs of mules.[36] Local rumors abounded about the ease of trafficking goods south beyond the Zona Libre. Moreover, Mexican customs duties outside the Zona Libre were such as to make even a couple of successful runs worth the costs of four or five unsuccessful trips.[37] With the profits from illicit trade high and the Mexican government unable to enforce its customs laws, smuggling along the border ran rampant.[38]

Smuggling's viability and lack of stigma led some border people to make it a family practice. U.S. Army Lieutenant Stephen O'Connor, who chased revolutionary Catarino Garza through the Rio Grande borderlands, complained that the

> Mexican population of the Rio Grande Valley is, as a whole, a criminal class. The tariff between the United States and Mexico has made smuggling profitable, hence the son has followed the father until now we have a hereditary class of criminals to deal with.[39]

O'Connor's racialized comment about "hereditary" criminality misses locals' moral economy while providing evidence that government tariffs altered habits among border people. By enforcing tariffs, the U.S. government made smuggling popularly accepted and lucrative. Thus, when it came to evading authorities, some families cultivated artifice rather than admonish it and chose smuggling as a viable way of life.

TRAFFICKERS AS STATE THREATS

Mariano Reséndez posed a threat to the Mexican state for several reasons. Mainly, Reséndez and other smugglers' unlawful importation of American consumer goods defrauded the Mexican government of significant customs revenues. Customs collections formed a critical part of the Mexican treasury, averaging over 50 percent of the public revenue between 1851 and 1885.[40] Imposts on foreign goods provided Mexico with over $23.6 million, or almost half its national budget, for the 1895–1896 fiscal year and averaged to 42 percent of its public revenue until 1910.[41] Customs returns from Mexico's maritime ports made up for some of the shortcomings in tariff collections along the U.S.-Mexico border, but were not enough to support the country. Foreign loans during Porfirio Díaz's modernization campaign cost Mexico greatly. In the summer of 1896 the country's national debt stood at over $200 million.[42] If the Mexican government could end traffickers' operations along the border, it stood to add significantly to its national revenue.

Reséndez's operations also exposed fundamental weaknesses in the Porfirian government. Mexico's control of its borderlands was not as complete as President Porfirio Díaz's propaganda portrayed.[43] Rather than exercising totalitarian control, Díaz ruled over a contentious northern borderland, with Yaqui uprisings, political disputes, and armed rebellions breaking out across Mexico in the closing decades of the nineteenth century. Catarino Garza's transnational anti-Díaz revolution emerged out of the Texas/Tamaulipas borderlands in 1891, just four years after Matías Romero asked U.S. officials for aid against Reséndez. Seen in this light, Mariano Reséndez and other armed smugglers posed a serious threat to the Mexican government. For instance, on February 11, 1881, an armed band of forty or more smugglers ambushed eleven Mexican Customs agents thirty miles west of Nuevo Laredo.[44] Smugglers killed the town *presidente*'s son-in-law in the engagement and escaped with a train of some fifty mules laden with contraband from the Texas side. Matías Romero's concern that Reséndez's resistance to Mexican authorities "upset the public order, causing other irreparable wrongs" illustrates Mexican officials' real fears of losing control of their border.[45] *Fronterizos* already regarded

Reséndez as a hero for his conflicts with Mexican federal forces.[46] Reséndez may not have issued political proclamations like regional revolutionary (and folk) heroes Juan Cortina and Catarino Garza, but like Cortina and Garza he led armed bands of men in skirmishes against the Mexican government. Although Reséndez did not seek to confront the state, but fought only when forced, the very boldness of his actions exposed weakness in the Mexican government and inspired others to similarly defy national authority and evade high tariffs. Given the Mexican state's tenuous hold over its northern borderlands, it is understandable why Reséndez seriously concerned Mexican officials, leading them to ask for U.S. assistance.

THE MORAL ECONOMY OF SMUGGLING

Smuggling tapped into popular local resentment toward excessive national tariffs. In 1884 locals complained of "too rigid enforcement" on the part of the Mexican customs collector in Nuevo Laredo.[47] Locals' complaints of stringent customs enforcement reveals that border people expected a certain amount of leniency in regard to their practice of illicit trade. Most borderlanders regarded smuggling as a "libertarian practice" or a just way around onerous government tariffs.[48] Locals even celebrated smugglers in song. In the popular late-nineteenth-century corrido "Mariano Reséndez," Reséndez challenges "cowardly border guards, who live off the government's bounty."[49] Reséndez's apocryphal challenge resonated with people of the time. Mexico's byzantine tariff system made crossing goods difficult, and minor errors in paperwork could lead to forfeiture and the loss of merchandise. Moreover, Mexican Customs agents received a portion of the fines they collected on tariff evasion. For example on December 5, 1899, Pedro Argüelles, the Mexican Customs administrator in Nuevo Laredo, received $4.98, or 37 percent, of a fine against a man who undervalued his import declaration.[50] Argüelles was not the only officer to profit from the practice. The *contador* received $2.29, or 17 percent, while the *vista*, or overseer, received $4.84, or 36 percent, of the same fine.[51] With money to be made imposing and collecting fines, Mexican Customs agents maintained a personal interest in being strict, and people reasonably viewed them as predatory. Indeed, fines composed a substantial portion of Customs officials' salaries. Although figures are unavailable for the border ports, in the 1890s fines constituted 70–90 percent of Customs officers' salaries at the port of Veracruz.[52] Mexican borderlanders did not see tariffs as protective instruments for national industry or legitimate sources of government revenue, Argüelles admitted, but as "simply tribute."[53]

Local contempt for official corruption played a part in trafficking-related violence. The corrido of Mariano Reséndez laments that Mexican authorities "let the big contrabands pass, while they catch the small timers," asserting that dishonest *fiscal* agents only pursued smugglers who failed to bribe them.[54] Traffickers like Reséndez could not, or refused to, bribe corrupt officials for the right to smuggle, especially considering they could pay these same Contraresguardo agents and transport their goods legally. *Fronterizos* had many reasons to resent Mexican customs duties and the men who enforced them. For instance, in 1888 agents reputedly opened each box of a shipment of sardines to check its contents.[55] Rather than credit the agents for their thoroughness, such scrutiny often stemmed from corrupt officers' attempts to solicit a bribe. Poorly paid government officers commonly supplemented their meager income with bribes known as *mordidas*, or bites. A pretense of decorum and officers' personal honor necessitated that bribes be less than overt; thus, experienced borderlanders avoided Mexican Customs agents ransacking their goods by leaving the bribe on top of the items to be inspected where it could be easily seen and discreetly collected. The Mexican Customs agents who checked every box of sardines in search of contraband may have simply been looking for their *mordida*. Moreover, corrupt agents likely used the threat of invasive inspections to coerce a bribe. As one American traveling in Mexico noted, by the late nineteenth century, Mexican Customs agents had forged a reputation for being "licensed brigands."[56]

Consumer goods such as the textiles that Reséndez trafficked fell inside the moral economy of smuggling in the borderlands. Aside from the money, Mariano and his band enjoyed other benefits of the trade. Because Reséndez provided consumer goods at affordable prices, he garnered public support and local prestige. Onerous Mexican tariffs made consumer goods so expensive that many borderlanders accepted smuggling as a common right. Moreover, Mexican borderlanders were wanting in material goods that their nation's domestic industries failed to supply. Mexican communities on the Rio Grande border stood on the periphery of a country focused on a distant capital seemingly unconcerned with their well-being. An American correspondent visiting Saltillo, Coahuila, in 1888 commented that even the finer homes were in a "condition of squalor" for want of fine furniture.[57] The little furniture wealthy Mexicans did have was reportedly so poorly made that tables and chairs overturned with the slightest touch, and its finished wood stained those who touched it.[58] With smuggling filling a basic need, the practice ceased to be a crime in the eyes of the community.[59]

Machismo further justified smuggling-related violence. Like other ballad heroes, Reséndez "no se dejaba" (would not suffer insults) and won honor by defying discredited authority and defending his "right" with force.[60] Reséndez and his men operated in armed mounted groups along lonely stretches of highway and backcountry trails. The group operated at night to avoid clashes with *fiscal* agents, but like other traffickers, Reséndez fought back when confronted. Ballad singers claim he was known to yell, "Gather round, my companions, or they will take our contraband!"[61] How Reséndez responded when Mexican forces finally succeeded in capturing him in November of 1887 is unknown. Border lore holds that Mexican forces surrounded his camp and took Reséndez by surprise. They executed him on the road to Monterrey shortly afterward.[62]

Although dead, Reséndez was far from forgotten. Reséndez had resisted unpopular laws through his trafficking and made a profit while also providing a service to his fellow borderlanders by selling less expensive smuggled American consumer goods. Whereas the Mexican government viewed Reséndez as a "wrongdoer" who challenged federal authority, rural borderlanders regarded him as a hero.[63] An anonymous minstrel composed the corrido of Mariano Reséndez shortly after the smuggler's death in 1887, and the song remains popular to this day. The Reséndez of the corrido is confident and suave, bragging of the quality of his contraband cloth and challenging Mexican Customs forces to take it if they can. Rather than vilifying him, Reséndez's smuggling and conflicts with the state gained him prestige and honor within the community to which he belonged.[64]

Common people regarded Mariano Reséndez as more than just a simple smuggler. His confrontations with federal authorities and the scale of his operations won him the title "the Smuggler" from ethnic Mexican borderlanders and even the Mexican government.[65] Ballad singers called him "don Mariano" out of respect.[66] It is noteworthy that some versions of the ballad place Mariano Reséndez's death in 1900, thirteen years after his actual killing by Mexican state forces. Although this inconsistency may be attributed to balladeers' creative license to make a rhyme, it also suggests a community's reluctance to give up a hero. Some borderlanders hold that Mexican forces never killed Mariano Reséndez at all, and that he bribed corrupt officials to have his body replaced with that of another,

FIGURE 2.3. *"Smugglers Attacked by Mexican Customs Guards,"* Collier's
Weekly, October 26, 1901. *Famed Western artist Frederic Remington's illustration
depicts the violence that occurred between armed smugglers and Mexican
Customs forces. The original caption beneath the image reads, "There is a great
deal of smuggling by water and land, from the gulf to the Pacific, into old Mexico,
and her custom house officers often have savage fights with the 'sneak thieves'
when they run them down. The severity of the Mexican government in dealing
with outlaws impels the wrong-doers to offer resistance to the death, and fatal
encounters are not uncommon along the Rio Grande." Amon Carter Museum
of American Art.*

leaving him to live out his days in peace near Laredo. Just how Mariano Reséndez died is not important; it is more significant that working-class, ethnic Mexican borderlanders chose to celebrate the exploits of a man who smuggled cloth for a living. By instituting high tariffs on basic goods that people needed, the Mexican government transformed smugglers into folk heroes.

Reséndez's death did not end trafficking or violent conflicts on the border. Although successful smugglers did not seek violence, traffickers' encounters with Mexican government forces invariably led to bloodshed. Traffickers clashed with Mexican Customs agents in the countryside outside Nuevo Laredo on three separate occasions in the summer of 1891. A typical confrontation occurred in late July 1891, when a band of fourteen smugglers making their way along the Camino de Guerrero learned that six *fiscal* agents were following them. The smugglers, unwilling to be arrested, prepared an ambush. Traffickers shot and killed two Customs agents who fell into the trap, and they fatally wounded another guard. The surviving Customs agents fled on horseback, barely escaping with their lives. Undaunted, the smugglers continued their journey without incident, the corrido of Mariano Reséndez possibly on their lips.[67]

If traffickers' victory over Customs men in late July were not enough evidence that the Mexican government could not stop illicit trade, then another battle in early August that took the lives of eight agents and four smugglers proved smuggling's persistence.[68] Mexico faced the impossible task of sealing its northern border against the illicit flow of desired goods. Aduana administrator Pedro Argüelles admitted that the only way to prevent smuggling would be to place a "line of guards whose elbows should touch, since the Rio Grande is fordable at all parts." [69] A Spanish language newspaper in Laredo echoed the Mexican customs collector's sentiments, reporting that "as long as there are high tariffs, there will be ambitious men that risk their lives to profit from contraband." [70] Indeed, Mexican authorities had more than hardened traffickers to contend with, as smuggling by common people persisted. For instance, in early August *fiscal* agents apprehended a young boy with two dozen cans of contraband tomatoes.[71] Borderlanders on both sides of the Rio Grande simply did not feel obliged to pay government tariffs, and state efforts failed to compel them otherwise. On May 1, 1896, Mexico finally abandoned the *alcabala* (interstate tariff) in an effort of curb smuggling.[72]

SMUGGLERS AND THE U.S. STATE

American officials faced similar difficulties combating popular smuggling. As the United States sought to assert its authority over the border in the late nineteenth century, locals on both sides of the Rio Grande found a way to adapt to the artificial barriers to international commerce—they smuggled. It is important to point out that not all who smuggled did so professionally, nor were all contrabandistas violent. Frank B. Earnest, U.S. customs collector for Laredo, complained that "petty smuggling is constantly carried on . . . and it is almost impossible to prevent."[73] Indeed, the U.S. government estimated three-quarters of the population smuggled in one form or another.[74] Women conducted a great deal of this petty smuggling by hiding things like lace, kid gloves, and silk hose under their clothes.[75] Aside from locals smuggling for personal consumption, a great many contrabandistas were nothing more than local merchants. Nuevo Laredo vendors seeking to sell their wares in the United States were required to pay a tariff on their imports. Many local traders simply smuggled their goods across the river to save the trouble of going through customs and the cost of paying a seemingly arbitrary tax. With average U.S. tariffs on dutiable imports never falling below 38 percent between 1871 and 1913, incentives to smuggle proved plentiful.[76] As on the Mexican side, merchants traded consumer items and staples that fit well within the moral economy of smuggling. For example, on January 17, 1885, U.S. Customs agents apprehended A. Alvarez attempting to evade tariffs on seven hundred oranges he unlawfully imported into the country.[77] Alvarez paid seven dollars for the appraised value of the oranges and waived his right to further proceedings.[78] Smuggling, to a degree, was an accepted part of life on the border.

Like Mexico, the United States placed tariffs on certain imports. Tariffs not only protected domestic industries; tariff revenue provided the U.S. Treasury over $182 million in 1880 alone.[79] The United States did not have a national debt equal to Mexico's, yet with most of its income derived from national tariffs, few U.S. Customs agents on the border proved willing to look the other way on tariff evasion. Most smugglers were unremarkable; very few posed a national threat. Mariano Reséndez was unique because his armed conflicts with the Mexican state prompted him to be mentioned by name in government correspondence and inspired border ballads in his honor, but most contrabandistas were far less colorful. For all his renown, Reséndez smuggled calico. With the exception of traffickers like Reséndez, smuggling was a mundane affair.[80] Ordinary people dealt mostly in textiles, livestock, produce, and mescal, or as one U.S. newspaper put it, "common pottery, [and] coarse Mexican sugar." [81] Take, for example, the two dozen cans of tomatoes that Mexican Customs agents caught the young boy smuggling in early August of 1891, or the lot of large and small doilies, napkins, and handkerchiefs U.S. Customs agents seized from Antonio Jacour on June 10, 1899.[82] Because the United States did not face armed bands of traffickers, the U.S. government could spend more time apprehending ordinary people evading tariffs on common household items.

The loyalties of Customs agents married to local women came into question when officers were called to administer justice on their neighbors and in-laws. Indeed, U.S. authorities worried that local ties posed an insidious threat to state power on the border. During his off-hours not spent actively pursuing revolutionaries through the brushland, Lieutenant Stephen O'Connor took time to grumble that U.S. Customs men were "both married to Mexican women and industriously engaged in raising half-breed families." [83] Fears of racial miscegenation aside, the lieutenant's principal anxiety was that this intermingling drew the very men charged to enforce state authority into the binds of the contrabandista community. Local women, O'Connor complained, shared bonds with their community and were "more or less connected by family ties with the revolutionists, smugglers and bandits of the border." [84] Just how warranted O'Connor's paranoia may have been is debatable, but his concerns highlight how the integration of federal forces into the community could undermine state objectives. Finding cases of officers looking the other way and allowing petty illicit trade proves an exceedingly difficult task for historians. Records fade and eventually crumble, not that tolerance or complicity was something participants would have wanted to write down. Still, officers enmeshed in their community through family connections undoubtedly felt pulled between strict and loose enforcement of the law.

Petty smugglers aside, by the late nineteenth century government tariffs prompted the professionalization of illicit trade. Mariano Reséndez was not the only borderlander who practiced smuggling as his "exclusive occupation." [85] Evidence for the rise of professional smuggling can be seen in local newspapers and U.S. federal court records repeatedly referring to "old smugglers." In 1899 federal authorities sentenced Antonio Peña, an old smuggler, to ten months in jail for unlawfully importing 250 pounds of dried meat valued at $25.[86] U.S. law enforcement arrested Francisco Flores, another old smuggler, in 1890 for evading tariffs on sacks of mescal he routinely imported.[87] Flores and other "old smugglers" such as

FIGURE 2.4. *After pleading guilty to smuggling $347 worth of assorted merchandise, particularly alcohol and tobacco, into the United States, Francisco Salinas was sentenced by the U.S. Western District Court of Texas to serve one year and a day in federal prison at Fort Leavenworth, Kansas. Francisco Salinas, Case File 2135, Inmate Case Files, 1895–1952, ARC Identifier 571125, Records of the Bureau of Prisons, Record Group 129, National Archives and Record Administration at Kansas City, Kansas.*

Francisco Salinas (fig. 2.4) earned their title by having appeared in court before on charges of smuggling, or by having witnesses testify that the accused smuggled as an occupation. Old smugglers were repeat offenders who smuggled professionally for profit to supply local markets, and their appearance in federal courts indicates that the enforcement of U.S. trade restrictions had the unintended effect of creating a new criminal profession on the border.

VIOLENCE

Unlike in Mexico, where authorities faced armed incursions by traffickers, violent confrontations between smugglers and American law enforcement in South Texas were uncommon and circumstantial, not indications of state weakness. When a U.S. Customs agent encountered Felipa Delesa smuggling three and a half gallons of mescal, she hit him and tore at his clothes in an attempt to escape.[88] Episodes like Delesa's scuffle with authorities occurred sporadically between contrabandistas and U.S. Customs agents, not recurrently as they did in Mexico. When violence broke out between smugglers and U.S. law enforcement it came suddenly. Jesse Perez, one of a handful of Mexican American Texas Rangers, recounted an instance when a Customs agent monitoring the bridge at Laredo stopped a suspicious man. The Customs agent confiscated a bottle from the intoxicated suspect who then drew a knife. The agent struck the suspect with a metal pipe he had handy, knocking him unconscious. Officers discovered a one-gallon bladder of mescal on the bleeding man and took him to the county jail.[89] The bloodiest encounter between smugglers and U.S. law enforcement came in the predawn hours of October 30, 1891, when Francisco Flores stumbled upon U.S. marshal George Wise and two deputies on the streets of Laredo.[90] Marshal Wise drew his gun, ordering Flores to stop. As the officer approached Flores, the man halted and stooped down to drop his sacks of mescal. Flores then sprung to his feet and plunged a knife into Wise and rushed Deputy Calixtro García, wounding him fatally. Wise fired twice at the fleeing man but missed as his killer escaped in the darkness.[91]

Flores's killing of two officers was a bloody anomaly in an otherwise nonviolent contrabandista culture north of the Rio Grande. At no other time between 1880 and 1910 did area smugglers confronted by U.S. authorities wound, let alone kill, officers in the line of duty. In contrast, mounted smugglers and Mexican Customs forces fought three armed clashes outside Nuevo Laredo in the summer of 1891 alone.[92] On the Mexican side of the border traffickers like Mariano Reséndez could ride the countryside confident of their ability to resist the government if confronted, but smugglers north of the border considered discretion the better part of valor and generally smuggled quietly rather than risk an intense state response. Marshal Wise and Deputy García were respected members of the community, and their murders shocked Laredo. Wise himself was a highly esteemed officer with a reputation for suppressing smuggling.[93] Moreover, local newspapers blasted the assailant, calling him a "cold blooded murderer" who practiced a "nefarious calling." [94]

Flores's actions afforded him little sympathy in local eyes. He did not kill in self-defense, but to evade capture. Rather than stand and fight, Flores feigned surrender and stabbed Wise with a concealed weapon before escaping. Although U.S. federal court records testify to the prevalent smuggling of mescal and provide evidence that many locals did not consider smuggling liquor as wrong, locals had tipped officers to Flores's operations because they did not want him in their community.[95] Wise's murderer stands out in his viciousness. Flores's smuggling may have fallen within the community's moral economy, but his violence made him a dangerous criminal and a pariah. No corridos sing his honor. Flores escaped to Mexico, but an "avenging justice" was reported hot on his trail.[96] Given the nature of his crime, and Flores's lack of public support, it is likely that "justice" in one form or another eventually found him.[97]

LIMITS OF THE MORAL ECONOMY

Local attitudes about gender shaped views toward women who smuggled. Whereas women's smuggling of consumer goods such as clothing for personal consumption or for their families was met with local acceptance, the amateur ferrying of mescal was objectionable because it violated *norteños'* views on proper female conduct and placed other women in jeopardy. In July 1884 an area newspaper reported that a Customs inspector in Laredo allegedly took "liberties" examining the bodies of "Mexican ladies" for contraband.[98] Although the article did not go into detail about the extensiveness of the inspection, the image of Anglo officers groping Mexican women's bodies outraged the community. Society, Anglo and ethnic Mexican, frowned on females running liquor under their skirts and resented the danger of suspicion it placed on other women.[99] Locals reported female liquor runners rather than put their loved ones at risk of search. Customs officers caught Felipa Delesa with five bladders of mescal after a local tipped them off about her.[100]

Contraband mescal supplied small local cantinas. Besides receiving smuggled goods, many, if not most, of these establishments did not pay federal and local taxes for selling alcohol and operated illegally. Women often worked as the principal managers of these underground establishments. The December 1899 docket of the U.S. District Court charged two Laredo women with failing to pay the necessary taxes for their cantinas.[101] In both cases, Mexican Americans provided the necessary information for the liquor raid. Although few Laredoans had qualms about cantinas, and mescal fit within the moral economy of the borderlands, these women's establishments exceeded local tolerance levels. Witnesses described Dolores Juárez's cantina as "one of the most notorious dives in the city."[102] Moreover, several witnesses claimed that Juárez sold to "all who wants [sic] to buy."[103] Locals did not look kindly on Juárez's seedy bar, nor did they esteem vendors who sold liquor to just anyone, including perhaps habitual drunks and children. Juárez's gender also contributed to her downfall. Laredoans did not want women working bars. Miguel Rosas's testimony that he visited Juárez's cantina "many times and paid her for it" strongly suggests that locals viewed Juárez's occupation akin to prostitution; such views contributed to the guilty verdict she received.[104] Brigida Hidalgo showed more prudence. She pled guilty after police raided her home, but told officers she sold liquor to "support her son." [105] The court set her bail at $200, which she could not afford, and she subsequently served time in jail.

Locals did not care for outsiders trafficking through their community either. On October 12, 1900, a U.S. Customs inspector discovered 255 cigars and 93 opals hidden in Thomas Bishop's baggage and on his body.[106] Bishop seems to have come to Laredo with intent to smuggle. He checked into a hotel and started a conversation with local Albert Kraff in order to gain more information and assistance in his scheme. Bishop claimed to be a member of the Odd Fellows fraternal order, as was Kraff, and Bishop persuaded his brother to go to Nuevo Laredo with him to visit a store he knew. At the store Bishop introduced himself to the manager, spoke to him for a while, and purchased 50 cigars. In the conversation the manager suggested that Bishop take the cigars out of the box in order to avoid problems with U.S. Customs officers at the bridge. Thinking the suggestion a good one, Bishop opened the box and hid the cigars under his clothes. Making it across the bridge successfully convinced Bishop that smuggling was easy money. Back in the hotel Bishop tried to talk Kraff into returning the next day for another run, but Kraff refused and asked Bishop why he did not just declare his cigars. Bishop's answer was surprisingly simple: paying "$4.50 was too high." [107]

As an Anglo outsider who trafficked for profit, Bishop fell outside the local moral economy of smuggling. Consequently, Kraff and other local witnesses testified against him. Borderland merchants may have provided Bishop with information on how to get around U.S. tariffs, but they did so to make a sale, not because Bishop's trafficking of luxury goods fell within local tolerance levels. Bishop did not risk his life or gain esteem for bravery the way mounted traffickers did. Many consumers, however, probably felt like Bishop did about smuggling goods to avoid tariffs. In fact, the store manager's advice to Bishop on hiding the cigars suggests the prevalence of tariff evasion. Still, outside smugglers were few and far between in Laredo at this time. Thomas Bishop is the only nonlocal professional smuggler in this period known to history, and that is because he failed.[108]

U.S. law enforcement used various tools to enforce the will of the state. Most, if not all, law enforcement officers working in Laredo lived in town and could identify professional smugglers.[109] Observant officers at times merely recognized "old smugglers" and stopped to search them.[110] Vigilant officers tipped each other off on whom to keep an eye on. Experience and simple luck also factored in successful arrests. Locals aided U.S. Customs in their duties by providing them tips on those who transgressed the moral economy of illicit trade.[111] In late September 1899 U.S. Customs agents acting on a tip arrested Victoriana Rodríguez with six quarts of mescal in bladders hidden under her clothes. Federal authorities had suspected Rodríguez for some time but did not have enough evidence to make an arrest. Local informant Juan Evins had reported Rodríguez's operation to authorities before, but they had failed to catch her. Having other orders, U.S. Customs inspector W. H. Gilmore could not act on Evins's information on another of Rodríguez's planned smuggling runs, so he gave Evins the "authority" to capture her himself.[112] The case of Victoriana Rodríguez is not unique. On March 10, 1900, Inspector Gilmore arrested Genevava Contreras for smuggling two gallons of mescal based on information provided by a local informant.[113] Although borderlanders resented state intrusions into their trade, to an extent locals and state officials enjoyed a reciprocal relationship of cooperation against those who transgressed the moral economy of illicit trade on the border. In fact, so important were tip-offs to contraband seizures that border people regarded cooperation as a "necessary qualification" for Customs officers and considered agents working without local aid as a "dead loss to the government and about as resourceful as a baby." [114]

At no time between 1880 and 1910 does the record show locals giving either U.S. or Mexican Customs agents information against persons who smuggled foodstuffs or staple household items like calico.[115] The community, however, did tip Customs agents off to dangerous individuals and "unsavory" female mescal smugglers to rid themselves of pariahs and enforce gender codes.[116] Outsiders like Bishop transgressed the local moral economy by trafficking luxury goods for profit. Whereas locals accepted saving a few dollars as just or sang the praises of professional smugglers of consumer goods like Mariano Reséndez, they resented Bishop's trafficking as shameless and criminal. For example, informant Albert Kraff testified that after Bishop successfully smuggled 255 cigars, Bishop tried to convince Kraff to help him traffic 8,000 or 10,000 more.[117] Ultimately, Bishop planned to leave town the same way he arrived: by rail. If other outsiders followed Bishop's example by attempting to use Laredo as a place to traffic, locals could expect more vigilant Customs agents, and that is something contrabandistas did not want. People like Bishop gave smugglers a bad name and threatened popular smuggling by provoking further government surveillance.

THE ZONA LIBRE AND U.S.-MEXICAN RELATIONS

Smuggling through the Zona Libre only mounted after Porfirio Díaz extended the free-trade zone across the length of the border in 1885. C. E. Hodson, an American correspondent working in Mexico in 1888, wrote that onerous Mexican customs duties led to a "flourishing contraband trade" that extended as far as Saltillo, Coahuila, some two hundred miles from the border.[118] Hodson noted that American-made goods in Saltillo sold for three times their original price, with basic goods such as nails, which cost five cents a pound in Texas, selling for fifteen cents a pound in Saltillo. Individuals like Mariano Reséndez and organized groups of smugglers made their living trafficking imports out of the Zona Libre south into Mexico. Reséndez, the "known smuggler" whom Matías Romero asked for U.S. assistance in apprehending, could speak for many traffickers in his apocryphal statement, "Come and get your calicos at the same price as on the other side, for my overhead is low and the profits great."[119]

The United States' lackluster response to Romero's request for aid against Mariano Reséndez revealed not only apathy to Mexico's dilemma, but a certain satisfaction in Mexico's struggle against smuggling. The State Department forwarded Romero's note to the governor of Texas, the U.S. Department of Justice, and the U.S. Treasury (which oversaw the U.S. Customs Service), but little seems to have happened. Although the Department of State instructed regional officials to prevent Mexico-bound smugglers from operating on U.S. soil, American agents on the ground claimed ignorance.[120] Texas Governor Lawrence "Sul" Ross wrote back to the U.S. Department of State saying that Romero's note was the first informing him of Mariano Reséndez. To add insult to injury, criticism of Romero's request appeared in American newspapers. In mid-May 1887 newspapers in San Antonio, St. Louis, and New Orleans carried articles stating that Romero was "wrong . . . and way off in his conclusions."[121] "None of the officers here have ever heard of [Mariano Reséndez] and . . . compared to ten years ago, there is no smuggling whatever on the Rio Grande."[122]

U.S. criticism over Romero's request for aid against Reséndez originated in American opposition of Mexico's free-trade zone along the border. Many Anglo merchants feared that the Zona Libre adversely affected their best interests in two important ways. First, it facilitated the smuggling of goods into the United States. Whereas low tariffs lured Mexican citizens to immigrate to Texas, many merchants north of the river moved

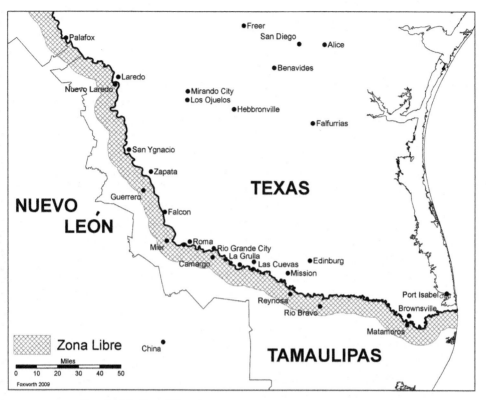

MAP 1. *Detail of the Zona Libre circa 1890.*

their operations south where they could sell their goods duty-free. Invariably, many borderlanders north of the river took their Mexico-bought wares illicitly into Texas. Secondly, the Zona Libre took away from U.S. exports by making European-made goods affordable to consumers on both sides of the Rio Grande. Exempt from U.S. and Mexican national tariffs, European goods could travel in bond to Mexico's border cities and compete advantageously with American-made goods.[123]

Contrary to American fears, the Zona Libre actually caused more smuggling into Mexico than the United States. American anxieties about the effects of the Zona Libre were almost entirely unfounded, with one U.S. commercial agent placing the value of goods smuggled into the United States at less than 5 percent of the value of products trafficked from the United States into Mexico.[124] Distance and transportation expenses kept most European goods out of the Zona Libre, while proximity ensured that most of the items imported into Mexico through the Free

Zone originated from the United States.[125] The U.S. government and merchants north of the border felt little concern at the unlawful trade in "red chili peppers, and a few articles of wearing apparel" and dismissed smuggling along the Zona Libre as petty consumption by poor border Mexicans.[126] Indeed, at the end of the nineteenth century Americans felt less threatened by smuggling along their southern border and regarded the moonlit river crossings of contraband silks, satins, and "gleaming cutlery from France" into the United States a thing of the past.[127]

Mexico also grew tired of the Zona Libre. Matías Romero himself advocated against the Zona Libre because the smuggling that occurred there denied the Mexican government substantial customs revenues. In fact, Romero convinced Porfirio Díaz to close the Tamaulipas ports of Mier and Camargo for a time because of rampant smuggling.[128] How Díaz and Romero hoped to stem contraband trade by making all international commerce across a thirty-mile stretch of the border illegal remains a mystery. The Zona Libre began in 1858 as an attempt by Mexican border states to stop the depopulation of their towns along the Rio Grande as their people fled onerous Mexican tariffs, but by the end of the nineteenth century the Free Zone no longer seemed necessary. The arrival of the railroad undermined proponents' arguments that Mexican border communities needed the Zona Libre because of their isolation from domestic markets. Moreover, in 1896 Mexico abandoned the *alcabala* on interstate commerce and the inflated prices on goods that came with it. President Díaz along with many of the country's leading economists also feared that the Zona Libre stifled domestic industry by making American manufactured goods so affordable. Feeling that the Free Zone had outlived its time, Porfirio Díaz abolished it by presidential decree on July 1, 1905.[129]

CONCLUSION

As the United States and Mexico attempted to consolidate their hold on the border and to raise vital national revenue, they continued to collect tariffs that interfered with local commerce on the borderlands. Many locals resisted what they regarded as arbitrary state barriers to free trade by smuggling. Anglo and ethnic Mexican locals accepted some forms of smuggling as just and continued to trade illicitly within a moral economy of smuggling. Mexico's and the United States' attempts to police their borders and enforce national tariff laws largely failed because smugglers benefitted from community support. State power consequently faced limits against a persisting transborder economy of illicit trade. Still, the U.S. and Mexican governments' efforts to impose and collect tariffs succeeded to a fault. While both governments failed to stop illicit trade, Mexican and U.S. tariffs and tariff enforcement were significant enough to make smuggling profitable and gave rise to traffickers like J. Archibald and folk heroes like Mariano Reséndez.

That contrabandistas continued to smuggle in spite of the state not only shows the limits of state power on the border, but also demonstrates border people's ability to bring the state into accommodation with local values. Border people formed their own ethics on acceptable and unacceptable illicit trade beyond the dictates of federal law. Communities along the Rio Grande may have existed on the "bordered lands" of state control, but border people on both sides of the river continued to routinely subvert government authority through smuggling.[130] Smugglers were neither "primitive rebels" who sought to engage the state, nor "social bandits," but rather acted more as consumers and merchants.[131] Despite his numerous outcries, Matías Romero himself believed Mariano Reséndez's motivations were primarily economic, not intentionally subversive.[132] Rather than being revolutionists, smugglers were opportunists who exploited state weakness to save money and entrepreneurs who filled a niche created by high national tariffs.

By 1900 contrabandistas succeeded in making illicit trade an accepted fact of life. In May 1906 all a local newspaper could say about the subject was that the U.S. federal court had a few minor smuggling cases to address, "no cases of importance."[133] Yet smuggling along the border was about to change. On July 27, 1909, the Mexican consul in Laredo warned his superiors that unknown persons had recently trafficked four hundred Mauser rifles into the country.[134] In the years to come, both the United States and Mexico would spend less effort enforcing tariff collection and concentrate more on preventing the smuggling of prohibited items that endangered the state.

PART II

Prohibiting Criminal Consumption

THREE

Smugglers in Dangerous Times

REVOLUTION AND WAR, 1910–1919

O n December 24, 1910, Robert W. Dowe, U.S. customs collector for the port of Eagle Pass, sat down and wrote a potentially career-ending letter to the U.S. consul in Ciudad Porfirio Díaz (present-day Piedras Negras). Although Customs had for years worked to protect American sovereignty on the border, its enforcement of U.S. neutrality laws interfered with the agents' traditional role as revenue collectors, and Dowe no longer felt comfortable seeing his men stray from their organization's founding mission. Rather than employ his agents in the task of preventing arms smuggling out of the country, Dowe chose to defy State Department wishes and ordered his men to "confine their efforts to the enforcement of the customs laws and the protection of the revenue."[1] For Dowe, keeping illegal arms out of Mexico became a secondary concern.

Collector Dowe's protests ran contrary to a shift in U.S. priorities on the border. Between the years of the onset of the Mexican Revolution and the First World War, the U.S. Customs Service on the border transformed from primarily being a revenue-collecting agency to being a national security force. Customs agents joined various federal and state units in border patrols guarding against revolutionaries, seditionists, and enemy aliens and treated their mission as tariff collectors as a secondary duty. Although Customs and other U.S. forces still maintained their vigilance against smugglers, they did so for different reasons than they had earlier. Rather than prosecute illicit traders for tariff evasion, courts tried smugglers for their violations of U.S. neutrality laws and for taking vital materiel needed for the war effort out of the country. Tariff collection gave way to neutrality enforcement as the U.S. government came to rely on internal taxes rather than tariff duties as its principal source of national revenue.

As the United States focused its energies to guard against new threats, the contrabandista community itself adjusted to the impact of international security concerns on local markets. Whereas the U.S. and Mexican governments viewed arms smuggling as a violation of neutrality, those in sympathy with the various movements bought arms and took them across the Rio Grande into Mexico with little regard for the law. Local U.S. merchants cashed in by selling arms to all buyers against the wishes of the federal government. Most of these illegal arms sales fell within the local moral economy of illicit trade on the border. World War I–related trade restrictions on foodstuffs such as sugar and lard, coupled with food shortages in war-ravaged Mexico, created a market for contraband consumables that entrepreneurial border people readily filled. Although many borderlanders benefited from food smuggling and accepted it as licit trade, the trafficking of foodstuffs and basic consumer goods worked to the detriment of law-abiding businesses that struggled to compete against the black market. Still, border people's economic and personal motives trumped U.S. prohibitions on arms and food exports and frustrated state efforts to regulate this trade on the border.

LOS DOS LAREDOS

In the fall of 1910 the people of Laredo could see signs of progress all around them. The railroads that had entered the community nineteen years earlier brought unprecedented growth and development. Laredo's population increased from 11,319 in 1890 to 14,855 in 1910.[2] Agriculture boomed as pumps carried river water to 1,200 acres of onions bringing forth twenty thousand pounds of produce per acre. Electricity, running water, and streetcars serviced downtown Laredo and promised to extend to the city's outlying areas. George Washington's Birthday was quickly developing into the community's main celebration, complete with parades and mock Indian battles. Laredoans celebrated another occasion on the sixteenth of September 1910 as they commemorated the one hundredth anniversary of Mexico's independence. One month after the celebration, as the sounds of the bullfights, baseball games, and twenty-one-gun salutes that marked the festivities faded, a disguised Francisco Madero entered Laredo on his way to ignite the movement that would oust Porfirio Díaz. The revolution Madero unleashed plunged Mexico into a civil

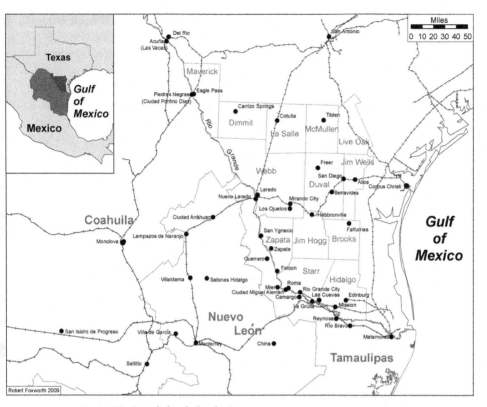

MAP 2. *Lower Rio Grande borderlands circa 1910.*

war that would ravage his country for years. Moreover, the Mexican Revolution did not remain within Mexico, but spilled north of the border with supporters of various factions scheming to aid their countrymen from their bases in the United States. In 1910, however, the arms trafficking and violence that would singe Laredo remained a year away. Madero's appeal in the Plan de San Luis Potosí did not cause a new day to dawn over the border, and casual smuggling continued.[3]

LICIT AND ILLICIT LIQUOR

Revolution and war did not change border people's desire for a drink, and mescal liquor smuggling's acceptance by the community continued to be contingent on the scale of the operation, the gender of the smuggler, and the way he or she chose to smuggle it. At about 10:00 p.m. on

November 2, 1910, U.S. Customs Inspector J. A. Burnett noticed local María Martínez crossing the international footbridge into Laredo. Perhaps because he thought it strange for a woman to travel alone at night, Burnett suspected her of smuggling. Whatever prompted Inspector Burnett to stop Martínez, his hunch proved correct. Upon being stopped and asked to declare her goods, Martínez removed a gallon of mescal hidden in a bladder underneath her skirt.[4] Nothing in the report indicates that U.S. Customs officials searched María Martínez, but male inspectors had regularly searched women before to great local disdain.[5] Customs Inspector Robert Rumsey did not give Felipe González the same courtesy that Inspector Burnett gave María Martínez. Rather than ask González if he had anything to declare upon crossing the footbridge into Laredo, Rumsey stopped and "searched him." [6] Even in the macho world of the borderlands, a certain decorum regarding women's bodies needed to be observed. Although agents had looked up women's skirts in search of contraband in the past, by 1910 Progressive-era concerns regarding professionalism mandated officers use greater discretion in apprehending female contrabandistas.[7]

Laredo's first female customs agents arrived in 1913. Unlike their male counterparts, female customs inspectors, or "inspectresses" as they were known, did not patrol for smugglers. Rather, their duties were limited to searching female suspects and writing up ads for auctions on seized goods.[8] On October 20, 1913, Juana Pequeño crossed the international footbridge into Laredo with two and a half gallons of mescal.[9] Customs Inspector Lyle Perkins made the arrest, but "Inspectress" Ada Pereira frisked the suspect.[10] Female agents did work in higher echelons of the Customs Service, however. Mary Devine, for instance, served as a deputy collector of customs. Unlike Ada Pereira, whose duties as an inspectress involved searching bodies, Mary Devine's job as a deputy collector included assessing customs duties and charging males and females suspected of smuggling. Late in January 1915 Deputy Devine wrote a judicial complaint against Miguel Castro for bringing five quarts of mescal illicitly into Laredo. Devine's actions led Castro to plead guilty, and the court ordered him to jail after he defaulted on his fifty dollar bail.[11]

Suspects' age and health mattered in the contrabandista community. Early in June 1910 U.S. Customs agents stopped Rosalio Escobedo at the international ferry at Eagle Pass with three quarts and two half-pints of mescal. Rather than arrest him, Deputy Collector Luke Dowe, Collector Robert Dowe's brother, released Escobedo because he was "old and apparently in bad health."[12] In a letter to his brother, whom he professionally referred to as "The Collector," Luke Dowe mentioned that he believed this to be Escobedo's first offense. Still, the officer gave Escobedo's clean past as only a secondary reason for his release. Instead of ordering Escobedo's arrest and trial for violations of U.S. tariff duties, Deputy Collector Dowe took pity on a sick, aged man and let him go. Evidence of Escobedo's age as a factor in his release is reinforced by Customs' harsher treatment of Serapio Martínez. Martínez lied about having dutiable merchandise, and when authorities discovered one gallon of mescal concealed in his pulled wagon, they seized his liquor and hack rather than overlook the offense.[13]

Copious mescal-smuggling charges in the U.S. District Court provide evidence of rampant liquor running along the border. Of the 122 cases examined from between 1910 and 1920, thirty-six concerned liquor smuggling.[14] Still, this does not mean that liquor smuggling fell outside the moral economy of illicit trade. Close scrutiny of mescal cases reveals that most arrests came without community aid. Arresting Customs agents were the most common witnesses when liquor cases came to trial. For instance, U.S. Customs agent Rumsey happened upon Felipe González smuggling one gallon of mescal and served as the sole witness against him.[15] Customs agents Ed Cotulla and John Chamberlain served as the only witnesses against Macedonio Martínez in his trial for smuggling one and a half gallons of mescal.[16] Locals rarely acted as witnesses against petty mescal smugglers. Of the dozens of liquor smuggling cases examined in the decade before Prohibition, only two involved a community witness and government tip-off.[17] Local juries gave not-guilty verdicts to four of the fourteen mescal smugglers who pleaded innocent. Even suspects who resisted government authorities could sometimes persuade juries to release them. At approximately 6:00 p.m. March 16, 1913, Customs Inspector Sam McKenzie noticed Ursulo Guzmán crossing into the United States and stopped to search him. According to Inspector McKenzie, Guzmán responded by attempting to draw a six-and-a-half-inch double-edged knife. Inspector McKenzie struck Guzmán with his gun and took from him three pints of assorted liquor. Guzmán pleaded innocent to Inspector McKenzie's charges, and despite the officer's testimony and the seized liquor as direct evidence, a local jury found Guzmán innocent. Perhaps locals sided with Guzmán because they did not believe McKenzie's story. Indeed, Guzmán may not have brandished a knife at all, but might merely have had one on his person. Guzmán, like other liquor smugglers, could also have pulled a knife to puncture the bladders that contained the evidence against him, not to slash at the arresting officer.[18] Moreover, seeing the visible signs of McKenzie's pistol whipping on Guzmán's face, the jury may have decided that he had suffered enough.[19]

Liquor smugglers' tendency to plead guilty is attributable to several factors. Law enforcement agents may have intimidated suspects into pleading guilty. Suspects caught red-handed could have simply acknowledged their guilt. Many petty smugglers also lacked money for a proper defense council and simply chose to throw themselves on the mercy of the court. Suspects knew that courts often showed leniency to petty offenders, with most convicted smugglers serving between ten days to six months in local jails. The court did not sentence any convicted tariff evader to the maximum two-year sentence and $5,000 fine.[20]

TARIFFS AND BORDER SECURITY

After decades of national debate between protectionist and liberal trade policy proponents, internal taxes came to replace tariff revenues as the principal source of U.S. government income in the early twentieth century. Tariffs served as the source of 40–60 percent of the U.S. government's revenue between 1865 and 1913, the year Congress approved the Sixteenth Amendment instituting a national income tax. Only about 2 percent of American households paid the income tax in 1913, and tariff and internal tax revenues on tobacco and alcohol continued to serve as the U.S. government's principal source of funds early in the 1910s. By 1920, however, tariffs composed only 5 percent of the national revenue, with personal and corporate income taxes supplying 57.9 percent of the U.S. government's budget during the 1930s. Customs revenue still flowed to the federal treasury, but increasing reliance on internal taxes, coupled with the Mexican Revolution's and First World War's simultaneous threats to U.S. neutrality, prompted the Customs Service to act less like an agency of economic security and more as a national security force.[21]

The U.S. Customs Service, although instituted to collect tariffs and gather federal revenue, had long worked in national security, but with revolution throwing the U.S. and Mexican borderlands into crisis, physical security trumped economics as a national priority. Customs officers' shift from principally being tariff collectors to being border security agents came gradually. In March 1911 Deputy Collector Luke Dowe and his fellow inspectors logged over 4,400 miles in their patrols. Dowe noted, however, that mounted Customs guards covered 1,744 of those miles serving as scouts for the U.S. Cavalry searching for neutrality violators, and only 2,679 patrol miles were devoted to "protecting the revenue." [22] In fact, Customs forces routinely abandoned their duties as tariff collectors to enforce neutrality. A typical neutrality enforcement operation occurred thirty miles west of Del Rio early in 1911. In January of that year, Deputy Collector Dowe and several other mounted inspectors left their jobs as tariff enforcers to investigate a report of a wagon carrying contraband arms into Mexico. Dowe and the other agents searched for several days before coming upon a partially burnt heap of empty U.M.C. cartridge boxes at the Rio Grande's edge. Inspectors' subsequent search of a nearby ranch uncovered one horse, two rifles, and 144 cartridges that they believed smugglers had left behind. [23]

As the United States turned to internal taxes as its principal source of revenue, it also cut certain tariffs, making many previously illicit trades licit. Democratic tariff reform enacted under President Woodrow Wilson in 1913 reduced duties on the "necessaries of life." [24] The *Laredo Weekly Times* pointed out that many of the items now duty-free were of "especial interest to housewives." [25] Basic foodstuffs such as milk, cream, flour, eggs, and meat could now be crossed free of charge, and rates on other household items like woolen and cotton clothing, blankets, and table linen were also greatly reduced. U.S. tariff reform dramatically altered the U.S. District Court's emphasis and notions of criminality in the borderlands. Prior to these changes, economics dominated court business in the southern divisions of Laredo and Brownsville. Tariff-evasion cases made up over 75 percent of the southern district's criminal docket at the end of the nineteenth century, but declined significantly in the first decades of the twentieth century. [26]

The few tariff-evasion cases that did go before the court largely concerned the gross fraud of revenue by traffickers of luxury goods. For instance, on August 12, 1914, Customs Inspector Robert Rumsey apprehended Julia Cárdenas and Gerónimo Villarreal attempting to evade import duties on an assortment of jewelry valued at $3,544. [27] Among the small treasure trove that Cárdenas and Villarreal illicitly introduced were a gold watch and chain, a pair of diamond earrings, and seven diamond rings. Villarreal and Cárdenas pleaded innocent, claiming that they had not bought the jewelry to resell in the United States, but instead for their "personal adornment." [28] Posing as affluent shoppers, they hoped to avoid trafficking charges. Whether their assertion was true or not is debatable. Customs officers saw Cárdenas and Villarreal as criminals regardless. Even if they intended the jewelry for their personal use, they failed to declare $3,544 of dutiable material, and therefore acted as traffickers. A similar instance occurred on March 1, 1916, when Customs Inspector Rumsey apprehended local merchant Naser Ach Hatem unlawfully importing an assortment of clothing valuing $150. Hatem's sheer audacity caught Rumsey's attention. Taking a few personal articles across the border was one thing, but Hatem tried to evade duties on thirteen silk scarves, thirty-nine shirtwaist fronts, twenty-four silk handkerchiefs, and thirty-seven hemmed table centerpieces, to mention but a few of the hundreds of items he sought to bring illicitly into the United States. Such brazen affronts to American law insulted federal authorities and contributed to Hatem's arrest.[29]

Hatem's, Cárdenas's, and Villarreal's arrests for tariff evasion on luxury goods are notable exceptions in a court record otherwise filled with petty smugglers, neutrality violators, and war trade offenders. Government prosecution of consumer item traffickers had more to do with smugglers' affronts to the "dignity of the United States" than their denial of needed customs revenue. The words "against the peace and dignity of the United States" that appear at the end of all smuggling charges are telling. Although tariff-violation indictments charged suspects with "intent to defraud the revenue" of the United States, the federal government no longer relied on tariffs as its principal source of income.[30] However, traffickers' audacity offended the government, motivating it to punish offenders.

REVOLUTIONARY SMUGGLING

U.S. and Mexican federal forces descended on their shared borderlands to protect their territories and police weapons trafficking arming the revolution. Additional U.S. Calvary units patrolled the South Texas countryside as early as January 1911, and on March 3 of that year a small biplane took off from Fort McIntosh on a surveillance mission along the border to Eagle Pass. The army pilots observed no signs of gunrunners or enemy movements that day, but more significantly, their flight was the first service mission for U.S. military aviation.[31] Arms smuggling in South Texas increased after the fall of Ciudad Juárez and Porfirio Díaz's resignation on May 25, 1911. The largest force of Texas Rangers assembled until that time arrived in Laredo that fall after hearing that former Díaz general Bernardo Reyes planned to use the American town as a base against Mexico's new president, Francisco Madero. On November 20, 1911, Texas Rangers captured a Mexican Army captain and discovered a cache of rifles and 60 dynamite bombs that he had amassed in town. Texas Rangers and other American forces would go on to seize over 152 horses, 21,000 cartridges, and more than 100 rifles during their heightened occupation of the community that fall.[32]

In lamenting locals' lack of cooperation in their investigation, Deputy Collector Luke Dowe complained that "ninety-nine percent of the Mexican population residing along the Texas border are in sympathy with the revolutionists as well as a great many of the American ranchmen." [33] This support led some individuals to manipulate U.S. federal forces to their advantage. Rival factions controlled Nuevo Laredo in 1911, but Madero's promise of a democratic Mexico gained him supporters in los dos Laredos and prompted Maderistas to tip off American authorities to their enemies' activities when they could. Late in November 1911 a young ethnic Mexican boy informed Customs Inspector Rumsey of a hoard of Mauser rifles and ammunition that Reyistas had hidden in a field outside of town. In the uncertain atmosphere of the Mexican Revolution, even the hated *rinches* (a term Tejanos applied generally to U.S. law enforcement) could prove allies.[34]

Government investigations into gunrunning through Laredo revealed the extent of arms trafficking within the community. Rather than finding mounted bandits or hardened criminals, authorities discovered local elites involved in arms smuggling. Suspect Amador Sánchez, descended from one of Laredo's founding families, served as Laredo's mayor from 1901–1910 and worked as the sheriff of Webb County at the time of his arrest. Sánchez's sympathies resided with his old friend, Mexican expatriate Bernardo Reyes, then plotting against Madero's government.[35] Authorities uncovered that Sánchez had used the county jail as a storehouse for weapons destined to be smuggled to Mexico, and on November 16, 1911, a local grand jury indicted him for conspiracy to violate the neutrality laws of the United States.[36] Sánchez pleaded guilty, but the former political boss never served time behind bars. The court fined Sánchez $1,200 for his role in the plot, which he promptly paid and returned to work as the county sheriff. Although several of Sheriff Sánchez's coconspirators could not afford to pay their fines and were ordered to jail, Sánchez used his power to grant them special privileges such as allowing them to go home at night.[37]

Political rivalries with other members of the local elite finally dethroned Sánchez in 1914, but it is significant that a convicted felon could remain county sheriff and president of the Webb County school board. Five months after his conviction, Sánchez's political ties secured him a presidential pardon. Still, Sánchez's recovery from his conviction for violating U.S. neutrality laws was more than an example of local corruption; it illustrates locals' acceptance of arms smuggling.[38]

NEUTRALITY VIOLATIONS

Arms trafficking may have captured headlines, but it is important to remember that U.S. neutrality laws affected ordinary borderlanders as well. National and international crises affected government border policies in ways that locals scarcely anticipated. Francisco Madero succeeded in ousting Porfirio Díaz in May 1911, but Madero's new government itself faced a series of revolts. Early in 1912 Pascual Orozco, a military commander who had once supported Madero, rebelled against the embattled president. Orozco based his rebellion in northern Mexico, plunging the border into further chaos. In response to the ongoing turmoil in Mexico, the U.S. Congress passed a resolution prohibiting the export of arms or ammunition to any country in the hemisphere where conditions of domestic unrest prevailed. Late in February 1913 Laredoan Pedro Villarreal knowingly or unknowingly violated the arms ban when he attempted to take a .22 caliber rifle and three hundred rounds of ammunition across the border into Mexico. Although it is highly unlikely that Villarreal took his .22 caliber Savage rifle in order to wage war in Mexico, American neutrality laws were strictly enforced, and the court ordered Villarreal to jail after he defaulted on his $500 bail.[39]

It is interesting to imagine Villarreal's thoughts over his quandary. Did he understand that by carrying a rifle and ammunition across the river he violated an American presidential proclamation and U.S. federal law? Records do not indicate how federal agents discovered Villarreal. Did he try to cross the border at the bridge, or did federal authorities arrest him as he tried to ford the river? Did he hide the rifle and the ammunition, or did he carry them openly, unaware that carrying arms across the border, even those for personal use, ran contrary to U.S. law? Villarreal did have approval from Nuevo Laredo's colonel *jefe de armas* (chief of arms) to take the rifle to his residence in Nuevo Laredo, but this permission did nothing to excuse his actions in the eyes of U.S. law. Villarreal may have felt his sentence an injustice, but he was pragmatic. A plea of innocent that ended in a guilty verdict would likely lead to a stiffer sentence than a plea of guilty. Lacking the money for attorney fees, he pleaded guilty of violating U.S. neutrality laws.[40]

Illicit Mexican arms came from established American merchants. Although U.S. law prohibited arms shipments to Mexico, gun orders for Texas towns boomed as local businessmen became international arms dealers. Hardware stores transformed into small armories as Anglo and Mexican American merchants became outfitters for anyone with money to buy.[41] Fighters' preference for the .30-30 Winchester carbine was such that the American rifle inspired its own popular corrido.[42] Because customs enforcement occurred at the border, Customs officers could do little but watch on as guns left shelves in broad daylight. Many buyers took their arms purchases to "out of the way places" and smuggled them after nightfall.[43] Arms sales along the border became so great that hardware stores struggled to keep up with demand.[44] Manuel Guerra, the proprietor of Guerra & Son of Roma, Texas, engaged in arms dealings so extensive the Mexican government took note. Late in September 1912 Alberto Leal, the Mexican consul in Rio Grande City, wrote his superiors that U.S. Customs had recently seized three thousand rounds of .30-30 shells consigned to "Manuel Guerra, a *mexicotexano* who is always involved in our civil difficulties to profit from the sale of arms and horses."[45] Aside from the seizure, Leal's informants warned that Guerra awaited another order of two thousand rounds of .30-30 shells and over ten thousand rounds of other assorted ammo.[46]

Personal sympathies factored in some arms sales, but legitimate businessmen's involvement in the arms trade kept weapons smuggling within the moral economy of the borderlands. While people died by the thousands in the chaos of the Mexican Revolution, U.S. gun merchants cashed in by running ads in border papers. A particularly colorful ad by an American arms company appeared in a prominent Spanish-language paper in the fall of 1910. Translated, the ad read, "Do you want a good rifle? Remember that an unarmed man is of no value. Write today[.] . . . It is our desire that each Mexican has a rifle."[47] Locals similarly exploited the booming gun market. Joseph Netzer decorated his show window in downtown Laredo with life-sized models of Remington Arms' trademark bear cubs, "armed to the teeth" with rifles they held in their paws.[48]

In the fall of 1913 an agent for the Bureau of Investigation (the precursor of the FBI) operating in Laredo looked deeper into Netzer's disturbingly large arms orders. Further sleuthing revealed that Netzer had sold nine thousand rounds of seven-millimeter ammunition to a Mexican citizen and that Netzer awaited an additional order for 160 .30-30 rifles and seven thousand shells. The .30-30s could be for sport, although they were more likely intended for war. Seven-millimeter rounds, however, were

FIGURE 3.1. *"Business is Business." Cartoon of a (cigarette?) smoking, sombrero-wearing Mexican buying ammunition from a shadowy figure across the border. In reality a great deal of illegal arms sales took place in stores during broad daylight. This 1917 clipping is part of a collection confiscated by U.S. military intelligence authorities in Germany following World War II. Library of Congress.*

strictly military-grade ammunition commonly used in machine guns. Nor was this the limit of Netzer's enterprises. An examination of Netzer's account books uncovered that he had sold twenty thousand seven-millimeter cartridges for $784,000 on a single day in October of that year. When questioned, Netzer claimed he could not remember the name of the man who made the purchases, only that the buyer had paid in cash. Bureau of Investigation agents delving into railroad shipping records revealed that in addition to Netzer's orders of guns and ammo, he also received blasting caps and explosives for which he could not account. Investigators further discovered that Netzer sold his arms to a local grocer who worked as a middleman for Mexican arms buyers.[49]

Jurors heard this seemingly compelling evidence against Netzer yet refused to indict him. Although Netzer had clearly broken federal law, he had not transgressed beyond the bounds of the moral economy of smuggling in the borderlands. Indeed, locals do not seem to have regarded Netzer as a criminal at all. After all, Netzer did not transport contraband across the border; he sold merchandise out of his establishment. He was a prominent businessman who served on the board of directors for the local chamber of commerce; breaking national laws simply made his business more profitable.[50] No matter what the law said, locals did not see selling prohibited arms destined to be smuggled as a punishable crime. Even Mayor Robert M. McComb reputedly sold arms to revolutionaries.[51] Indicted neutrality violators and suspected illicit-arms dealers not only evaded prison sentences, Netzer and others like him continued to live active community lives. In 1914 Netzer reprised his role as the president of the Washington Birthday Celebration Association (WBCA), the trustees of the community's largest and most lucrative festival, which he helped establish.[52] Subsequent federal investigations into Netzer's suspicious sales of pistol ammunition in 1919 did not prevent him from serving as president of the WBCA until 1923.[53] Charlie Deutz, whose gun advertisements routinely competed with those of Netzer, would go on to serve as the president of the WBCA in 1930.[54] That Netzer and others overcame their charges indicates that illicit trade and licit business overlapped in the borderlands and that smuggling, even in some cases gun smuggling, could be seen as acceptable in local eyes.[55] After a lifetime of community activity, Joseph Netzer's death in July of 1937 made front-page news. Among the many words of praise in the local newspaper, perhaps the most telling was the sentence stating, "He never turned down any proposition that was for the good of Laredo."[56]

Perhaps because President Wilson agreed to allow arms shipments to their enemies in February of 1914, retreating soldiers loyal to Mexican dictator Victoriano Huerta attempted to dynamite the international and railroad bridges leading across to Laredo. U.S. Army sharpshooters foiled the attempt, but exchanges of rifle fire across the border became increasingly common after the battle. Late in April of that year Huertistas put Nuevo Laredo to the torch rather than surrender the city to Constitutionalist forces loyal to former Madero supporter and northern strongman Venustiano Carranza. The greater part of Nuevo Laredo, including the city's archives, burned in the fire. Still, the worst was yet to come. In early 1915 Anglo authorities discovered a manifesto allegedly written by Mexican and Mexican American revolutionaries intent on reclaiming the U.S. Southwest. The Plan de San Diego, as the document came to be called for the Texas town in which it was supposedly signed, called for a "Liberating Army for Races and Peoples" comprised of ethnic Mexicans, African Americans, Japanese, and American Indians to attack and kill Anglo men over the age of sixteen and form an independent republic.[57] The plan, coupled with *sediciosos'* (seditionists) cross-border raids in the Lower Rio Grande Valley that summer sent shock waves among Anglo communities. Not to be outdone in terror, Texas Rangers and Anglo vigilantes struck back against any ethnic Mexican they perceived to be a threat, killing hundreds of Tejanos in a vicious counterinsurgency.[58]

The genocidal violence suffered in the Lower Rio Grande Valley, however, did not spread to communities farther west along the border. Ethnoracial tensions upriver were not as strained as those in the valley, where Anglos usurped Tejano ranches in order to create an economy based on commercial agriculture. Moreover, vigilante and Texas Ranger violence focused on areas of *sedicioso* activity, itself largely limited to the lower valley. Laredo's interethnic elite also helped prevent the worst abuses from spreading to the community.[59] Such was Tejano influence in the city that Laredo hosted El Primer Congreso Mexicanista in 1911. Meeting from September 14 to 21, the Congreso convened Mexican American representatives from throughout the state and Mexican consuls in Texas to discuss Mexican American civil rights. The ideas addressed that week took decades to bear fruit, but it is important to point out that ethnic Mexicans' position of strength in Laredo set it apart from the greater history of Mexican American marginalization in the Southwest.[60]

WHITE-COLLAR CONTRABANDISTAS

Even in the midst of revolution, the smuggling of luxury goods continued. Despite, or perhaps because of, the chaos surrounding the Mexican Revolution, trade between the United States and Mexico increased dramatically between 1911 and 1920. In 1911 documented U.S. imports from Mexico totaled to $57,450,111, and U.S. exports to Mexico amounted to $61,281,715. By 1920 the U.S. imported goods valuing $179,331,755 from Mexico and exported to Mexico $207,858,497 worth of material.[61] U.S. and Mexican federal forces rode the borderlands of their respective countries in search of revolutionaries and enemy aliens, but opportunistic smugglers continued to casually evade tariffs. State vigilance against tariff evaders, however, took a much different form than government efforts against neutrality violators. The occasional pistol whipping or shooting marked encounters with *mescaleros* (mescal smugglers) and arms traffickers, but elites did not accept violence against people smuggling luxury items. Take for example a local newspaper's suggestion to inspectors that rather than simply searching for and seizing prohibited aigrette feathers, inspectors "inform women . . . that the law forbids the introduction of such plumage . . . and that the trimmings must be removed . . . and turned over to the customs authorities." [62] Customs agents could stop and search men and women for mescal, but the community insisted that inspectors be "very courteous" to those bringing in luxury goods.[63]

Aside from the casual smuggler of articles for personal consumption, many border people's work involved smuggling. Illicit trade was simply part of business on the border. On about August 10, 1916, four men hatched an elaborate smuggling scheme of transatlantic proportions. Charles Levi and Harry Ahrens were two New Yorkers who wanted bird of paradise feathers and wanted them badly. Perhaps because the World War in Europe prompted U.S. Customs forces in New York to be extra vigilant, the easiest way for them to get an order from England was not through the port of New York, but from Laredo, Texas. Just how Levi and Ahrens hatched this plan is unclear, but it seems it helped to know someone with connections on the border. Using a middleman, Levi and Ahrens contacted John A. Nottonson of Webb County. Late in August of 1916 Levi and Ahrens provided Nottonson with $300 to make the proper arrangements in Mexico. Nottonson apparently spent the money bribing Mexican Customs officers and regional police captains between Nuevo Laredo and the port of Tampico. A month after Nottonson's entry into Mexico his financiers provided him with \$1,940.37 to cable Benjamin Williams & Co. of London, England, for an order of bird of paradise feathers. Nottonson smuggled over \$5,000 in plumage from Mexico to New York for Levi and Ahrens before Customs officials discovered the scheme and arrested the three conspirators. Whether or not Nottonson ever worked as a middleman for any other Eastern importers is unknown, but men like him served as entrepreneurial facilitators for transnational traffickers.[64]

John Bruni's role in the smuggling scheme is unclear, but his name is listed among those indicted for conspiracy. Unlike the others, however, Bruni belonged to a prominent Laredo family. John Bruni's father, Antonio Mateo Bruni, had immigrated to Laredo from Bedonia, a small village in the Apennine Mountains in northern Italy. A. M. Bruni founded a general store in Laredo in 1877 and did very well for himself and his family. Using the profits from the store, A. M. Bruni invested in city property and sheep ranching. Before he died in 1931 A. M. Bruni's accumulated holdings included 13,402 cattle, 468 horses, and almost half a million dollars in undervalued Depression-era real estate.[65] Through his hard work and prudent investing, Bruni elevated himself to the cadre of the *gente decente*, the Laredo elite. His money and his standing allowed Bruni to help his son John when he was indicted with Nottonson for conspiring to smuggle the feathers into the United States. What exactly the court accused John Bruni of doing is not mentioned in the docket, and this omission alone suggests that A. M. Bruni had some influence on the Laredo court. Whereas Nottonson did not have an attorney and pleaded guilty, Bruni's family money allowed him to hire a lawyer and plead innocent. A. M. Bruni paid \$2,000 for surety on his son's bond, and John remained free until trial. The presence of Robert F. Alexander and other members of the *gente decente* on the jury assured that John Bruni returned home at the proceedings' conclusion.[66]

John Bruni's involvement moving precious feathers into the United States shows how smuggling and legitimate business overlapped on the border. Because his family had money, Bruni did not need to smuggle. Still, evading government tariffs kept overhead low. Moreover, who did bringing in undeclared luxury goods hurt? Like Joseph Netzer, the hardware merchant who sold arms to revolutionaries, John Bruni was a businessman, but on the border illicit trade was part of business. Despite his indictment, the social status of the Bruni family remained intact. Bruni, Netzer, and indicted sheriff Amador Sánchez continued to live active political and social lives despite being accused of smuggling.[67] In fact, the Bruni name adorns one of Laredo's nicer downtown plazas. Although

Bruni, Netzer, and Sánchez broke the law, they did not violate community ethics on acceptable and unacceptable illicit trade.[68]

PETTY SMUGGLERS

That U.S. Customs forces shifted their focus from tariff collection to border security is evident in their treatment of petty smugglers. No cases came before the Southern District Court at this time for the evasion of tariffs on consumer goods worth less than $50. Although Customs guards could have avoided court proceedings by simply confiscating goods and letting smugglers continue on their way, given the reasonable argument that consumers intended purchases of less than $50 for personal use, it appears agents tolerated petty illicit trade. For instance, Juana Velendes's charge of petty smuggling had more to do with her bad luck than her offense. Velendes's crime consisted of illicitly transporting six Mexican tablecloths into the United States "valued at about $50," making her the most modest smuggler charged in this period.[69] The court set her bail at $200, which Velendes defaulted on, and the judge subsequently ordered her to jail. Court records do not reveal what effect this had on her personal life, livelihood, or family.[70]

Violating the border's integrity also got locals into trouble with the law. One month after Pancho Villa's raid on Columbus, New Mexico, left seventeen Americans dead and the United States and Mexico on the brink of war, U.S. Customs agents outside Laredo found time to charge individuals transporting one or two animals into the country with smuggling. On April 8, 1916, Benito Salinas entered the United States from Mexico with two horses and became a smuggler in the eyes of the law. It did not matter if the horses belonged to him or not, the two animals became dutiable once Salinas crossed into the United States. Salinas's arrest, however, was less related to his transportation of animals and prompted more by the way he chose to bring his horses into the country. Transporting horses clandestinely across the bridge was impossible, and officers would have turned him back without arrest had he tried to move his horses openly; this left crossing along an unregulated portion of the river as the only alternative for Salinas. When officers discovered Salinas, they charged him with smuggling, but his true offense was violating the integrity of the international border. Had Salinas been a Mexican national, U.S. federal authorities would have also charged him with unlawful entry. The Customs officers who arrested Salinas served as witnesses against him.

Salinas pleaded guilty to smuggling, and the court set Salinas's bond at one hundred dollars, which he failed to meet, and he subsequently went to jail.[71] Not all such cases ended unfavorably for the accused, however. Suspects who pleaded innocent could sometimes persuade juries to free them. Basilio Hinojosa refused to be bullied by the court or the agent who accused him. He pleaded not guilty to smuggling "293 pounds of fresh meat" because he did not consider shepherding a cow across the river without a declaration a crime. The jury agreed with Hinojosa and cleared him of all charges.[72]

Petty smugglers' arrests at this time were attributable more to their violations of U.S. national authority than suspects' denial of tariff revenues. Most judges considered petty smuggling a minor offense and tempered their obligatory law enforcement with lenient sentences. Although law enforcement agents prioritized preventing neutrality violations over policing low-level smuggling, officers did not tolerate affronts to national dignity or their personal honor. Juana Velendes and Benito Salinas were simply unfortunate enough to be caught, and Customs agents dutifully arrested them.[73]

WORLD WAR I EXPORT VIOLATIONS

State power not only worked to prevent the entry of contraband into the country, it also strived to keep certain things inside its borders. During the First World War, the U.S. government declared a litany of produce and consumer goods as material resources essential to America's war effort and thus illegal to export. As to be expected, the United States' prohibition on certain exports did not slake demand by consumers on the borderlands for these items, but rather made it more acute. Years of war had devastated Mexico's national infrastructure and left the country in chronic need of basic foodstuffs and material goods. Bureau of Investigation agents monitoring the border observed dire conditions on the Mexican side, particularly extreme prices for groceries of every kind.[74] Five days before Christmas 1917, one agent dispatched to Brownsville reported that forty-pound sacks of flour cost $7 in gold, two pounds of lard sold for $3.50, and sugar and corn were "very scarce."[75] On January 13, 1918, the *Laredo Weekly Times* commented there was "much need in Mexico. Almost every item of food is scarce and some articles cannot be had at all without importing them from this country."[76]

U.S. trade restrictions and Mexican shortages made trafficking consumables commercially viable. On February 12, 1918, U.S. Customs agents John Chamberlain and Robert Rumsey apprehended Mauricio Carreno smuggling six one-hundred-pound sacks of sugar out of the country without a license from the War Trade Board.[77] For this transgression, the court sentenced Carreno to serve ten days in the Webb County jail.[78] Carreno's operations were small compared to those of Juan Lozano and Jacinto Esquamia, who attempted to traffic one thousand pounds of sugar and four hundred pounds of lard out of the United States. The court's sentence of twenty days in county jail proved a small deterrent to determined traffickers.[79] Indeed, sugar smuggling's profitability inspired elaborate ruses to get goods across. Early in February 1918, U.S. Customs agents working in Laredo became suspicious of an ethnic Mexican man making frequent trips across the border in a wagon. Investigating agents stopped the suspect and discovered twenty-five pounds of contraband sugar hidden in a false compartment at the bottom of a can of gasoline. That the suspect claimed to have smuggled on behalf of another provides evidence that U.S. trade prohibitions and Mexican needs transformed the sugar trade on the border into a lucrative organized crime.[80]

Given the scarcity in Mexico, it is reasonable to assume that some people smuggled foodstuffs out of necessity or pity for those in need; however, Lozano and Esquamia's scale of operations make it more likely that they smuggled for profit. Although the illicit trade in sugar fit within the moral economy of smuggling on the border, commercial trafficking was another matter. Take for example the case of Macedonio García. García operated a wholesale grocery in Matamoros, Tamaulipas, across from Brownsville, and trafficked foodstuffs as part of his business. Unlike petty smuggling cases, which depended on arresting officers' testimonies, the government's case against García relied on local witnesses. Six Brownsville merchants testified that over the course of eleven days late in the fall of 1917, García unlawfully exported some $8,282 worth of rationed sugar and lard into Mexico by using a variety of third-party buyers so as not to arouse the inquiry of U.S. Customs. Further Treasury Department investigations revealed that the "malevolent practice" of crossing loads of foodstuffs as part of a larger trafficking operation could be "encountered anywhere there is a settlement between Eagle Pass and Point Isabel."[81]

Aside from foodstuffs, U.S. trade restrictions created a demand for prohibited American manufactured products in Mexico. Antonio Rojano and Anslemo Chapa saw a niche in the market, and on February 2, 1918, the two tried to smuggle a vast assortment of restricted goods including seventeen woolen suits, eighty-eight leather shoes, and 109 pieces of roofing tin weighing 214 pounds.[82] U.S. Customs agents apprehended José Guerra unlawfully exporting six leather purses, seven boxes of chewing gum, twenty-four yards of cotton mull, and three dozen silk ties out of the United States into Mexico in a similar case early that year.[83] Although the items that Rojano, Chapa, and Guerra attempted to export were harmless consumer goods that fell within the moral economy of illicit trade, state forces arrested them because the U.S. government believed this trafficking undermined the war effort on the home front. Moreover, the scale of their operations offended the government. Rojano, Chapa, and Guerra might have considered themselves entrepreneurs, but the government viewed them as greedy criminals. It is important to note that in the considerable boxes of case files examined, no petty smugglers of prohibited export items appear. Indeed, most of the cases were against Laredo and Brownsville merchants rather than average consumers. Customs officials and the court rarely, if ever, prosecuted individuals who smuggled prohibited items for personal use, but concentrated on those *exporting* restricted goods commercially in bulk. Locals did not consider Rojano and his companions' felony operations as wrong, however. Only the Customs agents involved in the case testified against him, and a local jury found the defendants not guilty.[84]

U.S. wartime restrictions adversely affected members of the pastoral economy as well. On February 1, 1918, area ranchers Pedro Benavides, Refugio Dominguez, and Eulalio Palacios became smugglers under the law when officers observed the three unlawfully transporting four bulls into Mexico. Bulls had been on the War Trade Board's conservation list since October 1917 and could not be taken out of the country without a license. Whether out of unawareness, fatigue, or spite, the three did not obtain the necessary license. U.S. Customs agents arrested the suspects, an examining trial held each of them on a $500 bond, which they failed to meet, and the three went to jail.[85]

In keeping with their traditional duties as U.S. Treasury agents, Customs forces also worked to prevent capital flight. On September 7, 1917, President Woodrow Wilson declared that Americans' "public safety" required that all gold coins stay inside the country's borders, and three days later it became entirely illegal to take any gold coins out of the United States.[86] Not surprisingly, people still tried to move gold coins across the Rio Grande. On January 3, 1918, U.S. Customs officers Robert Rumsey and John Chamberlain apprehended local Mariano Lozano trying to take two hundred twenty-dollar gold pieces out of the United States into Mexico. Lozano's intentions for the gold are unknown, but the court sentenced him to serve four months in the Webb County jail for his offense.[87] Lozano was not the only or boldest offender. Two weeks after Customs agents caught Lozano, they apprehended another local in the act of unlawfully taking $7,600 in American gold coins to Mexico.[88] Affluence among defendants in gold-smuggling cases allowed them to hire attorneys, and suspects usually pleaded innocent. Convincing a jury of one's innocence when caught red-handed could be difficult, however, especially considering that gold smugglers' wealth bought them little sympathy in local eyes. Three of the seven gold-smuggling cases examined resulted in guilty verdicts, while the state dismissed charges on two others. Although suspects could claim ignorance to their violations in the early days of the law's establishment, in January 1918 the Treasury Department placed notices by the international bridge in Laredo informing citizens of currency export restrictions.[89] These postings, coupled with word of mouth about export prohibitions, made currency smuggling a conscious, and in government eyes malicious, act to be punished. A federal judge fined Arcadio García $500 after a local jury found him guilty of attempting to unlawfully export $2,000 in Mexican gold coins.[90] Aside from gold, American authorities sought to keep other forms of liquid capital in the United States. Although her case was eventually dismissed, Rebecca Prado discovered that U.S. Customs would not permit her to casually leave the country with $4,000 cash and $700 in assorted gold and silver certificates. That the court dismissed the case a year later, after the war ended, attests to how governments afford leniency after a crisis has passed. That U.S. law enforcement arrested Prado at all, however, illustrates how states prioritized national security in times of emergency.[91]

VIOLENCE

Despite the U.S. government's worries about revolutionaries violating American neutrality and raiding into the country, violent encounters between smugglers and law enforcement occurred rarely in the early 1910s. It is important to note that most smugglers preferred discretion and did not seek to engage U.S. authorities. Smugglers at times carried arms, but they did so to protect themselves and their cargo, not for attack. Petty smugglers occasionally drew knives to resist authorities, and U.S. law enforcement did respond to these challenges with pistol whippings, but confrontations between U.S. law enforcement and smugglers were rarely fatal in the early years of the revolution. For instance, on April 14, 1911, mounted Customs inspectors A. H. Camp and G. U. Smith came across Máximo Martínez and his three companions camped twelve miles below Hebbronville, some sixty miles from the border. Suspecting Martínez and his companions to be a gang of smugglers, Inspectors Smith and Camp searched the men and discovered forty-six gallons of mescal packed upon their horses.[92] The inspectors confiscated the alcohol along with the *mescaleros'* horses and equipment and arrested the suspects. It is noteworthy that officers apprehended Martínez and his companions without bloodshed. Martínez and the men with him carried pistols, and they could have resisted Inspectors Smith and Camp had they wished, but they did not. Even if the inspectors surprised the *mescaleros* before they could draw their weapons, agents did not gun them down in cold blood. Still, law enforcement's arrest of the suspects came in 1911, before revolutionary violence made the bloody shootouts of the era acceptable. In 1911 ethnic Mexican smugglers and American law enforcement were not yet at war, but they would be.[93]

The spilling of revolutionary violence across the border, particularly after the bloodshed that followed the discovery of the Plan de San Diego in 1915, escalated tensions between American law enforcement and ethnic Mexicans so much so that by the end of the 1910s, U.S. forces on patrol in the brushland shot suspected smugglers on sight. At about ten thirty on the morning of May 5, 1919, U.S. soldiers on watch near Rio Grande City spotted a small group of people near the river. Sources differ as to what happened next. Sergeants John Smith and John Floyd claimed they ordered the men to halt and fired a warning shot in the air after the party ignored orders. According to the soldiers, riders on the Mexican side answered their calls with bullets, and a fierce firefight followed. A subsequent joint U.S. and Mexican investigation into the incident years later unearthed claims that no such engagement occurred and that the soldiers had simply shot unarmed suspects near the river. Discrepancies aside, Smith and Floyd shot Gregorio Falcón, wounding him mortally. Military authorities admonished the soldiers for shooting an unarmed suspect, but then allowed them to continue their duties without facing a trial.[94] Nor was this the only case of American forces shooting unarmed suspects. On a clear morning on April 8, 1919, Second Lieutenant Robert L. Gulley spied several persons pushing a raft across the Rio Grande during a cavalry patrol near Havana, Texas. Believing the raft carried contraband mescal, Gulley fired and mortally wounded Concepción García, a young girl. A court martial sentenced Lieutenant Gulley to be dismissed from service, but a presidential decision reversed the sentence and reinstated him. Seven years after their daughter's death, the U.S. government paid Teodoro García and María Garza $2,000 without interest for their loss.[95]

Perhaps the most striking example of U.S. authorities killing a group of ethnic Mexicans and calling them smugglers came in April 1920 when U.S. Customs agents engaged a group of mounted men forty-five miles southeast of Laredo. Crescencio T. Oliveira Jr., Dionisio Maldonado, and Vicente Aguilar died in the shootings. Area newspapers reported that the men were *returning* from smuggling liquor into the United States and elaborated that officers recovered "a small amount of ammunition . . . [and] several pair of new shoes" off the victims.[96] Although English-language newspapers dubbed the victims "smugglers," ethnic Mexicans remembered the deaths of the three quite differently. The corrido "Dionisio Maldonado," sometimes called the "Corrido de Oliveira," records the ambush and murder of the three men, but makes no mention of their involvement in smuggling. Rather, locals hold that the three constituted part of a wedding party on their way to Parras, Nuevo León, where Crescencio Oliveira planned to be married. Oliveira speaks the last lines of the song, lamenting the loss of his "betrothed whom he left behind."[97] The new shoes that law enforcement discovered were intended as wedding presents, whereas the two rifles and revolver the dead men possessed were nothing more than their sidearms. Ethnic Mexicans' version of events is indirectly supported by English-language newspapers, which inform that law enforcement recovered no alcohol from the victims. After a brief inquest by a justice of the peace, officers buried the three "near where they were killed," likely meaning a shallow grave.[98]

CONCLUSION

U.S. security concerns arising from the Mexican Revolution and First World War coincided with internal taxes' replacement of customs duties as the principal source of national revenue. This shift made national security, not tariff collection, U.S. Customs' priority on the border. Although casual smuggling continued, state efforts against petty smugglers decreased as Customs and other government agencies focused on keeping prohibited items out of or inside the country rather than on collecting tariffs on licit goods. Limited government resources, changing sources of revenue, and shifting priorities led to the state's virtual toleration of petty smuggling so long as it did not violate neutrality laws or hurt the war effort. Increased government vigilance against neutrality violations and war trade prohibitions, however, not only failed to prevent gun and rationed-food trafficking, it spurred a highly profitable illegal arms and rationed food-stuffs trade. Changing government priorities and regulations altered the nature of illicit trade in the borderlands as professional smuggling into the United States moved from the trafficking of consumer goods around tariffs to the trafficking of prohibited alcohol and narcotics. This change marked an escalation in smuggling to a more violent and overtly criminal activity outside the moral economy.

FOUR

Narcotics and Prohibition, 1914–1945

B e careful gentlemen, what I am about to sing to you about made
me gamble my luck." [1] So begins "El Contrabandista," the earliest drug-smuggling ballad of the borderlands, recorded in 1934
in San Antonio, Texas. "I began to sell champagne, tequila, and wine . . .
soon I bought a car, property," the singer recounts. [2] Life was good, until
the contrabandista expanded from bootlegging to drug running. El contrabandista bragged his routes stretched from El Paso to Houston, but
the profits of the drug trade were not without consequences, and authorities eventually caught up to him. "Because of selling cocaine, morphine,
and marijuana, they took me prisoner," the smuggler laments. [3] After suf-
fering in the hottest cells and from the loss of his mother, el contrabandista warns, "learn from my experience, because the law does not mess
around." [4] Although the song's lack of specifics make the account more
parable than oral history, the ballad reveals border people's attitudes
about the changing nature of smuggling through their community.

   In the early twentieth century demand and legal restrictions combined to produce a market for narcotics and alcohol in the United States.
Individuals responded to prohibitions by forming entrepreneurial alco-
hol- and narcotics-trafficking organizations. Narcotics and alcohol smuggling took a very different form than earlier illicit trade in the borderlands. Whereas locals largely condoned the smuggling of consumer goods
around excessive government tariffs, liquor and narcotics trafficking
brought with it an increase in violence that strained the moral economy
border people had created. Although the United States' war against liquor
traffickers led to a dramatic increase in smuggling-related violence on the
U.S. side of the border, popular acceptance of alcohol and sympathy for
certain smugglers kept liquor within the moral economy. The drug trade

had a more adverse effect on the borderlands, however. Borderlanders largely accepted the consumption of alcohol, but few accepted narcotics. Rather than support local consumers, drug trafficking supplied distant markets in major U.S. cities. This, coupled with the rise of violent cartels, helped create the impression of the U.S.-Mexico border as a criminal space and posed a threat to the moral economy of illicit trade.

NARCOTICS

Narcotics usage in the United States grew during the nineteenth century. Civil War veterans commonly received morphine to treat pain, leading to an untold number of addictions. Moreover, prior to 1900 opiates, cocaine, and marijuana could be purchased legally in the United States. Sears's 1897 mail-order catalogue advertised ready-to-go narcotics kits that included a syringe, several needles, and two bottles of morphine priced at $1.50. The popular beverage Coca-Cola contained cocaine until 1903. By 1900 some 250,000 U.S. residents were addicted to narcotics.[5] Domestic fears of social decay led to federal antinarcotics measures that inadvertently prompted drug trafficking across the U.S.-Mexico borderlands.

Although not directed at the border, it was not until the United States passed the Harrison Narcotics Act in December 1914 that authorities began to intercept drugs along the Rio Grande. The Harrison Act required that all drug transactions be registered with the federal government, imposed a sales tax on narcotics, and made it illegal to purchase drugs without a prescription. On March 26, 1915, Minnie Bishop became the first narcotics smuggler arrested in Laredo when Customs Inspector Ada Pereira caught her smuggling a small quantity of morphine and cocaine across the border from Mexico.[6] Records do not reveal the exact amount of narcotics that Inspector Pereira discovered, but it was far less than substantial. Bishop pleaded guilty, and the court set her bail at fifty dollars. Area U.S. Customs agents arrested three other persons on narcotics smuggling charges in 1915, but like Bishop, none of the suspects carried more than a few ounces.[7]

Within a year of the Harrison Act's passage, however, narcotics seizures in Laredo indicated modest drug trafficking. Customs Inspector Robert Rumsey apprehended Allen English trying to smuggle one thousand quarter-gram morphine tablets into the United States on July 6, 1916. English defaulted on his $250 bail and was ordered to the Webb

County jail.[8] Customs inspectors caught Charlie Williams with five hundred quarter-gram morphine tablets on December 16, 1916. Like English, Williams pleaded guilty, was given a $100 bond on which he defaulted, and subsequently went to jail.[9] Aside from its derivatives, smugglers took opium itself across the border into the United States. On February 17, 1917, Customs agents apprehended Vicente Calero and Eneas Levi with ninety-eight cans of smoking opium.[10] Although approximating the number of opiate addicts in the United States at the turn of the century is difficult, scholars of drugs in America estimate that in 1914 there were some 313,000 addicts in the United States out of a population of over 92,000,000.[11] With Laredo's population in 1910 standing at 14,855, it is highly unlikely that Levi and Calero smuggled ninety-eight cans of opium for local users.[12] Rather than supply local markets, Levi and Calero used the border to traffic opium north.

U.S. authorities confirmed drug traffickers operating through South Texas in early 1918 when law enforcement officers discovered a cryptic message concerning the movement of "Parras," or "Paars," across the border.[13] The letter began, "Dear friend . . . the man who want the Paars are still waiting to get the money from his people[.] . . . More Paars we can sell, more money for us."[14] The writer mentioned that it would take five days to bring the Parras from Monterrey, Nuevo León, and another day to get them across the border into the United States. U.S. Customs agents did not check the Laredo train station very well, and the writer assured the goods' safe shipment. If the buyer desired the goods to go to San Antonio, an additional $2 would be added to the price of each individual unit. It paid to buy in bulk. Parras sold for $40 in shipments of less than one hundred and $35 for shipments of one hundred and more. Difficulties such as distance only made the operation more profitable. Although the writer had to confirm with his contacts in Chicago and St. Louis, he heard that Parras sold for $80 apiece in Chicago. Finally, the writer mentioned that if the reader saw their rival Benito Salinas, "give him a good push in the nose."[15] Even if the reader bloodied Salinas, the writer considered reporting the competitor to authorities the next day.[16]

Parras turned out to be opium. Authorities arrested John Nixon, Francisco Alvarez, and Inez Stagner on charges of conspiracy to feloniously import twenty cans of smoking opium into the United States. Fritz Hoberg, another conspirator, escaped indictment by remaining across the river in Nuevo Laredo. Although their plan failed, Hoberg, Nixon, Alvarez, and Stagner's opium ring stretched from Monterrey, Nuevo León, to St. Louis, Missouri. Their method of operations worked thusly: Hoberg directed operations from Nuevo Laredo, beyond the reach of American authorities. He also made periodic trips to Monterrey to acquire the opium for the runs and reported rivals to Mexican authorities. John Nixon served as Hoberg's man in Laredo, receiving Hoberg's shipments and taking orders to their destination. Alvarez and Stagner worked as distributors or might have used Hoberg and Nixon as a source of opium for their own enterprises. Both Alvarez and Stagner corresponded with Nixon through code in the early months of 1918. On March 23, 1918, Nixon wired Stagner stating, "Your mother is here. Send the money."[17] That same day Stagner wired Nixon $405. Nixon took the opium by train to San Antonio where Alvarez and Stagner waited to collect it for probable shipment to St. Louis, and authorities arrested the three suspects as they made the drop-off. Despite the damning correspondence and twenty cans of opium as evidence, the suspects received surprisingly light punishment. The court ordered Stagner to serve sixty days in the Webb County jail and gave Nixon a four-month sentence. However, Alvarez and Hoberg seem to have escaped justice entirely. Hoberg's operation suffered a setback with Nixon's arrest, but he remained free in Mexico. In time, traffickers like him would develop increasingly sophisticated drug-smuggling syndicates.[18]

Unlike in the United States, where antinarcotics policies derived from moralistic and public health debates, Mexico's antinarcotics laws came partly from national security concerns.[19] Chinese immigrants excluded from U.S. shores in the late nineteenth century settled in large numbers in the Mexican states of Sinaloa and Sonora. Whether out of tradition or business, some of these Chinese settlers began cultivating poppies, thereby beginning opium production in the Americas. Mexico's first significant antinarcotics law came in 1916, when the revolutionary government prohibited the importation of opium.[20] Aside from curbing the crossing of U.S. narcotics dealers looking to purchase in Mexico, this measure went against powerful drug lords operating on the country's west coast. Between 1915 and 1920 Colonel Esteban Cantú ruled Baja California as his personal fiefdom on the proceeds from his arrangements with opium traffickers and the vice industry he oversaw. During his tenure Cantú sold concessions to opium traffickers in exchange for tens of thousands of dollars, which he used to outfit an 1,800-man-strong personal army equipped with American weapons and paid in U.S. dollars. The Mexican government's plans of a seaborne invasion to reincorporate Baja California sent Cantú fleeing to Los Angeles in August of 1920, but the specter of drug lords using the profits of the narcotics trade to resist state authority would continue to haunt the Mexican government.[21]

PROHIBITION

Liquor establishments throughout the United States gave their last *legal* calls for drinks near midnight January 16, 1920. Almost immediately, however, American disagreements with moralistic teetotalers expressed themselves as underground bars, moonshiners, and bootleggers across the nation quickly filled the niche that Prohibition created.[22] As with previous illicit trades, locals on the border negotiated the law with their own values. Prohibition made alcohol effectively illegal in the United States, yet most border people viewed the consumption of liquor as licit. The United States' "noble experiment" to end liquor consumption within its borders marked the triumph of decades of Waspish nativist activism and conflicted directly with the Mexican American Catholic majority of South Texas, which had few qualms about drinking and did not see it as wrong. Rather than obey laws contrary to their beliefs, Mexican Americans and other borderlanders accepted and celebrated certain groups of liquor smugglers as folk heroes within the moral economy.[23]

The prohibition of alcohol in the United States created new markets for controlled substances and further prompted the professionalization and criminalization of smuggling. During this period, mounted ethnic Mexican liquor smugglers, known commonly as *tequileros*, supplied Mexican liquor to thirsty American markets. U.S. law enforcement viewed tequileros' armed forays into the United States as transgressions against American sovereignty and resisted them with deadly force. Despite this violence, liquor smuggling in this period was interethnic in nature, with Anglo bootleggers and tequileros cooperating to profit from the circumvention of unpopular federal laws. Although Anglo bootleggers and ethnic Mexican tequileros both smuggled, U.S. law enforcement took a much higher toll on tequileros than on their Anglo counterparts, making Prohibition one of the deadliest decades for smuggling.

Prohibition came grudgingly to South Texas. Of the nineteen Texas counties still fully wet in 1911, eight were on the Rio Grande border.[24] Aside from a lack of local support, proximity to alcohol in neighboring Mexico made Prohibition almost impossible to enforce, and the region soon became a center for liquor trafficking. On January 5, 1919, a local newspaper commented how strange it was not to find any smugglers in court that Monday when so many were usually arrested over the weekend. Instead of naively believing that no illicit activity had occurred, the writer attributed the anomaly to smugglers being "very much on the *cuidado*" (being very careful).[25]

Cuidado or not, Prohibition ushered in a particularly violent era in smuggling along the border. On the night of May 8, 1919, mounted Customs inspectors Robert Rumsey and John Chamberlain and three immigration inspectors encountered four suspects crossing the Rio Grande by boat southeast of Laredo. Officers readied their weapons as they hid in the brush and waited for the suspects to land on the U.S. side. According to newspapers, what happened next was a shootout started by smugglers who refused to halt. A bullet struck Immigration Inspector Hopkins, killing him instantly. Two other immigration inspectors were wounded in the exchange, one fatally. When the smoke cleared, two officers had been killed, and four smugglers lay dead. Inspector Rumsey, a good shot under pressure, had killed two smugglers in the battle and walked away unscathed. Officers discovered deceased suspect Dorotéo Prado still clutching a U.S. Army automatic pistol, and in a troubling new trend, found rifles and sidearms among the other dead.[26] The shootout on May 8, 1919, marked the first of many violent confrontations between smugglers and American law enforcement during Prohibition.

TEQUILEROS

Prohibition created demand for contraband Mexican liquor in Texas, which ethnic Mexican entrepreneurs filled by loading their pack animals with illicit spirits and journeying north to American markets. Tequilero operations were simple, clever, and effective. Typically, tequileros operated at night in groups of three to five men, although some reports indicate that tequilero parties could swell to some twenty individuals.[27] Mexican nationals tended to work on the supply side of the operations and relied on Tejanos as guides, support, and go-betweens with Anglo bootleggers.[28] The tequila and mescal that smugglers transported they purchased on the border or deeper in Mexico. For example, a group of tequileros captured in La Salle County on September 21, 1921, claimed to have acquired their 550 quarts of tequila in a small town in Nuevo León, some seventy-two miles from the border.[29] If what the tequileros claimed was true, then they managed to cross over one hundred miles of territory between their pickup in Mexico and their capture in the United States without being detected. Because of the difficulties in crossing so much terrain, most tequileros operated closer to the border. Tequileros often worked out arrangements with local ranchers to cross through their land, and in exchange for a few bottles of tequila, cooperative ranchers left designated openings, or *falcetes*, in their fences for smugglers to cross. Consisting of nothing more than simple links of barbed wire that were hammered in such a way as to allow for easy removal and repositioning, *falcetes* provide evidence of smuggler/ranchero cooperation and tequileros' acceptance by the community.[30]

Tequileros used horses, mules, and donkeys in their operations. Horses carried the smugglers, while mules and donkeys served to convey their contraband cargoes. Tequileros proved adept at packing their draft animals. A skilled packer could fit fifty or more protectively wrapped bottles on a mature mule or donkey.[31] Layers of hay or grass helped prevent bottles from breaking, and, with the twine bags that carried them, muffled the telltale clinking of glass. Tequileros trained their animals well and used them expertly. Mules and donkeys traveled single file and could journey without tequileros' guidance along familiar paths. Trained draft animals could also wait for their handlers at watering holes or home in when separated from their masters. Texas Ranger Jesse Perez recounted that officers in the Lower Rio Grande Valley were continually frustrated by an animal they dubbed the "Lone Rum-Running Jackass of Starr County," whose special talent consisted of its ability to find its way home alone at night.[32] During the day the burro's handler guided the gifted animal across the river into Mexico, where it would be loaded with liquor at nightfall. After loading, smugglers "unhesitatingly" released the animal, confident it would make its way back home where its master waited.[33] Officers' morning discoveries of a lone pair of tracks emerging from the river provided silent testimony of the burro's success.[34]

Typically, tequileros' work consisted of transporting liquor across the Rio Grande into the United States. The agave plant from which tequila is derived flourishes throughout Mexico but was primarily distilled in Jalisco in the southern part of the country. Instead of producing the alcohol, business-savvy opportunists merely purchased it in Mexico to smuggle into the United States. Rather than sell the liquor themselves, tequileros often sold their cargo wholesale to bootleggers who then worked distribution. The degree to which tequileros and bootleggers worked together as part of an international trafficking organization is difficult to determine, but coordinated drops indicate planning and thus the actions of a criminal network (such syndicates are commonly called mafias). Indeed, liquor trafficking offered great profits. An apprehended group of tequileros claimed that they planned to sell their alcohol to bootleggers for $2.50 a bottle.[35] Given the men had 550 bottles of tequila, they could have earned $1,375 for their work. Divided by the number of tequileros in the party, each smuggler could hope to receive $137.50, less their costs. Had their venture succeeded, each tequilero stood to take away approximately $10,000 by modern standards.[36]

IDENTITY AND COMMUNITY PERCEPTION

Anglos and ethnic Mexicans had differing views on tequileros. U.S. law enforcement saw tequileros as criminal smugglers and armed invaders. William Warren Sterling, a Texas Ranger who fought against them, called tequileros "freebooters" who "would not hesitate to kill anybody who happened across their trail."[37] Maude T. Gilliland, a longtime resident of South Texas and the daughter of and later wife to a Texas Ranger, wrote that tequileros were "unbelievably ruthless and cruel . . . Mexican bandits."[38] Many Texas Rangers and mounted Customs officers saw tequileros' armed caravans and believed that the *sediciosos* of the Plan de San Diego had returned to kill more gringos.[39] Ethnic Mexican borderlanders, on the other hand, viewed tequileros entirely differently. The corrido "Laredo" sings of tequileros as individuals who "were not criminals," but men who had "distinguish[ed] themselves in that famed world war."[40] Indeed, some five thousand Tejanos fought for the United States in World War I, and it is a reasonable assumption that some returning veterans became tequileros.[41] Mexicans and Mexican Americans both rode the South Texas brush country with sacks of tequila. Leandro Villarreal of the famous corrido "Los Tequileros" offers a contrasting view of tequileros from that of U.S. law enforcement. In the corrido two professional tequileros, Gerónimo and Silvano, cross the Rio Grande into Texas and decide they need the assistance of another man whom they add to their party. Leandro initially refuses, claiming illness. According to local history, Leandro was not a professional trafficker like the other men, but a young man who had never smuggled before or otherwise broken the law.[42] Leandro, like most rural Tejanos, had only a few years of elementary education. He made some money from a little billiard hall he operated across the river in Guerrero, Tamaulipas, but not enough, apparently. Times had been hard for Leandro since his wife died, and the money he could make working with Gerónimo and Silvano would help him raise his three children. What Gerónimo and Silvano told Leandro to coax him out of his sickbed is unknown, but leave it he did. When the trio came across the *rinches*, as ethnic Mexicans commonly called murderous American law enforcement, he was the first to fall.[43] Leandro Villarreal's story shows that tequileros were more than the armed brigands that U.S. law enforcement portrayed them to be. Not all of them were hardened traffickers. Some were merely young men from rural backgrounds trying to get by.[44]

Tequileros were rural ethnic Mexicans who predominately came from poor ranching backgrounds. They were a mix of professional smugglers and novices. Tequileros might have been former *sediciosos* who turned to liquor running to continue their resistance to U.S. control, or they might have been entrepreneurs who saw liquor smuggling as a good way to make money. A few were desperate criminals who could kill indiscriminately, but most acted like prudent businessmen who avoided confrontation and turned to violence as a last resort. Tequileros were all these things and more. Whether they intended it or not, tequileros' smuggling and battles with U.S. law enforcement fell into the ethnic Mexican tradition of resistance to Anglo racism and American incorporation. Tequileros' actions in fact and song added to the *machista* culture of the border, and their courage, real or imagined, is enshrined in lore as exemplifying masculinity and honor. They are history and also legend.[45]

Decades after his death at the hands of U.S. law enforcement, family members disinterred Leandro from the unhallowed grave where Texas Rangers had left him. Rather than rebury him quietly, family members took pride in the legend that Leandro became in his last moments. On November 10, 2000, family members and locals celebrated Leandro's life in a memorial mass held at Our Lady of Lourdes Catholic Church in Zapata. Not only did information regarding Leandro's role in "Los Tequileros" appear in newspaper coverage of the event, family members chose to forever embrace Leandro's past as a tequilero by literally chiseling it in the stone above his grave. The fact that the artisan who completed the headstone took no pay for his labor, but provided the monument at cost, makes clear Leandro's reverence beyond his family and typifies tequileros' place of honor within the contrabandista community.[46]

Tequileros did not just traffic liquor illicitly into the United States; they also carried American foodstuffs and manufactured consumer goods south around onerous Mexican tariffs. Common items taken as contraband to Mexico included tobacco, sugar, flour, and bolts of calico, which smugglers either sold or enjoyed themselves.[47] Border people typically

FIGURE 4.1. *Gravestone of Leandro Villarreal with the corrido "Los Tequileros." Note the incorrect date for his death. Photograph by George T. Díaz.*

consumed more alcohol on the holidays, and tequileros worked to fill that demand, thus making smugglers' operations coincide with various festive occasions, particularly Christmas.[48] Material needs back home also prompted tequileros to return with clothing and shoes probably meant as holiday presents.[49] Government auctions indicate liquor smugglers' routine transportation of consumer goods for purposes other than sale, and it is not overly romantic to believe that tequileros smuggled items meant as gifts.[50] U.S. Customs agents destroyed liquor, but sold the rest of smugglers' possessions. Among newspaper reports of liquor seizures appear frequent advertisements of confiscated items set for government action. Part B of Section 593 of the Tariff Act of 1922 dictated that goods introduced contrary to law became forfeit and subject to sale by the Customs Service. Among the various rifles, pistols, and revolvers seized and sold were numerous other basic consumer goods. An advertisement that appeared on December 15, 1925, lists "1 baby's outfit, 8 cotton slips, 12 lace handkerchiefs, 2 gold rings, 7 baby dresses, 3 paintings, 4 ink pencils, 3 packages toys, 1 silk scarf, 3 embroidered quilts, 1 bottle perfume, 1 child's dress, . . . 1 baby cap[,] . . . 1 pair bootees."[51] U.S. Customs agents did not seize these items in one bust, but sold accumulated articles in regular auctions. Rather than the trafficking of consumer goods, the small scale of this trade indicates that liquor smugglers carried these items as presents for loved ones. Another possibility is that these consumer goods were not smuggled into the United States at all, but that officers used the law as a pretext to seize products that suspects legally possessed in order to punish them.

The way that the United States and Mexico perceived individuals as smugglers depended on whether they were coming or going. U.S. Customs viewed tequileros as smugglers when they took their contraband alcohol north, but American law did not consider these same men smugglers if they carried licit American goods back to Mexico with them. That American law enforcement engaged and at times killed these would-be merchants on their return trips had more to do with these same men's actions as tequileros than their lawful transportation of licit goods south. Similarly, Mexican law enforcement did not seriously attempt to prevent the flow of liquor north into the United States, but did seek to curb these same individuals from evading Mexican tariffs on consumer goods they trafficked south. For example, late in September 1929 Mexican authorities expressed concern over one Jorge Rodríguez of Laredo who made his living smuggling liquor into the United States and illegally introducing clothes and textiles into Mexico.[52] In the complicated world of business on the border, the difference between licit and illicit trade was contingent on what individuals sought to cross from one side of the border to the other.

VIOLENCE

Between May of 1919 and August 18, 1922, U.S. law enforcement agents operating in South Texas had six encounters with tequileros that left ten smugglers dead and another ten wounded. A typical confrontation occurred in southeastern La Salle County, some forty-five miles from Cotulla. For months law enforcement had received reports of cattle and horses being rustled from outlying ranches, and they suspected tequileros as the perpetrators. A party of Texas Rangers, mounted Customs inspectors, and county deputy sheriffs on patrol for the alleged offenders trailed and engaged a group of tequileros they found camped on September 12, 1921. Officers killed the reputed leader of the group, seized over five hundred quarts of tequila, and captured nine men and fifteen horses in the encounter. Authorities speculated that they came upon the tequileros as they waited to rendezvous with bootleggers who were to collect the alcohol and transport it north by truck. Officers placed the suspects in jail, where they remained because they were unable to pay their $1,000 bond.[53]

Entrepreneurial borderlanders readily filled the market Prohibition created, but U.S. state forces fought against this trade violently. Traffickers and contrabandistas did not wish violence. Rather, they merely sought to smuggle and make a profit. Smugglers were not "primitive rebels" or "social bandits," but circumstantial businesspersons or opportunists.[54] Tequileros did not attack Anglo land-grabbers or issue revolutionary proclamations, but tried to avoid the state, going so far as to ride for days through miles of thorny scrubland so as not to engage its forces in pitched battles.[55] During Prohibition, tequileros could scarcely avoid confrontation, because the U.S. government sought them out. In the aftermath of the Plan de San Diego, American law enforcement in South Texas had come to view tequileros with a greater wariness. Texas Ranger Captain William Warren Sterling put it simply: tequileros "had to be dealt with as foreign enemies, not as ordinary domestic bootleggers." [56] Some tequileros of the Prohibition era may have been former *sediciosos*, but even if they were not, they knew to fear the *rinches* who had killed so many ethnic Mexicans the decade before. Knowing the danger, tequileros armed themselves and resisted apprehension with force because they likely felt it was the only way to save their lives. With armed tequileros wary and mounted lawmen determined to stop smugglers' "armed invasion of the United States," it is not surprising that shootouts took place.[57]

Despite Texas and federal law enforcement officers' view of tequileros as desperate men who killed at whim, tequileros seem to have murdered only one rancher in the thirteen years of Prohibition. On June 28, 1923, an Anglo rancher's son went missing. Gregg Gibson's father knew that groups of tequileros traveled through their ranch in Duval County on their journeys north, and he suspected the worst. American law enforcement officers discovered Gibson's son's body the next day. Local Anglos claimed tequileros shot Gibson in the back and stole his horse. At least three publications by former U.S. law enforcement personnel point to Gibson's murder as an example of tequileros' savagery, but the tequileros may not have been as ruthless as Anglo memory insists.[58] Perhaps smugglers did not shoot Gibson in the back, but only after he drew his weapon. Gibson could have been patrolling his ranch in search of smugglers and found them. Even if tequileros did ambush Gibson, his case is the only one like it occurring in this period. Prohibition in South Texas was a violent time, but when blood spilled it spilled hot, not cold.

The stalking, ambush, and murder of the three smugglers in "Los Te-

quileros" is the exception that proves the rule. The corrido "Los Tequileros" narrates the deaths of three smugglers at the hands of American law
enforcement on December 18, 1922. On December 17, 1922, a group of
Texas Rangers and mounted Customs inspectors patrolling the Jennings
Ranch in Zapata County came across suspicious tracks. Officers followed
the trail early the next morning and came upon the smugglers at about
2:00 p.m. It was rough country, full of hills, rocky canyons, and arroyos.
Perched on a hilltop, the officers looked down at their targets. Ranger
Captain William Wright had fought smugglers before, and rather than
confront the smugglers, he prepared an ambush. Wright and one of his
men stationed themselves on the western side of the path, two others took
positions on the eastern side, and the rest of the officers hid in the southern end to block any retreat and "flush the game" to the barren northern
ridge where the smugglers would be cut down.[59]

Wright's ambush worked exactly as planned. The officer guarding
the southern opening fired his rifle, driving the three smugglers to where
Wright and the others waited. Smugglers ran pell-mell into the bush, and
others took to their horses, trying to escape. When the shooting ended
a few moments later, the three "Mexicans" were dead.[60] Officers found
a dead smuggler holding two ends of a broken rifle; a bullet had cut the
stock in half. After counting the bottles of tequila, the officers dashed
them against the ground. For good measure, they lit the pile and a long
blue flame reached into the darkening sky. The officers camped there that
night; the smugglers' uneaten lunch became their killers' supper. Gerónimo, Silvano, and Leandro were left where they fell until "a coroner
came out and said they were dead." [61] After a match-light inquest, officers
buried them in shallow graves. Ranger historian Walter Prescott Webb
quotes Ranger sentiments over such deaths starkly. In an unsigned dis-
patch to a Ranger captain, a recently bloodied private wrote, "the other
day we run on to some horsebackers and one of them thought he would
learn me how to shoot, so I naturalized him—made an American citizen
out of him." [62]

Texas Rangers' reputation for violence and racism against ethnic
Mexicans is well documented, but the callous nature of this particular
incident must be considered. Anglo newspaper articles described the killings with malicious glee. The *Laredo Weekly Times* headline read, "Three
Smugglers Killed . . . Captain Wright and Inspector Smith . . . Rid Country
of Three More Booze Smugglers." [63] Besides informing that officers "rid"
the country of the three smugglers, the paper reported that the tequileros had "bit the dust" under the Rangers' guns.[64] The probable reason

that the *Laredo Weekly Times* took such relish in describing the deaths of the tequileros is revealed in a headline on the same story from the *San Antonio Express*: "First Victory Over Border Gang Since Death of Customs Inspectors." [65]

On August 19, 1922, three months before the killing of the three tequileros, bootleggers murdered mounted Customs inspector Robert S. Rumsey. While returning from an arrest of two smugglers, Customs officers Rumsey, Frank Smith, and Will Musgrave passed two suspicious cars in eastern Webb County and decided to pull the suspects over. Rumsey exited his vehicle and approached the suspects when a tall, heavyset man shot him. The first bullet hit Rumsey in the stomach, knocking him off his feet. Two more shots struck him, hitting his left cheek and right leg. Officers Musgrave and Smith emptied their guns before the killers in the car fired on them, pinning them down. Rumsey's murderer stood over his dead or dying body and stripped him of his gun before rushing back to his car and speeding away, leaving the officers to return Rumsey's corpse to his widow.[66]

Officer Rumsey's loss greatly affected the community. Rumsey was born in San Antonio, but had lived in Laredo all his life. He had worked at Fort McIntosh outside of town and served as a Texas Ranger before becoming a Customs inspector. During his life in Laredo Rumsey also married María Herrera, a local ethnic Mexican woman, and the couple had started a family. Over the course of his life Rumsey had walked the streets of Laredo and made friends. Although perhaps a brutal officer of the state, Rumsey was also a local, and for weeks newspapers carried stories of his life, exploits, and death. Rumsey's murder particularly affected law enforcement officers. Mounted local police escorted his funeral procession. Texas Ranger Captain William Wright publicly remarked that the "customs service has lost its best inspector." [67] Privately, Wright's response to learning of his friend's death was more visceral; he reputedly "jerked out his pistol and exclaimed 'Wish I'd a been there, boom, boom.'" [68]

Captain Wright and the Texas Rangers had not been there to help Rumsey in August, but Wright was present at the killing of the three tequileros in December, and so was Frank Smith, the mounted Customs inspector who had transported Rumsey's body back to Laredo. Rumsey's murder was undoubtedly on the minds of many officers at the time. Wright and the other men there that day in December could have felt that justice was slipping away. Then they came upon the three tequileros. Perhaps the officers considered that these were the same men who had killed Rumsey. Or maybe it was simply revenge by proxy. Wright planned the attack well.

The officers surrounded the smugglers on all sides, preventing any escape. They flushed the tequileros out and cut them down in the crossfire. None of the men killed that day were found to be suspects in Rumsey's murder, but his death provoked the slaughter. James White, a deputy officer at the time, verified this in a letter to a friend when he stated, what "started the Rangers' . . . killing Tequileros was the murder of Rumsey." [69]

Mounted Customs inspectors and Texas Rangers responded to Rumsey's and other officers' deaths at the hands of smugglers by shooting first and asking questions later. Between 1922 and the end of Prohibition in 1933, mounted American law enforcement officers engaged horseback liquor runners in fourteen clashes that left nine smugglers dead. [70] Because most of the confrontations occurred in isolated rural locations, the exact number of clashes may be underrepresented. The state's war on smugglers took such a toll that corrido writers remembered it a generation later. The 1970s-era corrido "Pistoleros Famosos" begins, "On the banks of the Rio [Grande], from Reynosa to Laredo, there are no more bandits and no more smugglers. This is how the gunfighters are being wiped out." [71] The song goes on to list the names of the fallen, including Silvano [Gracia] of the corrido "Los Tequileros," "killed treacherously by the cowardly Rangers." [72] Dimas de León, Generoso Garza Cano, the del Fierro brothers, and one or two Americans, "all these brave men have been betrayed and killed." [73]

Tequileros stood little chance against the concerted power of the state. The most they could do was gather in larger armed caravans for better protection. On a Sunday evening in late September 1922, four Customs officers patrolling near Benavides in Duval County encountered a band of forty-five armed tequileros. [74] The large body of smugglers scared Customs agents into retreating, but state forces would not be dissuaded. In response to the officers' rout, the *Laredo Weekly Times* advocated using U.S. Army cavalry units to hunt down tequileros in order to prevent the "armed invasion of our territory." [75] Although no cavalry units are known to have taken the field against tequileros, the state did escalate its firepower in its campaign against them. In late 1922 and early 1923 Texas Rangers and Customs inspectors on the border received Thompson .45 and Browning automatic weapons. Brownings were too cumbersome to use on mounted patrol, and the ineffectiveness of Thompson submachine guns at longer ranges and in thickets minimized their usefulness. The guns nevertheless gave officers a profound psychological advantage over the inferiorly armed smugglers. [76] One night in early January 1924 a posse of eight mounted Customs inspectors and Jim Hogg County sheriff's deputies used one of their new Thompson guns in an engagement against approximately fifteen tequileros near Hebbronville. Officers believed they succeeded in wounding several smugglers, and they seized sixteen horses and more than 1,650 quarts of liquor as a result of the confrontation.[77]

Tequileros certainly fought when confronted, but surprisingly, tequileros operating in the lower Rio Grande borderlands failed to kill or even wound a single law enforcement officer in the years between 1919 and 1933. In contrast, mounted American patrols killed nine tequileros and wounded at least a dozen more. The reason for this disparity is more complex than Texas Ranger Captain Sterling's explanation that drunken tequileros were no match for the "superior skill of the American rifleman."[78] American law enforcement's victories over tequileros are best explained by their use of surprise. Texas Rangers, mounted Customs inspectors, and Border Patrol agents tracked tequileros and picked the most opportune moment to engage them. Mounted U.S. law enforcement rarely came across tequileros by accident. Rather, officers on patrol would search for tequileros' trails and then stalk them.[79] Just how law enforcement/tequilero shootouts occurred is unclear, but corridos' description of officers as "cowardly" has its basis in fact.[80] Officers tracking tequileros could have their guns drawn when they made their presence known. Law enforcement officers stalking horseback liquor smugglers could get ahead of their targets and lie in ambush as did the Texas Rangers and mounted Customs inspectors who killed the three tequileros on December 18, 1922.[81] Given the nature of state tactics, it is not surprising that the balladeer in the corrido "Los Tequileros" comments that the only way the *rinches* can "kill us is by hunting us like deer."[82]

Attrition and the ever-increasing incorporation of the region into the nation-state eventually ended the era of the tequilero. Liquor smugglers who did not lose their lives lost their property, and this confiscation of equipment helped drive tequileros out of business. Jesse Perez, a Texas Ranger who fought against tequileros, recorded that in three engagements tequileros' losses amounted to approximately $8,000, "a serious blow at the finances of the Smugglers."[83] Mounted Customs inspectors, Texas Rangers, and Border Patrol agents' campaign against tequileros wore them down, and their forays into the United States became less frequent as the danger mounted. The last five years of Prohibition saw only six reports of smugglers crossing overland through the brush in the counties adjacent to Laredo. Area law enforcement's last reported encounter with tequileros took place in Jim Hogg County in February 1927. Mounted Customs inspectors killed one smuggler and seized seven hundred bottles of whiskey and six horses in their final skirmish with tequileros.[84] Future years would see the occasional horseback liquor smuggler, but tequilero caravans came to an end six years before the repeal of national prohibition in 1933. Another, violent and more sophisticated, form of smuggler would come to fill the gap that tequileros left behind.[85]

BOOTLEGGERS

Bootleggers succeeded tequileros as the preeminent liquor traffickers of the Prohibition era. Unlike tequileros, who operated in rural areas on horseback, bootleggers were mostly urban Anglos and ethnic Mexicans who used automobiles. English-language newspapers of the period at times used the term "bootleggers" for tequileros, but U.S. law enforcement did designate bootleggers as those who smuggled liquor by automobile and tequileros as horseback liquor traffickers.[86] Rather than cut through ranches where mounted American law enforcement patrolled, bootleggers used the state's road system and consequently supplied a much larger network than tequileros. Whereas tequileros' animal-powered operations could only support local borderland markets, bootleggers drove their contraband cargoes to demand centers in San Antonio, Corpus Christi, Houston, Dallas, and beyond.[87] As in cases when practitioners of one methodology interact with adherents of another, rivalries, exacerbated by differing ethnic and class backgrounds between both groups of smugglers, invariably occurred. Still, bootleggers and tequileros generally worked together.

Although the state focused on combating tequileros, bootleggers took a greater toll on American law enforcement's ranks, killing two of the three officers who died in confrontations with liquor smugglers in South Texas during national prohibition. Bootleggers killed mounted Customs inspector Robert Rumsey on August 19, 1922, and ambushed and murdered prohibition agent Charles Stevens on the San Antonio highway on September 25, 1929.[88] Bootleggers killed more officers than tequileros because they could see the officers who pursued them. Unlike tequileros, who operated in dense cacti and mesquite thickets, the roads that bootleggers trafficked along provided a clear view to shoot. Cars also concealed bootleggers' hands, allowing them the opportunity to draw their weapons on approaching agents.

Community disdain for bootleggers reached such an extent that Tejanos eulogized officers who combated them. The 1920s-era corrido

"Capitán Charles Stevens" honors the life and death of prohibition agent Charles Stevens. Unlike the corrido "Los Tequileros," which described U.S. law enforcement officers as *rinches*, Stevens's ballad portrays him nobly. Stevens is described as "a man" who had "eagle eyes" and who in life was known as "the panther." [89] In contrast to the law enforcement officers in "Los Tequileros," who are depicted as cowards, Stevens is sung of as a brave man who "fought gallantly and without fear." [90] Charles Stevens served as a Texas Ranger captain before becoming a U.S. Customs agent in Laredo. At the time of his death, Stevens worked as a U.S. prohibition agent. In late September 1929, Stevens and two other officers were returning from raiding stills in Atascosa County when they spotted a woman on the roadside signaling someone with a spotlight. Stevens pulled over and decided to take the woman in for questioning. Several men then sprang from behind the foliage and riddled Stevens's car with shotgun blasts. Buckshot tore through Stevens's torso, killing him. Although the other officers returned fire and might have wounded two of the assailants, the killers escaped.[91] Stevens merited a corrido because he died valiantly fighting traffickers the community disdained. Moreover, he did not ambush and kill ethnic Mexicans like the Customs agents and Texas Rangers who murdered the three tequileros on December 18, 1922, but worked primarily against Anglo moonshiners and violently criminal bootleggers. Tejanos' eulogy of Stevens through song shows that Anglo and ethnic Mexican relations at the time were not always contentious. Ethnic Mexicans did not consider all U.S. law enforcement agents *rinches*, and some, like Stevens, could be viewed as brave and honorable.

Locals saw bootleggers as less honorable than the tequileros they succeeded. Tequileros' packing and driving of trains of animals through the brush country required a certain skill and hardiness that Tejanos esteemed.[92] Bootleggers in contrast simply hid alcohol in cars and drove. The border ballad "El Automóvil Gris" ("The Gray Automobile") captures bootleggers' greater inclinations toward violence. Unlike corridos about tequileros that celebrate their valor against *rinches*, "El Automóvil Gris" calls the members of the gray automobile gang the "hand that squeezes, that assaults, that kills and robs." [93] The bootlegger in the corrido is a decadent gangster who can be seen "drunk . . . smoking fine cigars, drinking cognac, sherry, beer to the sound of merrymaking." [94] He even claims to have enjoyed himself in Paris. Joe Hobrecht, Stevens's alleged murderer, fit bootleggers' image as gangsters. One newspaper published a mug shot of Hobrecht where the clean-shaven "dapper youth" is shown with his dark hair slicked back and wearing a suit and tie.[95] Like other bootleggers who used technology and highways to extend illicit trade networks beyond their regional communities, the smuggler in "El Automóvil Gris" boasts of his business in Matamoros, San Antonio, Laredo, and Belén.[96] Bootleggers' ability to smuggle at greater volumes increased trafficking's profitability, violence, and criminality beyond the moral economy.

Traffickers' sophistication and scale of operations increased as Prohibition wore on. The single largest alcohol seizure in the region occurred in early February 1927, when Customs inspectors discovered 471 pints of whiskey and 170 five-gallon cans of alcohol valued at $21,000 hidden under sacks of cabbages in a railroad boxcar.[97] Officers waited for E. M. Stevens to pick up his bill of lading and arrested him. The car had been destined for Fort Worth, Stevens's city of residence. Stevens paid his $2,000 bond and went free until his trial. For over a year the case was deferred, until April 1928, when the U.S. District Court sent Stevens to the federal penitentiary at Leavenworth, Kansas, for two years.[98] Nor were traffickers' schemes limited to the ground. In 1931 U.S. law enforcement suspected "a mysterious rider of the night skies" of trafficking liquor from Mexico to Kansas City by following airmail beacons.[99] Although somewhat laughable, the report may not have been far from the truth. As early as 1922 Laredo's customs collector, Roy Campbell, considered using an airplane to scout along the river for smugglers.[100] Aerial Customs patrols intercepted airborne bootleggers on five different occasions between September 1928 and the end of national prohibition in 1933. Mexican law enforcement captured two American pilots outside Nuevo Laredo in early January 1932. Authorities suspected Paul Davis and Joe Roubert of smuggling merchandise into Mexico and alcohol into the United States, but because officers did not catch the two red-handed, Mexican law enforcement instead charged them with unlawfully carrying firearms and entering the country without an airplane permit. The Americans' presentation of a flying certificate signed by Orville Wright failed to get them released or their plane *Low Money King* returned.[101]

As was the case with cars, horses, and mules, airplanes seized in liquor arrests fell under Section 3062 of the Revised Statutes of the United States, meaning that such articles employed in smuggling became the possessions of the Customs Service. Thus, the apprehension of an airborne rumrunner in Ohio in February 1932 provided federal agents a plane they put to good use. In May of that year a Customs pilot pursued an airborne smuggler 250 miles before forcing him down in McMullen County. The agent discovered more than 120 gallons of Mexican liquor in the plane and arrested the pilot, an American World War I ace. Nor was this the only case of airborne pursuit. Six months later Customs agents observed another plane crossing the border between Laredo and Eagle Pass and gave chase. The pursuit ended 150 miles later when the officer flanked the flyer and aimed a rifle at him. It seems the Customs aviator succeeded where no German could, for he caught William T. Ponder, an American ace credited with eleven kills behind the stick. Officers found more than eighty gallons of alcohol in the plane, and such successes prompted the Customs Service to establish a regular aerial patrol between Laredo and Eagle Pass.[102]

THE GROWING DRUG TRADE

Drug seizures were not uncommon during Prohibition. Mexican bans on the cultivation of marijuana and the Mexican government's severe restrictions on the distribution of cocaine and opiates in 1920 had the unintended effect of making the drug trade more profitable.[103] Between August 1922 and August 1928 U.S. law enforcement made eighteen narcotics arrests in the Laredo area. Morphine seizures predominated with thirteen captures, while cocaine confiscations came second with five. U.S. authorities also made opium, heroin, and marijuana busts. Drug smuggling occurred on a much smaller scale than liquor trafficking, with nineteen ounces of cocaine and seventeen ounces of morphine being large seizures for the time.[104] Still, Laredo was already making a name for itself as a nexus for narcotics traffic. Laredo made national headlines on February 26, 1928, when the *New York Times* described the "insuperable" difficulties that federal narcotics, Customs, and Border Patrol agents faced in preventing the flow of illegal drugs through the port.[105] Simply put, officers were so overburdened by the number of people crossing the border, they could not conduct effective searches. The article quoted an unnamed official as stating that Customs prevented a great deal of minor smuggling, but a "large amount of 'dope' gets by and unless we have a 'tip' or there is some suspicious action, we are obliged to let the travelers pass with just a superficial examination."[106] The article held that aside from lacking sufficient funds and manpower to effectively police drug smuggling, the greatest obstacle to keeping narcotics out of the country was the inability to reach the source of the supply, and until the Mexican government allowed undercover U.S. narcotics agents to track down ringleaders in Mexico, the "task of stopping the traffic is well-nigh hopeless."[107] National outcry would increase in later years, but as early as 1928 Laredo had an established reputation as a "transit point for [drug] smugglers." [108]

The drug trade brought with it new dangers to a community that had long accepted smuggling. Unlike earlier illicit trade that dealt in regulated or prohibited goods many people wanted, narcotics smuggling was viewed by most borderlanders as inherently criminal. Border people did not like the drug trade and feared that the lure of easy money it offered led to prison or death. Indeed, narcotics smuggling's dangers inspired cautionary border lore. The corrido "El Contrabandista" narrates the downfall of a former liquor smuggler who turned to the drug trade and subsequently ended his days behind bars in a Texas prison. "Carga Blanca," written in the 1940s and easily the most popular *narcocorrido* of the era, recounts the tale of José and Ramón, who cross the Rio Grande with "carga blanca" (white cargo, meaning either cocaine or in this case more likely heroin). The two sell the drugs for 2,800 pesos in San Antonio, but on their journey home a killer murders the pair and takes the money back to the buyer. Although José and Ramón's story cannot be traced back to a specific historical incident, the song reveals that as early as the 1940s, ethnic Mexicans of the borderlands knew the profits and dangers of the drug trade.[109] *Narcocorridos'* depictions of drug smugglers contrast sharply with the heroes of earlier ballads and serve as a warning against those who overstep the moral economy of illicit trade. Unlike the smugglers in "Mariano Reséndez" and "Los Tequileros," whom the corridos depict nobly fighting against discredited state agents, the protagonists in "El Contrabandista" and "Carga Blanca" come to inglorious ends. Texas law enforcement apprehend the smuggler in "El Contrabandista" without a fight and throw him in jail. After José and Ramón of "Carga Blanca" are murdered for their drug money, the balladeer closes, "Leave this crooked business alone, just see what has happened!" [110]

While booze running declined after Prohibition, marijuana smuggling rose. Marijuana of course was in no way new to the borderlands. Pancho Villa's Army of the North sang "La Cucaracha," a happy song about a marijuana smoker, during their free time.[111] Marijuana usage in the region was older still, but marijuana smuggling did not begin in earnest until after Prohibition. On October 12, 1938, U.S. Customs agents working in Webb County apprehended Miguel Salinas with four pounds of marijuana. Salinas pled guilty to unlawfully concealing and receiving smuggled merchandise and the court sentenced him to serve six months at the federal detention farm at La Tuna.[112] Salinas had the misfortune of being one of the first persons in Webb County prosecuted for violation of the Marijuana Tax Act of 1937. Passed August 2 of that year, the Marijuana Tax Act emanated from years of pressure by local police forces from southwestern states. Anti-Mexican sentiment in the United States had been on the rise since the Mexican Revolution first sent waves of refugees north across the border in 1910. Many Anglos living in the southwestern United States viewed the recent arrivals as competitors for unskilled jobs and as criminals. Local police in affected communities capitalized on the popular belief that marijuana contributed to Mexican criminality and helped lobby for antimarijuana legislation.[113] The new marijuana tax effectively made it impossible to lawfully possess the drug in the United States. A government-imposed occupational tax on individuals wishing to legally trade in cannabis drove many dealers underground. Those failing to register faced taxes of one hundred dollars an ounce on marijuana every time it changed hands. Persons transporting, selling, prescribing, or cultivating marijuana all fell subject to this tax. The U.S. District Court sentenced Miguel Salinas to serve six months of labor at La Tuna not for possessing or even smuggling a controlled substance. Rather, authorities imprisoned Salinas for a tax violation.[114] U.S. federal drug interdiction would continue to evolve out of economic measures throughout the twentieth century.[115]

Organized crime capitalized on networks created during Prohibition to escalate the drug trade, and by the mid-1930s Mexican-based narcotics traffickers usurped state offices and assassinated enemies across the borderlands. Under the protection of Rodrigo Quevedo, the governor of Chihuahua, the Quevedo family built a drug empire capable of wielding state power. Between 1933 and 1934 the Quevedos sent members of the state and local police to crack down on the rival Enrique Fernández drug gang. Authorities' raids weakened Fernández's organization, and police loyal to the Quevedos allegedly delivered seized drugs to the family, whose operations continued to expand. The Quevedos solidified their control of the Juárez drug trade with the assassination of Fernández in early January 1934. This pattern of narcotics trafficking, political corruption, and murder occurred along the length of the Rio Grande borderlands.[116] On June 19, 1934, narcotics smugglers assassinated Customs Inspector Loy C. Henry near his home in Del Rio. Inspector Henry was at home off duty that evening when he received a knock on the door asking for directions. Letting his guard down, Henry politely offered to drive the man at the door—Rafael Domínguez—to his destination. As the two drove off, Domínguez drew a Luger pistol and shot the officer three times. Domínguez fled the scene, but Inspector Henry lived long enough to identify the man who shot him. What troubled Stewart E. McMillin, U.S. consul for Piedras Negras, more than the murder of a U.S. Customs agent, was Henry's statement that the last words that Domínguez spoke to him before he ran were, "These are the thanks of Mr. Marcial Martínez." [117] Marcial Martínez was the mayor of Villa Acuña.

Prior to his death, Inspector Henry had learned of an attempt to smuggle an unspecified load of narcotics out of Acuña through Del Rio. Rather than try to seize the drugs before they shipped to Fort Worth, Henry crossed into Mexico to warn Martínez not to do it. Henry claimed Martínez offered him a monthly bribe to look the other way, but he refused and walked out. Rafael Domínguez shot Henry the next day. Domínguez confessed to shooting Henry, but denied Mayor Martínez's involvement in the matter. Still, U.S. authorities remained convinced of the mayor's complicity. In a letter to the secretary of state in Washington, McMillin wrote that a "drug smuggling ring" consisting of Marcial Martínez and his brother-in-law, Jesús Ramón, a deputy in the state congress for Saltillo, and several others ran the organization.[118] U.S. authorities had good reason to suspect Ramón. In 1929 the U.S. District Court in Del Rio had indicted Ramón for violating American tariff laws applicable to a cargo of liquor he sold San Antonio bootleggers, and two suspects in another case that term claimed to have purchased narcotics from him. Ramón, however, eluded U.S. authorities by remaining in Mexico. Frustrated, H. S. Creighton, the supervising U.S. Customs agent for the area, warned that because of his "political strength . . . Ramón and his organization are one of the most dangerous and vicious combinations we have to contend with." [119]

Assassinations like those plotted by Jesús Ramón and Marcial Martínez fell beyond the bounds of the moral economy of illicit trade. No *rinche*, Inspector Henry was well liked on both sides of the border and had served as a Customs agent for ten years. Indeed, Consul McMillin commented that sentiment was very strong against Rafael Domínguez in Del Rio and Villa Acuña, and Mexican Customs officials threatened to kill Henry's alleged murderer should they get the chance.[120] Although Mayor Martínez and Deputy Ramón used their power to protect themselves, Mexican federal authorities imprisoned Domínguez.[121]

Community outrage extended to the assassination of Mexican officers. In March of 1938 an assailant snuck into the Nuevo Laredo home of Mexican federal detective Ramón Pecina and murdered him by shooting him three times in the face as he slept. Authorities found the blood-stained and bullet-riddled taxicab that had carried the killer outside Pecina's home and discovered the body of the murdered driver in a ditch twelve miles outside of town. Over three hundred persons marched in Nuevo Laredo protesting the murders of Detective Pecina and taxi driver Julian Garza. Locals blamed Nuevo Laredo mayor Pablo Peña and other prominent municipal officials for orchestrating the murder to protect the drug smuggling "mafia" they operated.[122] Members of the taxi union to which Garza belonged even threatened that "if the guilty parties were not quickly brought to justice the people of this city would take matters into their own hands."[123] Fed up with corruption, locals believed that efforts to catch the guilty parties were nothing more than a "big show" while city administrators protected the real killers.[124] Protestors saved their most powerful speaker for last. An unnamed female teacher stated that if "Mayor Peña was incapable of finding the guilty persons he should leave the matter to women and they would undertake to find them."[125] The teacher's seriousness about organizing a search team composed of women is uncertain, but her harangue about the mayor's incapacity to perform his duty was clearly meant to be emasculating. Aside from her denunciation serving to enforce community ethics and condemn corruption and murder, the teacher's criticism could have been an avenue for gaining greater women's participation in local politics. Regardless of her intentions, her voice was one of the loudest at the protest.[126]

The murderers took these warnings seriously. U.S. immigration inspectors kept a lookout for suspects who feared for their lives on the Mexican side and might attempt to flee to the United States.[127] Although the suspects succeeded in eluding justice for two years, on August 2, 1940, U.S. consul for Nuevo Laredo Romayn Wormuth informed the secretary of state in Washington that "due to continued agitation on the part of the local population," a Mexican court sentenced murder suspects Jesús Lara Gómez and José Acosta Rodríguez to twenty-one and twenty-two years, respectively, in the state penitentiary at Ciudad Victoria.[128]

Escalating drug violence accompanied the increasing development of U.S. and Mexican highways. No longer isolated hamlets, by the early 1940s the two Laredos served as a bridge across a Pan-American network of movement and international commerce. Along highways, however, traveled an influx of narcotics traffickers who threatened popular smuggling by prompting further government surveillance and interdiction. Miguel Abed, a Syrian living in Puebla, Mexico, and one of the "largest dealers in narcotic drugs," entered the United States through the port of Laredo at least nine separate times between April 1931 and May 1940.[129] When U.S. Customs agents finally took note of Abed's crossings, they circulated his picture and passport number to increase vigilance. A U.S. draft board questioned Max Steiner, an Austrian-born naturalized U.S. citizen with a Long Island address as he crossed through Laredo early in February 1942. U.S. authorities had wanted to talk to Steiner since Mexican law enforcement arrested him with a "bulk of marihuana" in Veracruz on May 6, 1940.[130] Steiner admitted to being arrested by Mexican authorities for smuggling silk dresses from the United States, but nothing more. With no evidence to hold him Steiner walked free, but American law enforcement kept him under surveillance. In May of 1943 U.S. authorities became aware of one Gastón Baca Corella who regularly crossed one hundred to two hundred grams of heroin through Laredo in road trips between Mexico City and San Antonio, Texas.[131]

The outbreak of the Second World War disrupted overseas narcotics networks and prompted an increase in opium cultivation in Mexico. Trafficking naturally followed. On May 11, 1943, George S. Messersmith, U.S. ambassador to Mexico, noted the upsurge in the drug trade across the border and warned that "unless checked, [it] will probably become as large as that formerly existing between the Far East and the United States."[132] Indeed, the U.S. Treasury Department estimated Mexican opium production for 1943 to total sixty tons, a three-times increase from the previous year. Moreover, "owing to the ease with which opium may be concealed in automobiles and shipments of raw materials . . . our customs agents can be expected to seize only a portion of the total contraband."[133] Messersmith grimly concluded that "it would appear that Mexico . . . is fast becoming the principal source of opium illicitly entering the United States."[134]

CONCLUSION

Federal prohibitions on narcotics and alcohol separated drug and liquor trafficking from other forms of illicit trade. Unlike earlier illicit trade, which simply circumvented government tariffs, narcotics and Prohibition-era alcohol involved the professional smuggling of banned criminal substances. Criminals, not merchants or consumers, traded drugs and alcohol on the border. With the notable exception of tequileros, whose conflicts coincided with ethnic Mexican notions of honor, most traffickers of prohibited goods fell outside of the moral economy of smuggling. Organized criminals expanded on illicit networks created during Prohibition to traffic in drugs. Escalating sophistication, illegality, and profitability led to increased criminality as mafias corrupted and co-opted government employees or assassinated them when they threatened their underworld enterprises. Although corruption and drug violence fell outside the moral economy, locals could do little but protest against powerful criminal syndicates. National laws and domestic demands created a market for illegal drugs despite local attitudes and contributed to the border's reputation as a criminal space. Government bans not only failed to prevent the introduction of prohibited substances, they made the border a site of violent and professional smuggling.

FIVE

Smugglers and Seditionists

STATES CONFRONT ILLICIT TRADERS,

1920–1945

On February 24, 1920, J. Rábago, Mexico's vice consul in Hidalgo, Texas, sent a troubling report to his superiors in Mexico City. Rábago informed them that an "Association of Contrabandistas" dominated the border town of Reynosa, Tamaulipas.[1] While Rábago conceded that "[it is] certain that there is smuggling across all borders, in Reynosa, it is virtually the only profession." [2] In Reynosa, the consul continued, there is a "band of smugglers, an Association" made up of sixty-eight individuals led by four brothers. The association was well organized and for the most part operated just like a business, although an illicit one, making its money trafficking livestock, wax, cinnamon, whiskey, and other goods around federal tariffs and trade prohibitions. Rábago estimated that the association's activities defrauded the Mexican government of $200,000 worth of revenue annually. Moreover, the consul warned that in Reynosa "no one voted except those 68 in the band of contrabandistas; and in this way they control the municipality." [3] Simón González, one of the four brothers allegedly heading the organization, even served as the town's municipal president. With illicit traders wielding such influence and trafficking desired, popularly accepted items, Rábago wrote that along the border "it is not a discredit to be a smuggler even though they are wrongdoers." [4]

The Mexican Revolution unleashed decades of armed conflict and political instability in Mexico and the Rio Grande borderlands. As the Mexican government struggled to protect itself, federal border forces prioritized national security over collecting tariffs. Trafficking of arms across the border by revolutionaries, seditionists, and regional despots had to be stopped. With so much of its energy going to prevent arms trafficking, the Mexican government compromised with contrabandistas and their widespread petty smuggling on the border. Similarly, U.S. security fears regarding border integrity in the wake of the Mexican Revolution and the looming Second World War led to greater vigilance against perceived state threats, such as enemy aliens, and as the previous chapter has shown, alcohol and narcotics smugglers. While petty smuggling continued as a common practice, more and more trafficking inspired criminal activity beyond the moral economy.

MAFIOSO MERCHANTS

Unlike Mexico's war for independence, which devastated the national infrastructure, most of Mexico's industries survived the revolution intact. Rather than destroy refineries, plants, and breweries, occupying armies decided to operate or tax them to finance themselves. After the worst of the warfare ceased, most of these industries returned to their owners, who pressured the new government to continue the policy of high protective tariffs.[5] Intended to protect domestic industry, tariffs also served as a significant source of revenue and helped pay Mexico's debt, which stood at $700 million in 1922.[6] With tariffs high and less expensive products available in the United States, organizations specializing in the trafficking of consumer goods spread along the length of the Rio Grande borderlands.[7]

Illicit trade's increasing profits spurred sophisticated criminal networks whose members crossed the line between merchants and mafiosos. On June 12, 1922, over two years after word reached Mexico City of an association of contrabandistas operating in Reynosa, Francisco Pérez, the Mexican consul in Hidalgo, informed superiors that smugglers evaded consular duties on more than $100,000 worth of merchandise.[8] A year later in a report on illicit trade along the border, Pérez recommended the employment of secret agents to monitor the vast amount of smuggling taking place there.[9] The government needed secret agents because local witnesses did not step forward for fear of retribution. As an example, Pérez cited a group of traffickers apprehended on October 20, 1921, who attempted to defraud the government of over $250,000 worth of revenue and who "after a time were set free, had their merchandise returned, and now threaten the same authorities who apprehended them."[10] Mexican traffickers' willingness to intimidate and corrupt law enforcement illustrates their growing power beyond the customary moral economy of smuggling. State failures against organized smugglers in turn bred apa-

FIGURE 5.1. *The view entering Nuevo Laredo by way of the international bridge, Paso del Puente, Nuevo Laredo, Tamaulipas, early twentieth century. Photographer unknown. Special Collections, Laredo Public Library.*

thy among local authorities, who unsurprisingly proved uncooperative in federal investigations.

Mexican market restrictions on imports made the smuggling of consumer goods a profitable enterprise that invited organized crime. During the 1920s organized crime utilized an "army of women" to smuggle merchandise along Mexico's border with Texas.[11] Although the steady stream of female smugglers hiding stockings under their skirts added up to thousands of dollars of lost federal revenue and individuals continued to illicitly cross consumer items for personal consumption, by the 1930s violent traffickers overshadowed casual tariff evasion. Smugglers crossing a "grand cargo" of silk cloth and live poultry from the United States drew their guns and fired on Mexican Customs agents outside Nuevo Laredo in mid-March 1933.[12] Although no one was wounded in the encounter, confrontations between traffickers and Aduana agents could turn deadly. On January 21, 1933, traffickers smuggling pork lard and radio equipment killed two Mexican Customs agents as they crossed the Rio Grande near Ciudad Juárez. Mexican authorities succeeded in capturing four of the suspects, but believed that the four were just part of the "great business" of smuggling consumer goods into Mexico and liquor into the United States.[13] Nor was this the only case of blood being spilled by traffickers of consumer goods. Shortly after 2:00 a.m. on February 17, 1934, Mexican Customs agents stopped two suspicious cars carrying nine men near Nuevo Laredo. As the officers approached the vehicles, suspects drew automatic rifles, starting a five-minute shootout that left one of the agents dead. The suspects sped away or escaped on foot, but left behind a car loaded with forty large bundles of smuggled valuables.[14]

The trafficking of consumer goods adversely affected law-abiding Mexican businesses, which struggled to compete with illicit merchants who undersold them by selling smuggled products. Late in April 1932 members of Matamoros's Confederación de Cámaras de Comercio (Chamber of Commerce) appealed to Mexican Customs forces to combat the smuggling of consumer goods, which "defrauded finance, and caused a great prejudice against honorable business."[15] Members of the Confederación affirmed to local newspapers that they offered the lowest prices they could under import law, but could not compete with goods smuggled around tariffs. The chamber of commerce had reason for concern. Throughout the 1930s tariffs on most imports averaged 16 percent, but specific tariffs could be greater.[16] For example, the Confederación cited lard, which although valued at 5.50 pesos had a 4.50 peso duty.[17] With illicit businesses able to sell well under the legal price, the Confederación complained "many individuals are getting rich . . . while honorable merchants are ruined."[18] The Confederación's appeal against black-market merchants paid off a year later in March of 1933, when Mexican Customs forces investigated Andrés and Adrián Cisneros's business in Matamoros. The Cisneros brothers' establishment, aptly named "Zona Libre," raised eyebrows for selling staple consumer goods such as flour at prices that no competitor could match.[19] Suspecting smuggling, Mexican Customs forces delved into the origin of the Cisneros brothers' cheap products and discovered that they paid impoverished individuals to smuggle small amounts of flour to supply the store. Authorities estimated that the brothers' business cost the government over 12,000 pesos worth of revenue and that "commerce in Matamoros was truly at the mercy of the authors of contraband."[20]

GUNRUNNING

Mexican state concerns over the smuggling of consumer goods paled before its fears of arms trafficking. The accessibility of U.S. arms caused the Mexican government to exercise a great deal of vigilance guarding its northern border. In 1925 fifteen Mexican Special Service agents monitored the Texas border where the disaffected supposedly dwelled.[21] On December 17, 1925, local officials in Piedras Negras, Coahuila, warned the Mexican secretary of war that the border was "inhabited on both sides of the line by dangerous people set to smuggling."[22] Manuel T. Flores seems to have been one of these individuals. Flores operated a gas station in Rio Grande City, Texas, but he also reputedly trafficked arms into Mexico. On January 20, 1926, a Mexican Migración officer reported to superiors that Flores smuggled guns and ammo across the Los Ebanos ferry for rebels in Mexico whom he kept "constant contact" with.[23] Indeed, smugglers crossed guns along the length of the border. On December 3, 1926, Mexican Special Agent #2 warned that the government's enemies in northern Chihuahua had the resources to "pay people that are dying of hunger . . . to pass contraband," including arms and munitions.[24] The agent confirmed his suspicions on January 9, 1927, when he reported that "on the edge [of] the Río Bravo [Rio Grande] in the area of Villa Acuña . . . exist certain individuals of bad background that were in misery until recently and have ultimately dedicated their activities to smuggling arms and munitions for the revolutionaries."[25] It is noteworthy that the Mexican agent pointed out that the suspects "were in misery" prior to their involvement trading arms, because the observation indicates that poor *fronterizos* traded not only out of sympathy for the movement, but also out of necessity.[26]

Vicente Rendón Quijano, the Mexican consul in Rio Grande City, ventured into contrabandista communities while investigating reports of arms smuggling along the U.S. side of the border. On August 2, 1926, Rendón Quijano reported that there were various small ranches along the edge of the Rio Grande inhabited for the most part by settlers "almost totally Mexican . . . and related to people on the Mexican side."[27] Isolated and connected only by a cart road, this section of the river proved difficult to guard particularly because small Tejano ranches bordered similar ranches on the Mexican side. Although the consul informed superiors that locals for the most part sympathized with the government and could easily detect outsiders and report them to authorities, Rendón Quijano pointed out that it was "very easy in any of these ranches . . . to organize small groups of people" to "come and go without note . . . smuggling merchandise from one side to the other."[28]

BINATIONAL COOPERATION

The U.S. and Mexican governments cooperated when it served their interests. While the U.S. government worked to keep tequileros from unlawfully importing liquor during Prohibition, the Mexican government feared that liquor smugglers returned with contraband arms to Mexico. On January 4, 1924, Francisco Pérez, the Mexican consul in Rio Grande City, wrote his superior in San Antonio of one Eulogio Zárate of La Grulla, Texas. According to Pérez, Zárate made his living crossing tequila to the United States and smuggling arms and munitions into Mexico, even going so far as to lead armed men against the Mexican government. With Zárate and others like him breaking laws on both sides of the border, Pérez capitalized on Texas justice and informed Texas Rangers of the illicit activity in the area.[29] Whether U.S. law enforcement ever apprehended Zárate is unknown, but Consul Pérez proudly reported that mounted U.S. Customs inspectors later that month apprehended a number of tequileros near Hebbronville whom seditious elements had sought to employ in a revolutionary incursion into Mexico.[30]

In spite of the occasional success with binational law enforcement, the Mexican government believed liquor smugglers crossed weapons along the length of the Rio Grande. On September 23, 1926, a Mexican special agent monitoring the border near Langtry, Texas, reported that arms and munitions frequently passed as contraband in exchange for whiskey.[31] The agent went on to inform that the Mexican side of the border lacked permanent government vigilance and that Huertistas practiced their "secret work" there.[32] A. P. Carrillo, the Mexican consul in Del Rio, fueled government fears that December when he informed superiors that many liquor traffickers operated near Langtry, and "it is not difficult for those same smugglers on returning to Mexico, to bring cartridges in the same way they take liquor."[33]

INSURGENT MEXICO

Mexico's centuries-old conflict between church and state reignited in the late 1920s when President Plutarco Elías Calles began to enforce the anticlerical articles of the Constitution of 1917. In response to these measures, Mexico's archbishop declared that the country's Catholics could no longer in good conscience accept the Constitution. Elías Calles responded swiftly. The government ended public religious processions.

Foreign priests and nuns were deported. The doors of many convents, monasteries, and church schools slammed shut. In retaliation the Church declared a strike, refusing to celebrate the mass or perform baptisms, marriages, or last rites. Open warfare followed. Between 1926 and 1929 devotees attacked government outposts under the banner of "¡Viva Cristo Rey!," while government troops killed priests and burned churches.[34]

Although the majority of the fighting occurred in Central Mexico, the Cristero Rebellion directly affected contrabandistas in the borderlands. Most ethnic Mexicans on the border identified themselves as Catholics, and tales of church defilements exacerbated local Cristero sympathies. Indeed, churches along the U.S. border filled with the Mexican faithful who could not worship freely in their own land, and these hapless pilgrims doubtlessly fueled local outrage. Rural peasants could not withstand the military superiority of the Mexican army and needed guns to remain a viable movement; however, a U.S. arms embargo prevented Cristeros from acquiring American weapons legally. Mexican consuls believed that members of the Catholic fraternal organization the Knights of Columbus financed arms trafficking throughout the borderlands. Rumors ran rampant, but direct evidence proved scattered and fragmentary. For instance, one report stated that a Cristero sympathizer in Crystal City, Texas, loaned three planes to fly arms into Mexico.[35] Accounts of Cristero activity on the border peaked in the winter of 1927, when Cristero leader René Capistran Garza reputedly journeyed to Laredo to receive ten thousand shells.[36] Although Capistran Garza did travel to the United States on a fundraising campaign in the fall of 1926, it is unknown if he ever personally ran arms for the Cristeros. More troubling to the Mexican government than the suspicion of fraternal orders was the fear its officers were complicit in this smuggling.

On July 28, 1926, the Mexican consul in San Antonio sent a confidential letter to his superiors outlining disturbing reports that members of the Knights of Columbus had infiltrated important state positions on the border. The situation seemed particularly bad in Camargo, Tamaulipas, where the municipal president belonged to the order and the Mexican Customs administrator aspired to join its ranks. Moreover, directly across the river in Rio Grande City, the U.S. immigration inspector, his assistant, and the county sheriff all belonged to the Knights of Columbus. Worse still, the consul wrote that the Guerra family, "enemies of the actual government," controlled all the authorities in Rio Grande City, including the Mexican consul, whom they persuaded to join the Knights of Columbus.[37] With such local support, the consul worried it would be impossible to stop the seven boxes of ammunition an informant told him the Knights intended to smuggle to the Cristeros.[38]

Cristeros were just one of the many factions confronting the Mexican government. The more radical mandates of the Mexican Revolution came to fruition in 1934 with the presidency of Lázaro Cárdenas, who, aside from redistributing land, nationalized the petroleum industry in 1938. Cárdenas's revolutionary reforms prompted counterrevolutionary uprisings. In late August 1938 information circulated that los Dorados (the Gold Shirts), a fascist-like group dedicated to combating communists, planned to attack Reynosa, Tamaulipas. The Mexican government took such threats seriously. Investigators spent days looking into reports of secret arms caches in South Texas and pondering the "subversive propaganda" that los Dorados could spread in the event they seized the Reynosa radio station.[39] Although los Dorados' attack on September 16 (Mexican Independence Day) never occurred, rumors of gunrunning continued to run rampant. After conducting an investigation of arms trafficking on the border in August of 1939, one agent concluded that such activity could only have seditious purposes and indicated the preparation of an armed movement against the government.[40] Early in January 1940 the Mexican consul in Laredo reported to Mexico City that a former army officer tried to buy airplanes and other war materiel for the Cedillistas.[41] Six months later, Mexican federal authorities received information that $70,000 in U.S. arms destined for General Saturnino Cedillo's followers had entered the country illegally as part of a plot to "start a revolution in Mexico." [42]

Factional, regional, social, and religious conflicts in the wake of the Mexican Revolution destabilized Mexico for decades. Would-be insurgents sought weapons from the closest source, the United States, and Mexico did all it could to prevent rebels from gaining American arms. Mexico's Foreign Relations Service, the Secretaría de Relaciones Exteriores, investigated arms trafficking across the length of the U.S.-Mexico border. In December 1939 the Mexican consul in McAllen reported "persistent rumors" of large shipments of arms and munitions being smuggled into northeastern Tamaulipas.[43] These rumors proved to be well founded. On February 14, 1940, U.S. Customs agents working near Brownsville apprehended Esteban Loyola and Arturo Garza unlawfully exporting 2,300 rifle cartridges into Mexico.[44] Although U.S. authorities foiled Loyola and Garza's plot, the Secretaría de Relaciones Exteriores worried about their motivations. Why did Loyola, a resident of Brownsville, and Garza, a resident of Matamoros, attempt to traffic ammunition into Mexico? Mexican authorities wondered if the men were simply opportunists trying to make an illegal buck, or if they were seditionists.

Early in 1940 Mexican federal authorities suspected *norteño* presidential candidate General Juan Andreu Almazán's supporters, Almazanistas, of using smuggled American arms in a plot against the government.[45] The strength of these concerns were such that U.S. military intelligence observed that "around the [Mexican] War Department it is insistently rumored that an enormous quantity of arms, ammunition, and even machine-guns, have been introduced into Mexico from the United States."[46] Although Almazán and his followers did not rise up as Mexican authorities feared, the government's alarm highlights how loosely incorporated the Mexican north remained four decades into the twentieth century. Unable to effectively guard the border, Mexican authorities sought local assistance and turned to campesinos, the "natural allies" of the revolution.[47]

Despite the revolutionary government's reverence of the Mexican campesino (peasant) as the foot soldier of the revolution and the beneficiary of land reform, many of these campesinos placed local interests over national concerns and commonly smuggled. While investigating arms trafficking near Mier, Tamaulipas, Mexican agents discovered numerous contrabandista communities residing along the Rio Grande. The hamlets of Rancho Grande, Rincón de las Calabazas, and Las Mulitas were small agricultural communities peopled by campesinos, many of whom smuggled necessities such as flour and clothing to help make ends meet.[48] Rather than use boats that U.S. and Mexican forces could destroy or confiscate, locals crafted rafts known as *patos*, or ducks, out of little more than sheets of canvas and bound willows. Although crude to the untrained eye, locals' handiwork proved ideally suited to the cat and mouse game against border guards. U.S. officers investigating *patero* activity remarked that the canvas cover could be removed "in a moment, and then carried under a man's arm. The frame can easily be hidden in the brush, and if it should be destroyed, 15 minutes work with a machete (and no one ever saw a Mexican of this class without a machete) will construct another."[49] Contrabandistas' use of efficient, inexpensive methods to carry out their illicit trades would continually frustrate state efforts against them.

In the face of regional instability and the near impossibility of preventing illicit trade, the Mexican government decided to accept borderlanders' petty smuggling in exchange for their goodwill and cooperation in the state's effort to prevent arms trafficking. Rather than risk government interference in their own community-accepted contraband trades, locals reported transgressors of the moral economy. Early in February 1939 the Mexican consul in McAllen, Texas, received an anonymous tip of gunrunning in his district. On February 10 Mexican soldiers awaiting the transaction intercepted a load of 4,500 rounds of seven-millimeter machine gun ammunition they suspected belonged to los Dorados. Cooperative successes such as this led the Mexican government to seek a symbiotic relationship with contrabandistas. In 1940 Bonifacio Salinas Leal, governor of Nuevo León, accepted borderlanders' "way of life" and offered to tolerate their smuggling of consumer goods in exchange for contrabandistas' assistance in reporting arms traffickers.[50] For months afterward, authorities reported arms smuggling in the area "completely null."[51]

Governor Salinas Leal's deal with contrabandistas was brilliant. As Mexican government reports conceded, "it is easier to control smugglers than to chase them."[52] Leal's plan kept contraband within state-accepted levels. By allowing contrabandistas to smuggle necessities, he won their support against arms traffickers who posed a greater threat to the state. Instead of arresting petty smugglers, Mexican Customs agents could concentrate their limited resources searching for gunrunners. Indeed, the Mexican government could afford such concessions because it no longer relied on customs duties as its principal source of revenue. Although import and export duties continued to provide appreciable proceeds, the Mexican government prioritized keeping smuggled arms out of dangerous hands over collecting funds.[53] Contrabandistas benefited from Salinas Leal's plan too. Under the arrangement they did not have to worry about Mexican Customs agents' intrusions. Moreover, contrabandistas now had an interest in keeping arms traffickers out. Rumors of gunrunning would draw customs men, and locals did not want federal authorities disrupting their routine. Greater federal policing hurt petty smugglers and traffickers alike and intensified vigilance made it difficult for both gunrunners and contrabandistas to "work."[54]

Agreements between locals and the state proved mutually beneficial. Along the Rio Grande existed many small towns where trouble could grow. Some of these fears were realized in Río Rico, a community on Tamaulipas's northeastern border with Texas. A government inspector investigating arms smuggling in Río Rico commented that "most persons living there are not from good backgrounds."[55] Corruption, although in no ways unique to the border, seems to have taken root and thrived there. Word circulated that Bernardo García, a local Mexican Customs agent, took gifts in exchange for letting contraband pass. Given that García dressed well and drove a nice car for a lowly government worker, it stood to reason that the stories were true. García himself reputedly smuggled. Talk circulated that authorities discovered a great quantity of contraband women's stockings (*medias*) in García's car in 1939. García's activities became a threat to the state in November 1940 when Mexican Customs agents discovered two fifty-shell cases of .22-caliber ammunition in García's car as it made its way back across the border. He, however, was not behind the wheel. García's activities had escalated to the point of organized trafficking, though he himself no longer smuggled. Rather, he let two men borrow his car so they could cross the ammunition. The simple and effective scheme entailed the men hiding the ammunition in the car and García waving them through. García's associates crossed untold amounts of contraband while he stood duty in the eight months prior to the investigation, and were it not for a tip-off, García's trafficking might have gone on indefinitely.[56]

Río Rico slipped through the cracks in the Mexican state's defenses. Bernardo García represented one of the Mexican government's worst fears: a corrupt state agent who worked against its interests. García trafficked illegal arms commercially, and the Mexican government did not know whether individuals, organized criminals, or seditious elements like the Almazanistas hoped to buy them. García's motivations remain unclear. Although he may have trafficked arms to support fringe political groups, it seems more likely that he smuggled for personal gain. Rumors of his corruption and trafficking in consumer goods like women's stockings had circulated in the community for years. The difference between gunrunning and smuggling consumer goods was that the state viewed arms trafficking as a threat, and guns, unlike panty hose, fell outside most locals' bounds of acceptable contraband. Rumors that the local customs agent smuggled women's hosiery can be attributed to the pleasure people get from gossip. Gunrunning, however, was dangerous to both locals and the government. Not wanting arms smuggling in the community or the government's search for guns to upset local illicit trades, an informant reported García to Mexican authorities.[57]

ARMING MEXICO

Arms trafficking, however, continued despite the occasional denunciation. At about 9:00 p.m. on Friday, January 19, 1940, U.S. Customs agents arrested Francisco Del Valle Arispe and Gregorio Prieto at the international bridge in Laredo for attempting to smuggle twenty-eight thousand rounds of assorted .32-20 and .38 Special ammunition in their car into Mexico. Rather than believe the suspects' claim that they purchased the ten thousand pistol and eighteen thousand or so rifle rounds "solely for target practice," the U.S. and Mexican governments delved deeper into Del Valle and Prieto's case.[58] Further investigation revealed that both men served as officers in the Mexican army. Del Valle held a lieutenant colonel's rank while Prieto was a former major. Both held political aspirations. Prieto planned to run as a deputy congressman, and Del Valle campaigned for the position of federal deputy for Saltillo. Del Valle denied smuggling for revolutionaries or organized criminals and asserted that his arms purchases came from a poorly conceived effort to finance his political campaign. Given he invested three thousand pesos in the venture and hoped to sell the prohibited ammunition at three times the U.S. price, Del Valle could have mounted quite a campaign had he succeeded. Regardless of their motives, both suspects violated U.S. neutrality laws in efforts to cross arms.[59]

Del Valle and Prieto's legal defense argued that, not being registered with the U.S. secretary of state under the provisions of the Neutrality Act, the two could not have obtained an export permit had they applied for one. Moreover, Del Valle and Prieto claimed ignorance of needing an export permit. Although the ten thousand rounds of .38 Special ammunition the suspects attempted to export were most commonly used for police and military-grade service revolvers, the judge instructed the jury that if they believed the suspects purchased the ammunition "exclusively for sporting purposes," they should find the defendants not guilty.[60] Despite damning evidence, the U.S. government's prosecution failed to persuade locals to convict Del Valle and Prieto of conspiracy to violate the Neutrality Act of 1939 prohibiting the export of munitions to foreign countries without authorization, and a local jury found the defendants not guilty after a three-day trial. After the jury returned the verdict, the judge himself informed the jurors that he believed the defendants were "technically guilty," but admitted that the "law was inadequate to cover such cases as this one." [61] Given its failure to convict Del Valle and Prieto, the government abandoned its case against two other men charged with a similar offense in Brownsville.[62]

Del Valle and Prieto's acquittal reveals U.S. shortfalls in policing arms trafficking on the border. Although originally intended to prevent war materiel from reaching belligerent nations overseas, U.S. law enforcement attempted to use the provisions of the Neutrality Act of 1939 to prevent arms trafficking on the border. Despite being "technically guilty" of violating U.S. neutrality laws, local jurors allowed Del Valle and Prieto to slip through.[63]

Unlike their Mexican counterparts, many U.S. borderlanders accepted arms trafficking into Mexico. Although the suspects had received their ammunition from the warehouse of Joseph C. Netzer (the son of Joseph Netzer), neither the U.S. District Court, which tried Del Valle and Prieto, nor the court of public opinion indicted Netzer for his involvement in the conspiracy to smuggle stores of ammunition out of the country. In his defense, J. C. Netzer merely owned the bonded warehouse and may not have known the details of what went on in its daily operations. Still, Netzer's staff could not claim such ignorance. After Del Valle presented his paperwork for the order, Netzer's employees directed him to drive his car to the loading room. Rather than merely loading the wooden boxes into the vehicle, Netzer's workers opened the crates and placed the individual boxes of ammo in the car's trunk and in a suitcase. In the defense's own words, "Everything was done in the open . . . without trying to hide anything." [64] Netzer's staff did not ask questions, they did not know the buyers, and they silently "assumed" Del Valle had all the necessary papers.[65]

The Netzers, despite numerous accusations of their illegal arms dealing, continued to be active in community life. Aside from his warehouse where Del Valle and Prieto obtained their illicit ammo, J. C. Netzer operated a successful trucking company and a shipping firm with lines to New York, Philadelphia, and Chicago. During the late 1930s J. C. Netzer served as president of the chamber of commerce, Rotary Club, and the Washington Birthday Celebration Association. With such community involvement, it is no surprise a local paper closed its brief on Netzer's business by saying, "It is hoped he will continue his activities in Laredo." [66] On January 26, 1940, only seven days after Del Valle and Prieto took their ammo out of his warehouse, the *Laredo Times* informed that J. C. Netzer, then governor of the regional Rotary International, announced a series of forums on "international understanding" that included a talk titled "Organizing the World for Peace." [67]

That neither the court nor the public condemned Netzer or his workers for their complicity in arms trafficking shows the extent locals in the United States accepted illicit arms sales to Mexico. Furthermore, illicit trade's commonplace in border life made locals virtually blind to it. Netzer's workers removed the individual boxes of ammunition from their crates and placed them in Del Valle's car "in the open . . . without trying to hide anything." [68] Although Netzer's employees may have simply needed the pay, blatant acts such as this indicate that locals did not think that complicity with arms smuggling was wrong. Still, the suspects' discretion in placing the ammunition in the trunk and in a suitcase, rather than in plain sight, reveals that Del Valle knew that authorities would object to his arms trafficking.

CROSSING CUSTOMS

Los dos Laredos continued to develop as bustling border towns. In 1935 U.S. import duties in Laredo reached $1,235,104.[69] Nuevo Laredo kept its place as its country's most important port on the border and ranked as the third greatest port in Mexico the following year. By 1945 almost half of Mexico's trade along the border flowed through Nuevo Laredo.[70] The two Laredos' place along railroad linkages between the United States and Mexico, and the Pan-American Highway system that followed them, further spurred the communities' growth. Nuevo Laredo's population stood at 14,988 in 1920, while Laredo claimed a population of 22,710 that same year.[71] By 1940 Nuevo Laredo grew to host some 29,000 people and Laredo almost 40,000.[72]

Despite the spreading electrification and paved streets, communities along the Rio Grande remained loosely incorporated border towns where smugglers plied illicit trade. U.S. Customs officers working in the 1930s encountered the same problems that their predecessors endured a generation earlier. The Customs Service proved woefully understaffed, with only forty-five patrolmen regulating the district's 1,200 miles of river and coastline. Underbrush so thick it could "hide a man on horseback" stretched for miles along the riverbank, offering refuge to would-be smugglers.[73] Dense vegetation also made it impossible for Customs agents to patrol by car. Between La Grulla and Zapata lay some ninety miles of riverfront so impenetrable that an experienced officer lamented it would take "two men, working ten hours a day, 90 days" to patrol.[74] About sixty fords existed between Colombia and Guerrero at normal levels, and at its lowest stage, a U.S. military intelligence report informed, the Rio Grande could be "crossed almost anywhere."[75] In the game between smugglers and Customs, illicit traders had the advantage. Experienced smugglers decided when and where to cross and had local knowledge of the terrain that officers could not match.[76]

Mexican officers were no more successful at policing their side of the border. Some three hundred Mexican Customs agents monitored Nuevo

Laredo and its outlying areas, but significant security gaps persisted. "Mere trails" linked Nuevo Laredo to Guerrero and Mier, making the border difficult to patrol.[77] On May 11, 1940, a Mexican inspector checking the border for arms trafficking reported to his superiors in Mexico City that although he received information of arms and ammo being smuggled at a place called Paso del Charco, the crossing could not be located. Although only thirty miles separated Camargo and Mier, Tamaulipas, the space where the site supposedly lay, Mexican investigators speaking to locals could find no one who admitted knowing the ford.[78] Along the border lay a web of river crossings and paths that only locals knew. The Mexican inspector complained that "close to 40 kilometers from Camargo is a ranch called 'Rancho del Charco' but it lies closer to the interior" and could not be the suspect site. The Mexican inspector went on to mention three other locations with similar names, but concluded that "a place called 'Paso del Charco' close to the Río Bravo [Rio Grande] . . . could not be found." [79] Aside from the inadequate roads and lack of information, poor economic conditions among the inhabitants worked against the Mexican government's efforts to secure the line. In December of 1940, U.S. military intelligence noted a poor standard of living in Nuevo Laredo and listed "underworld characters" amongst the common occupations of hotelmen, waiters, and saloonkeepers typical of border towns.[80] With vigilance weak and incentive strong, smuggling continued as both necessity and as a business.

CONTRABANDISTAS IN A SECURITY STATE

Contrabandistas continued to evade U.S. tariffs. Late in October 1942, a woman from Tampico known only as Elena wrote her friend in San Antonio complaining that shopping in Mexico was too expensive . . . Could she please buy her three pairs of shoes? Elena enclosed a check for twenty-two dollars and suggested that a friend take the shoes to her in Mexico next time she visited. Before Elena's friend in San Antonio could read her letter, U.S. Customs agents intercepted and transcribed it under the title "MEXICAN WOMAN MAY ATTEMPT CUSTOMS EVASION." [81]

The Second World War greatly increased the power of the U.S. government. Fearful of spies, saboteurs, and other subversives undermining the war effort, the government monitored the border like never before and inadvertently uncovered evidence of the popular acceptance of petty smuggling. Elena's letter discussing smuggling was just one of hundreds

FIGURE 5.2. *U.S. Customs building, Laredo, Texas, early twentieth century. Photographer unknown. Special Collections, Laredo Public Library.*

of similar correspondences that U.S. Customs agents intercepted in their national security efforts. Early in November 1942, Goza Ayala of Monterrey, Nuevo León, wrote Antonia Pérez in San Antonio asking for help getting a doll for a friend's daughter. The doll did not have to be expensive. A dollar or a dollar and a half would be fine, but Ayala warned Pérez to "be careful bringing things you should not bring because they are not going to let you pass them." [82] Like Elena, Ayala was not a criminal trafficker, but a binational consumer who felt no scruples about evading government tariffs. Not criminals who smuggled professionally, Ayala and other contrabandistas like her merely saw smuggling as a victimless crime and a way to save money. A doll would make a good present for Día de los Reyes on January 6, the day Mexican children get their Christmas presents. Indeed, gift giving served as a common reason for petty smuggling. On Halloween 1942 a woman from Ciudad Victoria, Tamaulipas, wrote Azucena Guitérrez in Laredo asking for a ten-dollar black suit for her husband's birthday. The U.S. Customs Service intercepted the letter and transcribed it under the title, "MEXICAN PLANS POSSIBLE EVASION OF CUSTOMS." [83]

Periods of heightened national security like World War II allowed the federal government the resources to uncover mundane smuggling on the border, but despite its founding principle as a revenue-collecting agency, the U.S. Customs Service did not prioritize tariff enforcement at that critical time. Instead, Customs agents focused their efforts on national security and the war effort and were more and more becoming agents of border security rather than agents of economic security. This shift in Customs' emphasis came largely from the decline of tariffs as the principal source of federal revenue. Customs receipts constituted less than 10 percent of total U.S. federal revenue in 1941. By war's end less than 5 percent of the government's money came from tariff duties.[84] With tariff revenue no longer the principal source of government funding, tariff collection ceased to be a government priority. That is not to say that Customs agents did not apprehend tariff evaders when they could, only that collecting tariffs, especially in minor amounts, came after national security and the prevention of neutrality violations.

EXPORT CONTROL

The U.S. government also worked hard to keep certain items from leaving the country. As in World War I, the United States placed restrictions on the exportation of items necessary to the war effort. Government bans prohibiting exports went beyond obvious war materiel such as guns and ammunition. Rubber, gasoline, and sugar, for instance, could not lawfully leave the country because the government needed these products for the war. Government restrictions did not end popular demand, and many U.S. citizens resorted to smuggling to get what they desired. Rather than do without conveniences such as soap, sugar, or coffee, many consumers on the borderlands merely crossed into Mexico for these goods. The casual smuggling of consumer goods for personal consumption, even if contrary to the war effort, largely fell within the moral economy of illicit trade. Ramiro Rendón of Laredo recalled that as a teenager in 1942, he and his friends routinely crossed into Mexico to buy rationed goods. Typically, Rendón and his friends purchased these items for women whose husbands or sons were away at war. That locals condoned Rendón's activity is shown by his mother's instruction that he "go to Mrs. Casiano's house because she has five sons in the Armed Forces, and that's the least we can do for her."[85]

Government rationing made basic staples expensive or difficult to acquire, and many people smuggled because they could not afford or lawfully obtain their basic needs. In 1945 Vernon Fluharty, U.S. vice consul for Nuevo Laredo, complained that sugar was scarce and sold at "speculation prices."[86] The cost of bread continued to rise, but the quality and weight per loaf fell. In Reynosa another U.S. consul observed that the "high cost of the barest necessities of life is entirely out of proportion to wages and salaries."[87] Indeed, one U.S. consul estimated that the cost of living in Nuevo Laredo had risen "350% for Mexicans and 500% for foreigners."[88] For many, the price proved too much to bear. Even members of the Mexican Customs Service quit their jobs in droves and went into business for themselves out of "sheer economic necessity."[89] The need to acquire essentials like medicines similarly compelled people to smuggle. On October 13, 1944, Rosario de Zambrano of Monterrey, Nuevo León, phoned Dr. Francisco Canseco in Laredo about getting two bottles of penicillin for her sick son. Dr. Canseco responded that the U.S. government did not allow any penicillin to go to Mexico, but he would send it via her chauffeur if he could, and call if he could not.[90] U.S. rationing of penicillin caused such shortages in Mexico that in February 1944, U.S. Treasury officials directed border customs agents to keep a lookout for a chemist named Mann, first name unknown, who intended to smuggle vials of penicillin culture on his person in order to cultivate the drug in Mexico.[91]

War-era trade restrictions also created ample opportunities to smuggle for profit. Of all the goods trafficked to Mexico during the war years, few were as lucrative as automobiles. In a personal letter to her son in the army, one mother revealed that aside from things being well at home, "Arthur has been doing a kind of black market business in cars new and used."[92] Using fictitious names, Arthur Graham purchased numerous vehicles in the United States, swearing he would not resell them. Graham, being an enterprising individual, took the cars to Mexico where he sold them for "about 100% profit."[93] U.S. Customs struggled to catch illicit car traders. Although Customs agents carefully recorded vehicle model numbers, license plates, and even the serial numbers of individual tires including the spare, persons driving to Mexico had only to leave their car behind.[94] Still, car traders knew that Customs agents watched for them, and they hatched elaborate conspiracies to get their vehicles across the river. Early in November 1944 two men plotted how best to sneak a car into Mexico. Ricardo Pérez, the traffic manager for Braniff Airways living in Laredo, phoned his friend Douglas Stockdale in Mexico City. They exchanged greetings and moved on to the matter at hand. Pérez informed Stockdale that if he wanted the car, Stockdale would have to fly to Laredo and get it himself. Pérez could not cross the car himself because he was already too well known. Like the time they crossed the Ford, Pérez would arrange everything on the U.S. side, and as soon as Stockdale arrived, they would go to the Mexican Customs office and say the car belonged to

Stockdale. Pérez told Stockdale if he did not come, they would have to go through the trouble of obtaining manifests, etc.[95]

Stockdale conspired to smuggle a car that really belonged to him because lying to Mexican Customs agents about the duration of his stay saved the burdensome paperwork required to cross the car legally. Whether Stockdale and Pérez intended to sell the car in Mexico or not, lying about the vehicle made the two smugglers. Pérez served as the traffic manager at the local airport, but he had also smuggled cars to Mexico before, and bridge guards recognized his face. Because he worked a steady job and did not plan to sell the car he crossed, it is interesting to wonder if Pérez even considered himself a smuggler. He may simply have thought of himself as a man who knew how to get things done on the border.[96]

Contrabandistas accepted the circumvention of unpopular federal laws, but it is important to point out that aside from denying states tariff revenue and undermining national aims, illicit trade harmed law-abiding businesses. On November 16, 1943, Joseph Tanous, a mining engineer working in Laredo, phoned his friend Rubén Moreno in Guadalajara. After exchanging greetings, Tanous told Moreno that he planned to visit him in Mexico and asked if he needed anything. Moreno said he needed about a *metro* (approximately three feet) of wire for an electric stove, but the U.S. government needed it too, so Tanous would have to conceal it.[97] Moreno may have saved some money getting smuggled wire, but illicit trades such as his undercut businesses that operated within the law. The week after Tanous called Moreno, Gonzalo Pérez, a Mexico City businessman, wrote the U.S. embassy reporting the trafficking of electrical material across the border. Pérez detailed that an employee of the Southern Electric Company of San Antonio, Texas, broke U.S. law by giving false invoices for purchases of switches. The "bad employee" apparently made multiple manifests for $23.93, just under the $25 limit.[98] Multiple buyers then purchased these switches and pooled them together into a lot of one thousand. Mexican residents traveling to San Antonio would then collect batches of these switches and take them to vendors in Mexico for a small fee.[99]

Trade fraud greatly concerned Gonzalo Pérez. In his letter to the U.S. embassy Pérez pointed out that conspirators wrote fraudulent invoices in pencil, making it easy for the names to be changed as needed and that in the future the Customs Service should insist forms be completed in ink to deter fraud. Pérez went on to suggest that if U.S. Customs agents checked their records, they would find that the same person had taken multiple shipments of wire declared at $23.93 through the ports of Del Rio, Eagle

Pass, Laredo, McAllen, and Brownsville. Pérez closed his letter with the plea, "I do not have to tell you that this makes a lot of trouble for the working man, who earns his living by the sweat of his brow." [100]

Pérez's letter to the U.S. embassy reflects the cost of contraband trade on law-abiding Mexican businesses. While consumers of contraband benefited from the evasion of tariffs and the acquisition of rationed goods, illicit trade harmed commercial ventures that paid tariffs and adhered to government rationing. Pérez's reporting of consumer traffickers reveals a consequence of the moral economy of smuggling. Honest merchants like Gonzalo Pérez found it difficult to compete against illicit merchants who undersold them with cheaper smuggled goods or goods they could not acquire at all. Despite its benefits to consumers, illicit trade undermined law-abiding business.

CONCLUSION

Illicit trade flourished in the decades after World War I, as Mexico and the United States placed border security above tariff collection. Mexican tariffs inadvertently made the traffic in consumer goods a profitable organized crime, but greater state threats, such as the introduction of guns by seditious elements, compelled Mexico to acquiesce to contraband consumption in order to concentrate its limited resources on combating arms smugglers. Although deals with contrabandistas won Mexican borderlanders' support against the unlawful flow of arms into Mexico, the toleration of arms trafficking north of the border worked to frustrate Mexico's effort to prevent guns from entering the country. While the smuggling of consumer goods benefited many border people, it undercut law-abiding businesses, which could not compete against cheaper black-market items. Moreover, illicit trade defrauded the Mexican government of significant revenue. Similarly, U.S. efforts to enforce its neutrality laws and prevent the unlawful exportation of rationed material created a market for contraband arms and restricted products that traffickers exploited. Ultimately, U.S. and Mexican trade restrictions not only failed to prevent the illegal movement of articles across the border, they created a market for desired contraband goods that many borderlanders and outsiders exploited for self-gain.

Good Deals and Drug Deals

Since 1848 the United States and Mexico strived to police trade on their shared border, and a great many border people resisted state interference in their commerce by smuggling. Sometimes border people acquiesced to government regulations and trade restrictions, while at other times they took an active role in shaping customs policies. Border people's disregard of tariff laws they deemed detrimental forced the Mexican government to concede the establishment of a free-trade zone on the border in 1858. Aside from dramatic concessions such as the creation of the Zona Libre, by 1940 contrabandistas succeeded in prompting the Mexican government to accept petty smuggling in exchange for information on arms trafficking by organized criminals and revolutionaries who challenged the state. Smugglers' persistence north of the border similarly forced the U.S. government to tolerate petty illicit trade in order to focus its limited power on combating armed liquor and narcotics traffickers who posed a greater state threat.[1]

Beginning in the nineteenth century border people formed their own concepts on what was and was not acceptable smuggling, rather than accepting state dictates on criminal activity. Members of the contrabandista community supported illicit traders by not reporting them to authorities, finding them innocent when tried, and honoring them in song. Those who violated the parameters of community acceptance faced denunciations to authorities, testimony by local witnesses, and protests by the community. Smugglers succeeded when they crossed without being caught or when, as with the case of Mexico's creation of the Zona Libre, they brought national law into synchrony with their regional values.

Locals' tolerance of certain forms of illicit trade persisted into the twentieth century and allowed some smugglers to operate almost openly, and in some cases to virtually co-opt the state. Illicit arms dealers in Laredo could be charged with violating U.S. neutrality laws but remain in public office and as leaders of civic organizations. In Reynosa and other Mexican towns along the border businessmen formed associations dedicated to the trafficking of consumer goods and ran for local and regional offices, which they often gained. Without community support, state agents on the border could do little but complain to superiors in their capitals that local values did not coincide with those of the government. Smugglers within the moral economy continued in their illicit activities regardless of state condemnation of their transgressions. Knowledge of the ubiquity of illicit trade along the border even seeped into popular culture. *On the Road* heroes Sal Paradise and Dean Moriarty stop in Laredo only long enough to eat, but notice that "contraband brooded" in the air.[2] Like many outsiders, Jack Kerouac painted smuggling in lurid terms, but he was correct about illicit activity pervading the atmosphere of the border. Despite damning evidence, indicted arms dealers could be found innocent and continue their roles as community leaders, and many border merchants engaged in illicit trade as part of their businesses. In speaking to Alicia Dewey, a fellow historian researching commerce in the borderlands, I once asked if she had come across Joseph Netzer. She responded, yes, he was a businessman who filed for bankruptcy. I responded that her businessman was my smuggler.[3] Although Netzer may not have dirtied his hands, he and other merchants like him engaged in illicit trade as part of their enterprise while maintaining their roles as prominent members of society.

The shift from collecting tariffs to prohibiting the flow of narcotics and arms across the border set the stage for border people's modern ethical parameters for smuggling, which endured after 1945. Never monolithic, the contrabandista community continued to be shaped by borders and national security issues. Smugglers exploited the prohibitions and concerns in one state by taking advantage of apathy in neighboring nations. For instance, Americans' common acceptance of U.S. guns being smuggled to Mexico worked against Mexican efforts to combat arms trafficking. Indeed, despite firearms' practical illegality in Mexico, guns were so common in 1946 that Mexican authorities in Matamoros took measures to abolish "pistolerismo," or the "promiscuous carrying of arms."[4]

Illicit arms in Mexico most often came from complicit American merchants. Arms orders far in excess of what communities their size could reasonably absorb flabbergasted sales representatives in border towns. The border's ability to soak up guns so shocked Rex Applegate, a representative and sales agent working in the late 1940s for an American arms and ammunition manufacturer, that he confessed to the U.S. Department of State that the weapons he sold Laredo dealers were virtually destined to be smuggled to Mexico.[5] Edward A. Beckelhymer, owner of the Buffalo Finance Company, sold some of these guns. U.S. Customs caught a glimpse of Beckelhymer's day-to-day operations in an interview with one of his Mexican buyers. On February 4, 1952, Rogelio Villarreal walked into Beckelhymer's store looking for a .22-caliber rifle for his son. Villarreal looked around before finding a rifle he liked, asking the price, judging it fair, and buying it for $30.90. While handing Villarreal a box of shells, Beckelhymer called over an employee to make the invoice, but when Villarreal looked at the slip of paper, he noticed it had a name other than his. Beckelhymer never asked Villarreal for his name or address; he knew better and did not want to deal with anything that might hamper his business. Rather, he simply made the invoice to a straw buyer in Laredo, Texas.[6]

Edward A. Beckelhymer sold arms to Mexican buyers contrary to U.S. law, and like many businessmen on the border, he did so for self-gain. When someone came into his store, Beckelhymer looked to make a sale. He did not ask questions, because inquiries were bad for business. Beckelhymer turned a blind eye to the law and continued his enterprise because he wanted the money and did not think selling guns was wrong. Rather than ask Villarreal for his identification, all he asked for was his money. Beckelhymer's name comes up periodically in U.S. Customs investigation records. On July 7, 1948, U.S. Border Patrol agents apprehended a Mexican citizen with over $2,000 worth of assorted ammunition he had purchased from Beckelhymer. Unable to cross it all in one trip, the suspect claimed Beckelhymer offered to cache the arms in his home for pick up later.[7] Although U.S. Customs investigators never managed to prove it, they suspected Beckelhymer used the excess black powder from his massive orders to produce reloaded ammunition for illicit export to Mexico. Because laws at the time did not require a record of the powder's use, Customs agents could only look on as Beckelhymer's mammoth orders vanished from his store. In June 1952 Customs investigators seized two hundred .38-caliber pistols addressed to Beckelhymer in a Laredo truck depot.[8] The bust was part of what U.S. Customs later learned to be a sizeable arms shipment to Mexico.

Beckelhymer died a respected businessman in 1957, but his son Edward A. Beckelhymer Jr. continued his father's practice of selling arms to Mexican buyers. Early in November 1963 U.S. law enforcement raided a building in east Laredo they suspected served as a storage and transfer point for American arms being smuggled to Mexico. Inside the building they found 154,000 rounds of various calibers, 100 boxes of .30-caliber Luger ammunition, and 486 packages of .38-caliber bullets. Authorities also discovered a number of vehicles with false compartments they believed smugglers used to cross weapons. Investigators traced the building to José Manuel Ruiz, Beckelhymer's store manager. The court sentenced Ruiz to three years' confinement and a $10,000 fine but could not prove any conspiracy charges against Beckelhymer. Ruiz later claimed he pled guilty to protect members of his family from charges of driving the loaded vehicles into Mexico. Still, Ruiz admitted he had sold many weapons to Mexican citizens during his time with Beckelhymer and had even arranged the smuggling of the purchases. Beckelhymer did not take part in the actual smuggling, but Ruiz informed authorities that his boss "was just pleased" that weapons sold so well.[9]

Authorities finally caught up with the Beckelhymer family in August 1972, when the U.S. District Court found E. A. Beckelhymer Jr. guilty of making unlawful gun sales, falsifying entries, and engaging in conspiracy to violate the Federal Gun Control Act. The prosecution's break came when Guadalupe Fernández, the manager of a taxicab company adjacent to Beckelhymer's store, testified to routinely signing false forms for Beckelhymer's customers in exchange for a five-dollar gratuity.[10]

Beckelhymer's arms sales made him a criminal under U.S. law, but his fellow Laredoans did not share their government's views and saw him as a local businessman who ran a family store. Indeed, locals knew that Edward Beckelhymer Jr. had inherited the store from his father and shared the business with his mother and three sisters. Beckelhymer may not have bragged about setting a national pistol record for the Army in 1954, but his neighbors knew he was a veteran and a family man with a wife and three children. Dozens of letters of support poured into the judge's office after his conviction. Sister Dorothy Salazar, the principal of the school his children attended, wrote that Beckelhymer, although not a Catholic, was a member of the Parent Teacher Association who gave generously of his time and energy and was an "honest and respectable man."[11] J. C. Martin Jr., the mayor of Laredo and *patrón* of the local political machine, asked the judge to show leniency on an upstanding citizen who had served in numerous civic organizations and community events for years. To cement Beckelhymer's image as an honest businessman, Mayor Martin informed the judge that Beckelhymer provided technical assistance to local law en-

forcement regarding firearms and on a number of occasions had even testified as an expert on their behalf.[12]

Public sympathy stemmed in part from the fact that Beckelhymer's
felony conviction took away his right to handle firearms. Guns were
Beckelhymer's life, and he could hardly conceive of an existence outside
his family's trade. He swore he had never knowingly broken the law, but
had only sold guns to Mexican police officers with proper credentials.
Beckelhymer's appeals came to naught, however, and at age forty-two he
was forced to retire from the gun business. Still, the contrabandista community's appeal for leniency did not go unheard. The judge suspended
Beckelhymer's sentence of five years' imprisonment and allowed him to
walk free.[13]

Since the 1840s illicit trade has formed an integral part of business
in the borderlands, and it remains essential to regional commerce. Mexicans' demand for consumer goods they could not find or afford domes-
tically led to a boom in sales along the U.S. side of the border. In 1982
Laredo's per capita income was $5,109 and the second lowest in Texas.
That same year, however, Laredo recorded $20,149 worth of sales per
household—the second highest in the U.S.—due to international commerce.[14] As a child growing up in the 1980s, I recall seeing the streets and
parking lots of Laredo littered with crushed boxes and empty packaging
material that Mexican consumers left behind in their attempt to smuggle
new American goods across. Rather than be burdened by cumbersome
and conspicuous packages of new clothing, Mexican buyers wore (often in
multiple layers) their purchases as they crossed the bridge so as to evade
their national tariffs. What began over a century ago as petty smuggling
for personal consumption became a business due to restrictive Mexican
tariff rates and exorbitant bribes demanded by corrupt Mexican Customs
agents. Demand for electronics climbed so high in the 1980s that dark-
ened cargo planes loaded with televisions and stereos left border airports
nightly for points south. Mexican demand for American-bought goods
led to the rise of *chiveras/fayuqueras*, women who make a living buying
clothing and other consumer goods from U.S. merchants in bulk for re-
sale in Mexico.[15] The smuggling of consumer goods continues in spite of
the North American Free Trade Agreement, and U.S. merchants are hap-
pily complicit in these sales and depend on them for survival. During my
interviews with downtown border merchants in 2008, one businessman
remarked that "today *chiveras* call or fax orders."[16] He then gestured to
his workers, who were busy packing brand-new watches in plastic Ziploc

bags, and commented, "About 1,800 to 2,000 watches can fit in a box that holds 50 or so originally."[17]

Consumers in the borderlands feel they have a right to trade freely and will smuggle, protest, or riot to defend it. As one border businessman simply said, "Mexicans don't like to pay taxes [import duties], because their government steals."[18] Such sentiment was probably behind an uprising that devastated Mexican Customs offices in Nuevo Laredo in 1992. On November 29 of that year a 6,000-strong protest against prohibitive trade restrictions turned violent when demonstrators reached the Aduana offices at the international bridge. Protestors began mocking officers as they attempted to search southbound cars, and a fight broke out that sent Mexican Customs agents fleeing for safety on the U.S. side. Demonstrators then rushed the undefended Aduana building, raiding files and destroying a computer the Mexican attorney general's office claimed would have put an end to smuggling on the border. Mexican officials admitted the profitability of smuggling electronics and other consumer goods around Mexican tariffs and estimated that $15 billion in duties slipped through Nuevo Laredo alone. While Mexican authorities placed the blame on *fayuqueros* (professional smugglers of consumer goods) and union radicals, Nuevo Laredoans claimed the riot resulted from the Mexican government limiting border residents to returning with no more than fifty dollars in U.S. merchandise.[19]

When states shifted from taxing trade to prohibiting illegal flows at the border, they fundamentally altered their view of their international boundaries as ports for collecting revenue and came to see borders as spaces of subversive criminal activity. Although both the United States and Mexico have always strived to preserve their national security, state actions on the border reflect their changing security concerns. Commercial tariff evasion hurt law-abiding businesses and defrauded the U.S. and Mexican government of significant proceeds, but as federal sources of revenue diversified in the early twentieth century, national security came to trump tariff collection as a state priority on the border. Though never abandoning their duties as tariff collectors, U.S. Customs forces transformed from primarily being agents of economic security to serving as agents of border security. Similarly, the Mexican government conceded to the smuggling of consumer goods in order to gain contrabandistas' cooperation against arms traffickers. By the mid-twentieth century, states focused on the interdiction of threatening prohibited goods, particularly arms and drugs, rather than on collecting tariffs.

BLACK LEGENDS AND TERRIBLE TRUTHS

Black legends surround smuggling on the border. I remember U.S. Border Patrol agents coming to my elementary school as part of the Drug Abuse Resistance Education (DARE) and "Just Say No" programs. Before seated children, the agents relayed the story of a young family trying to cross the international bridge into the United States. After stopping the car and asking the parents their nationality, officers noticed something wrong with the baby. The child did not stir, nor did the infant seem to be sleeping. Officers informed my classmates and me that upon further investigation they discovered that the baby was dead and that the suspects had gutted its corpse to use as a vessel for smuggled drugs. This story and others like it are common on the border. When I told this story at a gathering in McAllen, Texas, in 2011, lifelong border residents nodded their heads in troubled agreement, acknowledging that these things happen. Although these and other black legends concerning smuggling along the border persist, in the course of my investigation I have yet to find a single documented case of smugglers using dead babies as conduits for crossing drugs.[20]

Similar stories circulate regarding organ trafficking. Despite numerous tales of tourists and other victims of kidney theft waking up in ice-filled bathtubs, no credible evidence of organ trafficking on the border exists.[21] One of the earliest examples of this legend's appearance came in April 1974, when the Mexican newspaper *El Mundo de Tampico* reported that government special agents were investigating stories of a mafia that specialized in the smuggling of human blood.[22] Although the organization reputedly earned as much as a million pesos per ton of plasma they trafficked out through Nuevo Laredo and Reynosa, Mexican agents uncovered no proof of the vampire mafia's existence.[23]

Recently, terrorism and the all-too-real violence of the drug war in Mexico have come to overshadow the contrabandista community. U.S. security fears after the terrorist attacks of September 11, 2001, led to a centralization of American federal police forces. The Customs Service was transferred from the Department of Treasury to the Department of Homeland Security in 2003, cementing the agency's transformation to one whose focus is primarily that of border security rather than economic security.[24] In Mexico the end of the Institutional Revolutionary Party's (PRI) seventy-one-year reign in July of 2000 upset the decades-old custom of quiet corruption and limited drug violence. With their former associates out of power, cartels increasingly fought amongst themselves for a place in Mexico's new political climate. On September 6, 2006, several men brandishing machine guns and dressed as commandos broke up a party in Uruapan, Michoacán, dumping the severed heads of five of their rivals on the dance floor.[25] In response to brazen assaults against the peace, Mexican President Felipe Calderón sent the military on the offensive against the nation's drug cartels. Although the Mexican government succeeded in capturing or killing a number of cartel leaders, the crackdown had the unintended consequence of dramatically escalating violence as destabilized organizations fought for dominance. This escalation can be felt across the borderlands as U.S. Predator drones (operated by Customs and Border Protection, no less) have come to replace the mounted patrols of a century before.[26]

I grew up in Laredo at a time when it felt safe to go across for drinks on the weekend. One of my classmates at United High School was Edgar Valdez, whom I remember as an outgoing football jock who liked to joke around and typically dressed in Red Wing work boots, jeans, and a polo shirt. Edgar's fair complexion and green eyes earned him the nickname "Barbie," which he took in stride. After finishing high school, Edgar got involved in the drug trade, and through a mixture of opportunism, entrepreneurship, and ruthlessness became the only American to lead his own independent Mexican drug cartel. I next saw Edgar on television when Mexican authorities presented him as a trophy after capturing him in an extensive manhunt. Flanked by masked federal police commandos, Edgar stood handcuffed, wearing one of the polo shirts he was so fond of, smiling and defiant to the end.[27]

Smuggling on the border has changed a great deal since 1848. On the early morning of September 13, 2011, the bodies of a man and a woman in their twenties were found hanging from a pedestrian bridge in Nuevo Laredo. Both corpses showed signs of torture, in particular the female victim, whom killers left topless, disemboweled, and hogtied. Killers left a sign by the bodies saying a similar fate awaited anyone bold enough to denounce *narcos* on social networks. In an otherwise largely nonconfrontational tradition of smuggling along the border, recent spectacle violence and narco-terrorism are bloody anomalies. As of 2013 over seventy thousand people have fallen victim to the drug war in Mexico. Given the U.S. and Mexican governments' increased policing of the border and Americans' ceaseless demand for drugs (not to mention undocumented migrants' desire to work in El Norte), the profits from trafficking drugs and people will continue to prompt professional criminality from organizations willing to defend their ventures with deadly force.[28]

Like the stories of dead babies and kidney thieves, smuggling along the U.S.-Mexico border has been conflated and overshadowed by recent images of headless bodies and the real horrors of the drug war. Drugs and guns were and are smuggled across the border, and this trafficking has led to greater criminality and violence, but gun and drug trafficking are just part of a larger process of illicit border trade. On any given day people fail to declare bottles of liquor and cartons of cigarettes they hope to enjoy in the United States, while others cross perfectly licit consumer goods illicitly into Mexico. Drug busts and *narco* violence grab headlines, but petty smuggling is the unrecorded norm. Smuggling is typical, not atypical, the rule rather than the exception. Indeed, successful smugglers seek to be nondescript rather than attract attention.[29]

Violence is better understood as a sign of smugglers' failure rather than their strength. Historically, few smugglers sought violence or notoriety, either of which could damage business. Those that did enter into confrontations did so as a last resort or when they thought they could win. As criminal syndicates gained ground in Mexico and became, in effect, institutions, cartels turned to assassinations to do away with uncooperative government authorities or intimidate them into submission. The U.S. government's reputation for swift and violent responses to attacks has so far deterred criminal syndicates from engaging American authorities to the extent that cartels challenge the Mexican state. With the major exception of the abduction, torture, and murder of U.S. Drug Enforcement Agency agent Enrique "Kiki" Camarena Salazar in Guadalajara in February 1985, traffickers have avoided confronting U.S. forces directly because they do not wish to provoke an intervention they cannot withstand.[30]

U.S. and Mexican regulatory and restrictive trade policies not only failed to prevent illicit flows, they created a market for trafficked goods. Smuggling not only persisted, it became professionalized in the midst of states' border-building projects. Aside from criminalizing what had once been customary local commerce, government laws pushed criminal activity to their nations' edges by prompting the trafficking of goods through the borderlands on their way to interior U.S. and Mexican markets. Although many borderlanders participated in the moral economy of illicit trade and capitalized on black markets by forming enterprises that involved smuggling, border people also found their communities becoming sites of organized and violent crime. Borderlanders' petty smuggling persisted, but state responses to violent trafficking have transformed the border into a criminal space where border people are seen as suspects more than citizens of their respective countries. Greater regulation and interdiction transformed smuggling from a low-level mundane activity in which many border people participated, to a highly profitable professional criminal enterprise. Despite this, the contrabandista community has adapted and persisted in the wake of states' best efforts to combat it.

Songs as Sources

MARIANO RESÉNDEZ

Entre las diez y las doce,
miren lo que se anda hablando,
éste es Mariano Reséndez
pasando su contrabando.

Éste es Mariano Reséndez,
el hombre contrabandista,
sesenta empleados mató
y allí los traía en su lista.

Año de mil novecientos
dejó recuerdos muy grandes,
a don Mariano Reséndez
lo aprehendió Nieves Hernández.

Salía Nieves Hernández
divisando por el llano,
y le pregunta a un ranchero:
—¿No me has visto a don Mariano?

—Pues sí señor, sí lo vi,
se fue rumbo a La Sierrita,
diciendo que si lo alcanza
quinientas balas le quita.—

Decía Mariano Reséndez,
gritaba de vez en cuando:

—¡Arrímense, compañeros,
nos quitan el contrabando!—

Decía Mariano Reséndez:
—Muchachos, éntrenle al toro,
vengan a llevar indianas
que son de la Bola de Oro.

—Vengan a llevar indianas
al mismo precio de allá,
que son muy pocos los gastos
y grande la utilidad.

—Eso de pasar indianas
no se me quitan las ganas,
traigo la vida en un hilo
por las malditas indianas.—

Decía Mariano Reséndez
con esa boca de infierno:
—Éntrenle, guardas cobardes,
engreídos con el gobierno.

—Traigo una pana muy fina
y un casimir de primera,
y un buena carabina,
éntrenle ora que hay manera.—

Empleados de San Fernando,
no son más que alburuzeros,
dejan pasar contrabandos
por agarrar maleteros.

Empleados del Encinal
y también de La Sierrita,
que nomás llega Reséndez
y hasta el hambre se les quita.

Empleados de Matamoros,
esos de banda primera,
aquí les traigo licores
dentro de mi cartuchera.

La pólvora es la cerveza,
las balas vino mezcal,
los casquillos son las copas
en que se lo han de tomar.

Avísenle a ese gobierno
que cumpla con sus deberes,
que cuando ponga acordada
no la ponga de mujeres.

Y lástima del destino
que ellos traen entre sus manos,
hasta lástima es que digan
que son puros mexicanos.

De Santa Cruz para abajo
de Santa Rita pa' arriba,
pelearon fuertes combates
don Mariano y su partida.

De Santa Cruz para abajo,
murieron los dos Meléndez,
por defender las indianas
de don Mariano Reséndez.

Decía Mariano Reséndez
con aquella voz divina:
—No me queda más amparo
que Dios y mi carabina.—

Decía Mariano Reséndez
como queriendo llora:
—¡Ay, alma mía de mi hermano,
quién lo pudiera salvar!—

Decía Mariano Reséndez
debajo de unos nogales:
—A mí me hacen los mandados,
los puños y los ojales.—

Decía Mariano Reséndez:
—Éntrenle, no sean cobardes,

no le teman a las balas
ni se acuerden de sus madres.

—Este es Mariano Reséndez,
que lo querían conocer,
les ha dar calentura
para poderlo aprehender.—

En su rancho, que era El Charco,
día martes desgraciado,
no pudo el hombre salvarse
porque amaneció sitiado.

Fueron a romper las puertas
cuando llegó el otro hermano,
con ansia le preguntaban:
—¿Dónde se halla don Mariano?—

Don José María Reséndez,
su contestación fue buena:
—Señores, yo no sé nada,
yo vengo de Santa Elena.—

Luego que ya lo aprehendieron
dispuso la autoridad:
—No vayan muy descuidados
Que de un tosido se va.—

El carro 'onde iba Mariano
iba rodeado de lanzas,
decía Mariano Reséndez:
—No pierdo las esperanzas.—

A la Heroica Matamoros,
para allá lo condujeron,
no le valieron influencias
ni dinero que ofrecieron.

En La Bota y San Román
en puro oro lo pesaban,
galantías a la tropa
por ver si lo rescataban.

Pues lo pesaban en oro
y lo evaluaban en plata,
¡quién les ha dicho, señores,
que un hombre bueno se mata!

Las fuerzas de Tamaulipas
a Nuevo León lo entregaron,
luego que lo recibieron
en el acto lo mataron.

Porque le tenían miedo,
que recibiera algún cargo,
lo mataron entre medio
de Agualeguas y Cerralvo.

Empleaditos de Guerrero,
a todos los traigo en lista,
ya no morirán de miedo,
se acabó El Contrabandista.

Empleados de El Encinal,
de San Fernando y de Méndez,
duerman a pierna tendida,
ya mataron a Reséndez.

Quédense con Dios, empleados,
acompañen a Morfeo,
y para que no se asusten
acostumbren el poleo.

Ya con ésta me despido,
cortando una flor de mayo,
aquí se acaban cantando
los versos de don Mariano.[1]

MARIANO RESÉNDEZ

Between ten and twelve o'clock,
look at what people are saying;
this is Mariano Reséndez
smuggling his contraband goods.

This is Mariano Reséndez,
the smuggling man;
he killed sixty officers
and carried their names on a list.

The year nineteen hundred
left us many vivid memories;
Don Mariano Reséndez
was captured by Nieves Hernández.

Nieves Hernández went forth,
looking out across the plain,
and he asked of a ranchero,
"Have you seen Don Mariano?"

"Well, yes sir, I have seen him;
he went toward La Sierrita,
saying that if you catch up with him,
you can take his five hundred bullets."

Then said Mariano Reséndez,
he would shout now and then,
"Gather around, my companions,
or they will take our contraband!"

Then said Mariano Reséndez,
"Boys, take the bull by the horns.
Come and get your calicos;
they come from the Bola de Oro.

"Come and get your calicos
at the same price as on the other side,
for my overhead is low
and the profits are great.

"I can never get enough
of this business of smuggling calico;
my life hangs on a thread
because of these damned calicos."

Then said Mariano Reséndez,
in a malevolent voice,

"Come on, you cowardly border guards,
who live off the government's bounty."

"I'm carrying some very fine corduroy,
and some first-class cashmere,
and also a good rifle;
come try your luck now there's a chance."

The officers at San Fernando
are nothing but noisy braggarts;
they let the big contrabands pass,
while they catch the small-timers.

You officers of El Encinal,
and those of La Sierrita too,
as soon as Reséndez appears,
you even lose your appetite.

You officers of Matamoros,
who are said to be first-class men,
I am bringing you some liquor
inside my ammunition pouch.

The gunpowder is beer
and the bullets are mescal,
the cartridges are the glasses
in which you will drink it up.

Send word to the government
that it should meet its obligations,
that when it sets up an *acordada*,
it should not staff it with women.

What a pity that such responsibility
should be put into their hands,
and it is really a pity
that they should call themselves real Mexicans.

Downriver from Santa Cruz
and upriver from Santa Rita,
hard battles were fought
by Don Mariano and his band.

Downriver from Santa Cruz,
the two Meléndezes died
while defending the calicos
of Don Mariano Reséndez.

Then said Mariano Reséndez,
in that divine voice of his,
"I have no protection left
except God and my rifle."

Then said Mariano Reséndez,
as if he was going to cry,
"Oh, brother of my soul,
how I wish I could save you!"

Then said Mariano Reséndez,
underneath some pecan trees,
"You can run my errands for me,
and make my cuffs and buttonholes."

Then said Mariano Reséndez,
"Stand and fight, do not be cowards;
don't be afraid of bullets,
and do not think of your mothers.

"This is Mariano Reséndez,
you wanted to know him;
you are likely to catch a fever
before you can capture me."

In his ranch, which was El Charco,
on an unfortunate Tuesday,
the man could not save himself
because he woke up surrounded.

They went to break down the doors
when his other brother arrived;
they anxiously asked him,
"Where can Don Mariano be found?"

Don José María Reséndez's
answer was an honest one,

"Gentlemen, I know nothing;
I have just come from Santa Elena."

After they had captured him,
the authorities decreed,
"Do not be very careless with him,
or he'll be gone in a wink."

The cart in which Mariano rode
was surrounded by picked men;
Mariano Reséndez said,
"I have not lost hope."

To Matamoros,
that is where they took him;
his connections were of no avail,
and neither was the money that was offered.

At La Bota and San Román
they offered his weight in pure gold;
there were courtesies done to the soldiers,
to see if they would ransom him.

They offered his weight in gold
or the same value in silver.
Who has told you, gentlemen,
that a good man like that must be killed!

The soldiers of Tamaulipas
handed him over to Nuevo León,
and as soon as they had received him,
they killed him out of hand.

Because they were afraid of him,
afraid he might be given some office,
they killed him on the road
between Agualeguas and Cerralvo.

You policeman of Guerrero,
I have you all on my list;
you no longer will die of fright,
because The Smuggler is dead.

Police of El Encinal,
of San Fernando and Méndez,
now you can sleep soundly,
for they have killed Reséndez.

God be with you, you policemen,
and may Morpheus accompany you;
and so you won't get fright sickness,
make it a custom to drink pennyroyal tea.

Now with this I say farewell,
plucking a flower of May;
this is the end of the singing
of the stanzas about Don Mariano.[2]

CORRIDO DE OLIVEIRA/ DIONISIO MALDONADO

Año mil novecientos veinte
mes de abril día primero.
Mataron a tres Tejanos
esos rinches de Laredo.
Mataron a tres Tejanos
esos rinches de Laredo.

Cuando llegaron a Bruni
las puertas tenían candado.
Él que fue a traer las llaves
fue Dionisio Maldonado.
Él que fue a traer las llaves
fue Dionisio Maldonado.

Si te preguntan los nombres
no los vayas a negar.
Fueron Dionisio Maldonado,
Oliveira y Aguilar.
Fueron Dionisio Maldonado,
Oliveira y Aguilar.

El rinche que estaba allí
corazón de una gallina.
Se puso descolorido

nomás vio mi carabina.
Se puso descolorido
nomás vio mi carabina.

Cuando oyeron el descargue
se oyeron tres tiros más.
Fue cuando cayó Oliveira,
Maldonado y Aguilar.
Fue cuando cayó Oliveira,
Maldonado y Aguilar.

Oliveira como era hombre
le dio rienda a su caballo.
Salgan rinches del gobierno
a pelear con este gallo.
Salgan rinches del gobierno
a pelear con este gallo.

Cuando su padre llegó
se encontraba en agonía.
Fuerzas son las que me faltan
valor tengo todavía.
Fuerzas son las que me faltan
valor tengo todavía.

No siento a mi caballo prieto
ni siento a mi silla plateada.
Lo que siento es a mi Chucha
que deje pedida y dada.
Lo que siento es a mi Chucha
que deje pedida y dada.[3]

BALLAD OF OLIVEIRA/
DIONISIO MALDONADO

In the year 1920,
on the first of April,
those *rinches* of Laredo
killed three Tejanos.
Those *rinches* of Laredo
killed three Tejanos.

When they got to Bruni,
they found the doors padlocked;
The one who went to ask for the key
was Dionisio Maldonado.
The one who went to ask for the key
was Dionisio Maldonado.

If they ask you for their names,
do not deny they were Dionisio Maldonado,
Oliveira, and Aguilar.
They were Dionisio Maldonado,
Oliveira, and Aguilar.

The *rinche* who was there
had the heart of a chicken;
He lost all color
when he saw my rifle.
He lost all color
when he saw my rifle.

When they heard the blast,
they heard three more shots.
That is when Oliveira,
Maldonado, and Aguilar fell.
That is when Oliveira,
Maldonado, and Aguilar fell.

Oliveira, because he was a man,
gave rein to his horse:
"Come on, you cowardly *rinches*,
tangle with this fighting rooster."
"Come on, you cowardly *rinches*,
tangle with this fighting rooster."

When his father arrived,
he found him in agony.
"Strength is what I lack,
I still have my courage."
"Strength is what I lack,
I still have my courage."

"I do not feel the loss of my dark horse,
or my silver-plated saddle.

"What I do feel for is for my Chucha
whom I leave betrothed and left behind."
"What I do feel for is for my Chucha
whom I leave betrothed and left behind."[4]

LAREDO

Ese pueblo de Laredo
es un pueblo muy lúcido,
donde es encuentra la mata
de los hombres decididos.

Y ese puerto de Laredo
es un puerto muy mentado,
los agentes de la ley
andan siempre con cuidado.

En ese rancho de Lule
varios casos han pasado,
contrabandistas y rinches
sus vidas las han cambiado.

Pero también en el frente,
porque no eran criminal,
¡decir que no se lucieron
en esa guerra mundial!

Debemos de recodar
que muchos jamás volvieron,
por cumplir con su deber
en esa lucha murieron.

No solamente en la frente
demostraron ser humanos,
por eso en Laredo, Texas,
se aprecian los mexicanos.

Y el que le guste pasearse
nunca lo podrá negar,
nomás que cruce el Río Grande,
hay mucho en donde gozar.

Y el que le guste pasearse,
gozar de toda alegría,
que pase a Nuevo Laredo
y gozará noche y día.

Ya con ésta me despido,
tomándome un anisado;
adiós, lindas morenitas
de ese Laredo afamado.[5]

LAREDO

That town of Laredo
is a very distinguished town,
where is found the cradle
of resolute men.

That port of Laredo
is a very famous port;
the officers of the law
always go about with care.

In that ranch known as Lule,
several incidents have taken place;
smugglers and *rinches*
have taken each others' lives.

But they have also been at the front,
because they were not criminals;
Let no one say they did not distinguish themselves
in that famed world war!

We should remember
that many never came back;
they died in that conflict
while doing their duty.

Not only at the front
have they demonstrated their humanity;
that is why in Laredo, Texas,
Mexicans are held in esteem.

And he who likes to go out
it never can be denied,
let him just cross the Rio Grande,
where there is much he can enjoy.

And he who likes to go out,
and enjoy all kinds of merrimaking,
let him cross over to Nuevo Laredo,
and he will enjoy himself night and day.

Now with this I say farewell,
while drinking an *anisado*;
Farewell, beautiful dark girls
of that famed Laredo.[6]

LOS TEQUILEROS

El día dos de febrero,
¡qué día tan señalado!
mataron tres tequileros
los rinches del otro lado.

Llegaron al Río Grande,
se pusieron a pensar:
—Será bueno ver a Leandro
porque somos dos nomás.—

Le echan el envite Leandro,
Leandro les dice que no:
—Fíjense que estoy enfermo,
así no quisiera yo.—

Al fin de tanto invitarle
Leandro los acompañó,
en las lomas de Almiramba
fue el primero que murió.

La carga que ellos llevaban
era tequila anisado,
el rumbo que ellos llevaban
era San Diego afamado.

Salieron desde Guerrero
con rumbo para el oriente,
allí les tenían sitiado
dos carros con mucha gente.

Cuando cruzaron el río
se fueron por un cañón
se pusieron a hacer lumbre
sin ninguna precaución.

El capitán de los rinches
platicaba con esmero:
—Es bueno agarrar ventaja
porque estos son de Guerrero.—

Les hicieron un descargue
a mediación del camino,
cayó Gerónimo muerto,
Silvano muy mal herido.

Tumban el caballo a Leandro
y a él lo hirieron de un brazo,
Ya no les podía hacer fuego,
tenía varios balazos.

El capitán de los rinches
a Silvano se acercó,
Y en unos cuantos segundos
Silvano Gracia murió.

Los rinches serán muy hombres,
no se les puede negar,
nos cazan como venados
para podernos matar.

Si los rinches fueran hombres
y sus caras presentaran,
entonce' a los tequileros
otro gallo nos cantara.

Pues ellos los tres murieron,
los versos aquí se acaban,
se les concedió a los rinches
las muertes que ellos deseaban.

El que compuso estos versos
no se hallaba allí presente,
estos versos son compuestos
por lo que decía la gente.

Aquí va la despedida
en medio de tres floreros,
y aquí se acaba el corrido,
versos de los tequileros.[7]

THE TEQUILA RUNNERS

On the second day of February,
what a memorable day!
The *rinches* from the other side of the river
killed three tequila runners.

They reached the Rio Grande
and then they stopped and thought,
"We had better go see Leandro,
because there are only two of us."

They asked Leandro to go with them,
and Leandro said he would not:
"I am sorry, but I'm sick.
I do not want to go this way."

They kept asking him to go,
until Leandro went with them;
in the hills of Almiramba,
he was the first to die.

The contraband they were carrying
was tequila *anisado*;
the direction they were taking
was toward famed San Diego.

They left from Guerrero
in an easterly direction;
two cars with many men
were waiting for them there.

When they crossed the river,
they traveled along a canyon;
there they stopped and built a fire
without any regard to danger.

The captain of the *rinches*
was saying, speaking in measured tones,
"It is wise to stack the odds
because these men are from Guerrero."

They fired the volley at them
in the middle of the road;
Gerónimo fell dead,
and Silvano fell badly wounded.

They shot Leandro off his horse,
wounding him in the arm.
He could no longer fire back at them,
he had several bullet wounds.

The captain of the *rinches*
came up close to Silvano;
and in a few seconds,
Silvano Gracia was dead.

The *rinches* are very brave,
there is no doubt of that;
the only way they can kill us
is by hunting us like deer.

If the *rinches* were really brave
and met us face to face,
then things would be quite different
for us tequila runners.

So all three of them died,
and these stanzas are at an end;
the *rinches* were able to accomplish
the killings they wanted.

He who composed these stanzas
was not present when it happened;

these verses have been composed
from what people are saying.

Now here is my farewell,
in the midst of three flower vases;
this is the end of the ballad,
the stanzas of the tequila runners.[8]

CAPITÁN CHARLES STEVENS

Parte I

Oigan señores los que voy a cantar,
estos sucesos yo los canto y no lo olviden,
Pues ya murió el jefe prohibicionista
y que en vida se nombraba Charles Stevens.

Este que tiene de "águila los ojos"
y que dio medida en dondequiera,
Es el retrato mismo los despojos
de él que en vida le nombraban "la pantera."

Él no por eso perderá su alma,
no maldijo jamás su ingrata suerte,
Como hombre soportó con toda calma
En el horrido campo de la muerte.

Más debido al valor que éste tenía,
Charles Stevens el jefe que yo nombro,
Cuando buscaba la cerveza hacía
que todo el mundo le tuviera asombro.

Cayó herido y entonces con denuedo,
siguió Murphy con igual valor,
Pelió intrépido y sin miedo,
sostuvo aquella lucha con honor.

Al lado siempre de su fiel amigo,
él mismo lo llevó hasta el hospital,
Debatió para hacer que otro enemigo
moviera el auto en el Camino Real.

Un mexicano, luego sin más cosa
lo meten en un lío porque oyó
como muere de pronto en Santa Rosa,
En silencio el secreto se incognó.

Parte II

Ahora en confusión queda pendiente
la esposa de Guajardo en el condado,
Si es que compruebe así ser inocente,
o la encuentra culpable el gran jurado.

Oír esta tragedia y triste historia,
por Dios que esto huele ya muy mal,
Si la falta de un padre es tan notoria
la de una madre en prisión no tiene igual.

Lo de siempre sucedió, lector querido,
los hechos a la historia ya pasaron,
Solo un pobre mexicano se ha perdido
y los otros matadores se han pelado.

La muerte del valiente Charles Stevens
ha venido a descubrir que en San Antonio,
No son los *bootleggers* los que solo viven,
son de otra parte los que crían el demonio.

Y seguirá la ley haciendo esfuerzos
para evitar las bebidas embriagantes,
y yo continuaré cantando versos
aunque perezca mal a los pedantes.

Aunque se quiebren todas las botellas
por agentes de la ley que a todos pasos,
relucirán las ilusiones bellas
a través de los vidrios y los vasos.

No olviden, por lo tanto estos alardes,
no hay a quién no le duela su pellejo.
Los mismos son valientes que cobardes
y tal como el refrán lo dice un viejo.[9]

CAPTAIN CHARLES STEVENS

Part I

Listen, men, to what I am about to sing,
these events, I sing about and don't forget them,
Because the head prohibitionist is dead
and who in life was named Charles Stevens.

He who has "eagle eyes"
And who lived up to his name everywhere,
It's the same picture as the despoilers,
He who in life was known as "the panther."

Not for that will he lose his soul,
nor will he ever curse his ungrateful luck,
Like a man he withstood all calmly
In the horrible camp of death.

Owing to the courage he had,
Charles Stevens, the man to whom I am referring,
When looking for beer, he astonished
everyone in the whole world.

He fell injured and then with boldness,
Followed Murphy with equal courage.
Who fought gallantly and without fear,
continuing the struggle with honor.

At his side, always his faithful friend,
he took him to the hospital.
He fought to make the enemy
move the car out of the way.

A Mexican, then, without further ado,
got into a fix because he heard
how suddenly he dies in Santa Rosa.
In silence the secret was kept safe.

Part II

And now in confusion what is pending,
Guajardo's wife in the county jail,

Was waiting to see if proven innocent
or if the grand jury will find her guilty.

Listen to this tragedy and sad story,
for God's sake, this smells bad,
If the lack of a father is so notorious,
That of a mother in prison has no equal.

The usual thing happened, dear reader,
these deeds have now become history.
Only one poor Mexican has been lost
while the other killers have gotten away.

The death of the brave Charles Stevens
has made it known that in San Antonio,
it's not just the bootleggers who live there,
These troublemakers come from another place.

The law will continue to make efforts
to prohibit intoxicating drinks,
and I will continue singing verses,
even though the pedants don't like it.

Even if all the bottles are broken
by the agents of the law, in any case,
all the beautiful illusions will shine
through the glassware and the glass.

Meanwhile, don't forget this display,
there is no one whose skin won't hurt.
The same who are brave are cowards
just as it's said by this old man.[10]

EL AUTOMÓVIL GRIS

En Matamoros me verán, borracho, fumando buenos puros,
tomando coñac, jerez, cerveza al son de la alegría,
y estos pendientes que tengo, los tengo en San Antonio,
Laredo, Texas, y allá en Belén.

Yo soy la mano que aprieta,
que asalta y que mata y roba,

y por dondequiera que ando
a todos les doy la coba;
yo pertenezco a la banda
de ese Automóvil Gris,
me llamo Higinio de Anda
y me he paseado en París.

En Matamoros me verán, borracho, fumando buenos puros,
tomando coñac, jerez, cerveza al son de la alegría,
y estos pendientes que tengo, los tengo en San Antonio,
Laredo, Texas, y allá en Belén.

Y allá en la penitenciaría
donde doce años duré
en compañía de otros hombres
y del Chato Bernabé,
y en esa celda del once
donde murió el Negro Frank,
donde mataron a Udilio,
lo mataron a traición.

En Matamoros me verán, borracho, fumando buenos puros,
tomando coñac, jerez, cerveza al son de la alegría,
y estos pendientes que tengo, los tengo en San Antonio,
Laredo, Texas, y allá en Belén.

Y ese don Pablo González,
que la vida nos salvó,
que estando formado el cuadro
su pistola disparó;
yo pertenezco a la banda
de ese Automóvil Gris,
me llamo Higinio de Anda
y me he paseado en París.

En Matamoros me verán, borracho, fumando buenos puros,
tomando coñac, jerez, cerveza al son de la alegría,
y estos pendientes que tengo, los tengo en San Antonio,
Laredo, Texas, y allá en Belén.[11]

THE GRAY AUTOMOBILE

In Matamoros you may see me, drunk and smoking fine cigars,
drinking cognac, sherry, beer to the sound of merrymaking;
I have things I must do; they'll be done in San Antonio,
Laredo, Texas, and over in Belén.

I am the hand that squeezes,
that assaults, that kills and robs,
and everywhere I go,
I smooth-talk everyone;
I belong to the famed
Gray Automobile band;
my name is Higinio de Anda,
and I have enjoyed myself in Paris.

In Matamoros you may see me, drunk and smoking fine cigars,
drinking cognac, sherry, beer to the sound of merrymaking;
I have things I must do; they'll be done in San Antonio,
Laredo, Texas, and over in Belén.

And over there in the penitentiary,
where I spent twelve years
in the company of others
including Chato Bernabé,
and in that cell number eleven,
where El Negro Frank died,
where they killed Udilio,
he was treacherously killed.

In Matamoros you may see me, drunk and smoking fine cigars,
drinking cognac, sherry, beer to the sound of merrymaking;
I have things I must do; they'll be done in San Antonio,
Laredo, Texas, and over in Belén.

And that Don Pablo González
was the one who saved our lives;
the firing squad was at the ready, when he fired
his pistol in the air;
I belong to the famed
Gray Automobile band;
my name is Higinio de Anda,
and I have enjoyed myself in Paris.

In Matamoros you may see me, drunk and smoking fine cigars,
drinking cognac, sherry, beer to the sound of merrymaking;
I have things I must do; they'll be done in San Antonio,
Laredo, Texas, and over in Belén.[12]

CARGA BLANCA

Cruzando el Río Bravo
y casi a la anochecer
con bastante carga blanca
que tenían que vender.

Llegaron a San Antonio
sin ninguna novedad
y se fueron derechito
a la calle Navidad.

En una casa de piedra
entraron José y Ramón
y en la troca se quedó
esperándolos Simón.

Dos mil ochocientos pesos
les pagó don Nicanor
y le entregaron la carga,
eso sí, de lo mejor.

Apenas iban llegando
a la calle Veracruz
cuando les cerró el camino
un carro negro y sin luz.

"No hagan ningún movimiento
si no se quieren morir,
entréguenos el dinero
que acaban de recibir."

Varios tiros de pistola
y unos gritos de dolor
se escucharon de repente
esa noche de terror.

Dos muertos y tres heridos
la ambulancia levantó
pero el rollo de billetes
de allí desapareció.

Ahora, según se dice,
ya ven la gente lo que es,
que el dinero completito
volvió a su dueño otra vez.

Despedida se las diera
pero ya se me perdió:
¡Dejen los negocios chuecos,
ya ven lo que sucedió![13]

WHITE CARGO

They crossed the Rio Grande
almost at nightfall
with a big load of white cargo
that they had to sell.

They arrived at San Antonio
without any problem
and went straight
to Navidad Steet.

José and Ramón went
into a house made of stone,
and Simón waited for them
in the truck.

Don Nicanor paid them
2,800 pesos
and they delivered the cargo,
the very best of its kind.

They were just arriving
at Veracruz Street,
when a black car with its lights turned off
blocked their way.

"Don't move
if you don't want to die!
Hand over the money
you have just received!"

Suddenly, several shots
and some painful screams
were heard during
the horrible night.

The ambulance picked up
two dead and three wounded people,
but the roll of bills
had disappeared.

Now, according to what they say,
you know how people are,
all the money went right back
to its original owner.

I would give you a farewell,
but I have lost it.
Leave this crooked business alone,
just see what has happened![14]

Notes

INTRODUCTION

1. Warner P. Sutton to Honorable William J. Wharton, Nuevo Laredo, Tamaulipas, April 25, 1890, *Despatches from U.S. Consuls in Nuevo Laredo, Mexico, 1871–1906* (Washington, D.C.: National Archives Microfilm Publications, 1959), microfilm, M280.

2. Américo Paredes, *Folklore and Culture on the Texas-Mexican Border*, ed. Richard Bauman (Austin, T.X.: CMAS Books, 1993), 23; and Oscar J. Martínez, *Border People: Life and Society in the U.S.-Mexico Borderlands* (Tucson: University of Arizona Press, 1994), 23.

3. E. J. Hobsbawm, *Bandits* (London: Weidenfeld & Nicolson, 1969); and Hobsbawm, *Primitive Rebels: Studies in Archaic Forms of Social Movement in the 19th and 20th Centuries* (New York: W. W. Norton, 1959).

4. Willem van Schendel and Itty Abraham, eds., *Illicit Flows and Criminal Things: States, Borders, and the Other Side of Globalization* (Bloomington: Indiana University Press, 2005), 4.

5. Moisés Naím, *Illicit: How Smugglers, Traffickers, and Copycats are Hijacking the Global Economy* (New York: Anchor Books, 2005), 2.

6. Ibid., 8.

7. Howard Campbell, *Drug War Zone: Frontline Dispatches from the Streets of El Paso and Juárez* (Austin: University of Texas Press, 2009), 6, 8.

8. Eric Tagliacozzo, *Secret Trades, Porous Borders: Smuggling and States Along a Southeast Asian Frontier, 1865–1915* (New Haven, C.T.: Yale University Press, 2005), 3.

9. As my book was going into print, Peter Andreas's *Smuggler Nation* hit the stands. Given Andreas's expertise and *Smuggler Nation*'s scope, his book is destined to become the standard text on the history of smuggling in the United States. Andreas, *Smuggler Nation: How Illicit Trade Made America* (New York: Oxford University Press, 2013); Andreas, *Border Games: Policing the U.S.-Mexico Divide* (Ithaca, N.Y.: Cornell University Press, 2000); James A. Sandos, "Northern Separatism During the Mexican

Revolution: An Inquiry into the Role of Drug Trafficking, 1919–1920," *Americas* 41, no. 2 (October 1984); and Gabriela Recio, "Drugs and Alcohol: US Prohibition and the Origins of the Drug Trade in Mexico, 1910–1930," *Journal of Latin American Studies* 34, no. 1 (February 2002).

10. Rachel St. John, *Line in the Sand: A History of the Western U.S.-Mexico Border* (Princeton, N.J.: Princeton University Press, 2011), 8.

11. Robert Chao Romero, *The Chinese in Mexico, 1882–1940* (Tucson: University of Arizona Press, 2010).

12. Elaine Carey and Andrae Marak, eds., *Smugglers, Brothels, and Twine: Historical Perspectives on Contraband and Vice in North America's Borderlands* (Tucson: University of Arizona Press, 2011).

13. Kelly Lytle Hernández, *Migra! A History of the U.S. Border Patrol* (Los Angeles: University of California Press, 2010), 148.

14. Jeremy Adelman and Stephen Aron, "From Borderlands to Borders: Empires, Nation-States, and the Peoples in Between in North American History," *American Historical Review* 104, no. 3 (June 1999): 816.

15. Tagliacozzo, *Secret Trades, Porous Borders*; Friedrich Katz, *The Secret War in Mexico: Europe, the United States, and the Mexican Revolution* (Chicago: University of Chicago Press, 1981); Elliott Young, *Catarino Garza's Revolution on the Texas-Mexico Border* (Durham, N.C.: Duke University Press, 2004).

16. Samuel Truett, *Fugitive Landscapes: The Forgotten History of the U.S.-Mexico Borderlands* (New Haven, C.T.: Yale University Press, 2006), 9. For other excellent examples on the limits of state power see Patrick Ettinger, "'We Sometimes Wonder What They Will Spring on Us Next': Immigrants and Border Enforcement in the American West, 1882–1930," *Western Historical Quarterly* 37, no. 2 (Summer 2006); Karl Jacoby, *Crimes Against Nature: Squatters, Poachers, Thieves, and the Hidden History of American Conservation* (Los Angeles: University of California Press, 2001); and Deborah Kang, "Peripheries and Center: Immigration Law and Policy on the U.S.-Mexico Border, 1917–1924," in *Bridging National Borders in North America: Transnational and Comparative Histories*, ed. Andrew Graybill and Benjamin Johnson (Durham, N.C.: Duke University Press, 2010).

17. Paul Nugent, *Smugglers, Secessionists & Loyal Citizens on the Ghana-Togo Frontier* (Athens: Ohio University Press, 2002).

18. Paredes, *Folklore and Culture*, 24.

19. Ibid., 26.

20. Jacoby, *Crimes Against Nature*; and E. P. Thompson, *Customs in Common: Studies in Traditional Popular Culture* (New York: New Press, 1993).

21. Deborah Kang, "The Legal Construction of the Borderlands" (unpublished manuscript, 2006); St. John, *Line in the Sand*; and Truett, *Fugitive Landscapes*.

22. Truett, *Fugitive Landscapes*, 86.

23. Andreas, *Border Games*, 8.

24. Phillip W. Magness, "From Tariffs to the Income Tax: Trade Protection and Revenue in the United States Tax System" (Ph.D. diss., George Mason University,

2009), 266; and Don Whitehead, *Border Guard: The Story of the United States Customs Service* (New York: McGraw-Hill, 1963), 25.

25. Graciela Márquez Colín, "The Political Economy of Mexican Protectionism, 1886–1911" (Ph.D. diss., Harvard University, 2002), 202–203; and Matías Romero, *Mexico and the United States: A Study of Subjects Affecting Their Political, Commercial, and Social Relations, Made with a View to Their Promotion* (New York: G. P. Putman's Sons, 1898), 146.

26. Adelman and Aron, "From Borderlands to Borders," 814.

27. John A. Adams Jr., *Conflict and Commerce on the Rio Grande: Laredo, 1755–1955* (College Station: Texas A&M University Press, 2008), 103, 129.

28. Customs House, Collector's Office, Laredo, Texas, February 23, 1895, in Romero, *Mexico and the United States*, 489.

CHAPTER 1

1. Edmund Ned Wallace, Deputy Collector, Eagle Pass, Texas, to Hon. James Guthrie, January 21, 1856, *Letters Received by the Secretary of the Treasury from Collectors of Customs ("G," "H," "I" Series), 1833–1869* (Washington, D.C.: National Archives Microfilm Publications, 1969), microfilm, M174A.

2. Paredes, *Folklore and Culture*, 23; and Martínez, *Border People*, 23.

3. *Oxford English Dictionary*, s.v. "contraband," accessed May 28, 2013, http://www.oed.com/.

4. El Paso de Jacinto (or El Paso de los Indios) and El Paso de Miguel Garza are both near Laredo; however, El Paso de los Indios was and remains the more widely used of the two. Seb. S. Wilcox, "Laredo During the Texas Republic," *Southwestern Historical Quarterly* 42, no. 2 (October 1938): 84.

5. Although documents of the time refer to the now U.S. side of the Rio Grande as the left bank and the Mexican side as the right bank, I will refer to the U.S. side as the north bank and the Mexican side as the south bank. J. B. Wilkinson, *Laredo and the Rio Grande Frontier* (Austin, T.X.: Jenkins, 1975), 46.

6. Gilberto M. Hinojosa, *A Borderlands Town in Transition: Laredo, 1755–1870* (College Station: Texas A&M University Press, 1983), 12; and Robert D. Wood, *Life in Laredo: A Documentary History of the Laredo Archives* (Denton: University of North Texas Press, 2004), 30.

7. Stanley C. Green, *Tilden's Voyage to Laredo in 1846*, vol. 14 of *The Story of Laredo* (Laredo: Border Studies, 1991), 69; and Hinojosa, *A Borderlands Town*, 62–63.

8. Green, *Tilden's Voyage to Laredo*, 69.

9. Jerry Thompson, *Laredo: A Pictorial History* (Norfolk, V.A.: Donning, 1986), 149.

10. Howard J. Erlichman, *Camino del Norte: How a Series of Watering Holes, Fords, and Dirt Trails Evolved into Interstate 35 in Texas* (College Station: Texas A&M University Press, 2006), 81; and Robert S. Weddle, *San Juan Bautista: Gateway to Spanish Texas* (Austin: University of Texas Press, 1968), 418.

11. During the *Major Brown*'s journey up the Rio Grande in 1846, Lt. Bryant Tilden repeatedly commented on the frequent visits by curious locals and the "courtesy" and "cordiality" they showed the Americans. Cited in Green, *Tilden's Voyage to Laredo*, 65.

12. Stanley C. Green, *A Changing of Flags: Mirabeau B. Lamar at Laredo 1846–1848*, vol. 5 of *The Story of Laredo* (Laredo: Border Studies, 1992), 48.

13. Mirabeau B. Lamar to Major Gen. Zachary Taylor, Laredo, Texas, 1846, in Green, *Lamar at Laredo*, 55.

14. For a fascinating examination of Indians' role in weakening Mexico's northern borderlands, see Brian DeLay, *War of a Thousand Deserts: Indian Raids and the U.S.-Mexican War* (New Haven, C.T.: Yale University Press, 2008), 74–75.

15. Mirabeau B. Lamar to Major Gen. Zachary Taylor, Laredo, Texas, 1846, in Green, *Lamar at Laredo*, 56.

16. Wilkinson, *Laredo and the Rio Grande*, 52.

17. Mirabeau B. Lamar to Major Gen. Zachary Taylor, Laredo, Texas, 1846, in Green, *Lamar at Laredo*, 56. Although Native Americans' role in illicit trade across the U.S.-Mexico borderlands is not the focus of this book, it is important to point out that Indian raiders at this time did cross national borders with stolen dutiable property. Ethnic Mexican smugglers seeking to profit from the illicit trade in cattle and horses led some of these later raids. See Adams, *Conflict and Commerce*, 97. The last Indian raid near Laredo occurred in September of 1871, when some seventy-five Comanche descended on the community stealing seventy horses and abducting two children. Charles Winslow, Commercial Agent U.S., to William Hunter, September 26, 1871, *Despatches from U.S. Consuls in Guerrero, Mexico, 1871–1888* (Washington, D.C.: National Archives Microfilm Publications, 1964), microfilm, M292.

18. Mirabeau B. Lamar to Major Gen. Zachary Taylor, in Green, *Lamar at Laredo*, 57.

19. Ibid., 56–57.

20. Bryant J. Tilden, "Notes on the Upper Rio Grande," in Green, *Tilden's Voyage to Laredo*, 65.

21. Inhabitants of Santa Rosa to Lamar and American Officers, May 20, 1848, in Green, *Lamar at Laredo*, 54–55.

22. Lamar had reasons to exaggerate his statements about most Laredoans' favor of the Americans, but his assertions have their basis in fact. Local memory does not recall Americans' arrival with bitterness. Mexican insurgents did not strike American caravans outside the city, nor are any disturbances, such as the writing of anti-American graffiti, known to have occurred. Aside from reports that the garrison's quartermaster failed to pay local merchants for their goods, relations between the garrison and the town were fair. Edwin R. Clay's Statement, Laredo Garrison, December 6, 1846, in Mirabeau B. Lamar, *The Papers of Mirabeau Buonaparte Lamar*, ed. Charles A. Gulick Jr. and Winnie Allen, vol. 4, part 1 (Austin, T.X.: Pemberton Press, 1968), 31; and José M. Gonzalez, Laredo, Texas, December 9, 1846, in Lamar, *Papers*, 151.

Local ethnic Mexicans claim Laredo did not suffer the virulent racism that other communities in the Lower Rio Grande Valley experienced. Historians Elliott Young and Gilberto Miguel Hinojosa have provided evidence to support locals' popular memory. Other scholars such as Beatriz de la Garza and Roberto Calderón dispute this claim. Although Calderón and de la Garza are correct in insisting that incidents of ethnoracial discrimination did occur, their scholarship focuses more on the exception rather than the norm. See Elliott Young, "Deconstructing *La Raza*: Identifying the *Gente Decente* of Laredo, 1904–1911," *Southwestern Historical Quarterly* 98, no. 2 (October 1994); Young, "Red Men, Princess Pocahontas, and George Washington: Harmonizing Race Relations in Laredo at the Turn of the Century," *Western Historical Quarterly* 29, no. 1 (Spring 1998); Hinojosa, *A Borderlands Town*, 71; Beatriz de la Garza, *A Law for the Lion: A Tale of Crime and Injustice in the Borderlands* (Austin: University of Texas Press, 2003); Roberto R. Calderón, "Mexican Politics in the American Era, 1846–1900" (Ph.D. diss., University of California Los Angeles, 1993); and Adams, *Conflict and Commerce*, 78.

23. Ana María Alonso, *Thread of Blood: Colonialism, Revolution, and Gender on Mexico's Northern Frontier* (Tucson: University of Arizona Press, 1995), 15–16.

24. Thompson, *Laredo: A Pictorial History*, 103.

25. Stanley C. Green, *Laredo, Antonio Zapata, and the Republic of the Rio Grande*, vol. 8 of *The Story of Laredo* (Laredo: Border Studies, 1992), 109.

26. Alexander Mendoza, "'For Our Own Best Interests': Nineteenth-Century Laredo Tejanos, Military Service, and the Development of American Nationalism," *Southwestern Historical Quarterly* 115, no. 2. (October 2011): 129; Andrés Reséndez, *Changing National Identities at the Frontier: Texas and New Mexico, 1830–1850* (Cambridge: Cambridge University Press, 2005); and Wilcox, "Laredo During the Texas Republic."

27. For a classic Chicano examination of Anglo intrusions, see Rodolfo Acuña, *Occupied America: The Chicano's Struggle Toward Liberation* (San Francisco: Canfield Press, 1972).

28. Adams, *Conflict and Commerce*, 75–76; and Green, *Lamar at Laredo*, 49.

29. Representative Commission of the People to Gen. Wool, Laredo, Mexico [Texas], April 10, 1848, in Green, *Lamar at Laredo*, 64.

30. Ibid.

31. Mirabeau B. Lamar to Town Commission, Laredo, Texas, April 11, 1848, in Green, *Lamar at Laredo*, 65.

32. The earliest U.S. Customs records for the port of Laredo begin in 1851, five years after Lamar's arrival. Impost Books for Laredo, Texas, 1851–1914, vol. 1, E 1700, A-32-48-4, Records of the United States Customs Service, Record Group 36, National Archives and Records Administration (hereafter NARA)–Fort Worth, Texas.

33. Lamar mentioned in a letter that Lt. Bee was out on "collectorial duties," but otherwise his papers are silent on the subject. Mirabeau B. Lamar to Lt. Chas J. Helm, Laredo, Texas, June 17, 1848, in Green, *Lamar at Laredo*, 67.

34. "Special Order," Mirabeau B. Lamar, Laredo Garrison, May 5, 1847, in Green, *Lamar at Laredo*, 60.

35. Asst. Adjt. Gen. W. W. J. Bliss to Gen. M. B. Lamar, October 15, 1846, in Green, *Lamar at Laredo*, 50.

36. Lamar to Senr. Dn. Andrés Martínes, Laredo, Texas, October 20, 1847, in Green, *Lamar at Laredo*, 61.

37. Juan Mora-Torres, *The Making of the Mexican Border: The State, Capitalism, and Society in Nuevo León, 1848–1910* (Austin: University of Texas Press, 2001), 31–32.

38. The United States did collect Mexican tariffs at the country's principal port of Veracruz, but this was the exception. Treaty of Guadalupe Hidalgo, Art. III, February 2, 1848, cited in Oscar J. Martínez, ed., *U.S.-Mexico Borderlands: Historical and Contemporary Perspectives* (Wilmington, D.E.: SR Books, 1996), 21–22.

39. LeRoy P. Graf, "The Economic History of the Lower Rio Grande Valley, 1820–1875" (Ph.D. diss., Harvard University, 1942), 306–307.

40. Magness, "From Tariffs to the Income Tax," 266.

41. Impost Books for Laredo, NARA–Fort Worth, Texas.

42. Ibid.

43. Hinojosa, *A Borderlands Town*, 57–58.

44. Carl E. Prince and Mollie Keller, *The U.S. Customs Service: A Bicentennial History* (Washington, D.C.: Department of the Treasury, U.S. Customs Service, 1989), 121.

45. At least three men living in Laredo worked as U.S. Customs agents in the 1850s. Two were Anglo immigrants and one, John Leyendecker, was a German native. Edmund Davis, future Radical Reconstruction governor of Texas (1870–1874), served as an inspector and deputy collector in Laredo from 1849–1853. Adams, *Conflict and Commerce*, 45–78. U.S. customs enforcement along the desert border between California and Presidio in West Texas may have been worse. Only twenty-five agents worked the nine-hundred-mile stretch in the 1880s. See J. Evetts Haley, *Jeff Milton: A Good Man with a Gun* (Norman: University of Oklahoma Press, 1948), 165.

46. Hinojosa, *A Borderlands Town*, 74.

47. In his seminal examination of the economics of the lower Rio Grande borderlands, LeRoy Graf concludes that although "irregularities" likely occurred under the system of mounted Customs inspectors, mounted inspectors were the most effective means of tariff collection the United States could muster. See Graf, "The Economic History," 305. Corruption by the very men charged with enforcing customs regulations was also a problem. On January 28, 1867, Commissioner of Customs Nathan Sargent reported that along the Rio Grande "almost every officer of customs is either engaged in or permits smuggling." Sargent singled out the officers of the Brownsville station as "most corrupt," with "no regard for God, man, or the devil, and . . . think it no harm to defraud the government . . . provided they . . . can be paid for so doing." Commissioner N. Sargent to M. B. Marshall, U.S. Consul, Matamoros, January 28, 1867, *Letters Sent by the Commissioner of Customs Relating to Smuggling, 1865–1869* (Washington, D.C.: National Archives Microfilm Publications, 1963), microfilm, M497.

48. Deputy Collector and Inspector Edmund Reed Wallace to Collector of Customs La Salle, February 1, 1855, *Letters Received by the Secretary of the Treasury*, Series G, Roll 57.

49. Ibid.

50. Impost Books for Laredo, NARA–Fort Worth.

51. Ibid.

52. Ibid.

53. Deputy Collector Edmund Wallace at Eagle Pass to Collector of Customs, La Salle, Texas, February 7, 1855, *Letters Received by the Secretary of the Treasury.*

54. José Herrera to Collector of Customs of this Place, undated letter, *Letters Received by the Secretary of the Treasury.*

55. Collector Caleb Sherman, District Paso del Norte, to Hon. James Guthrie, Secretary of the Treasury, Washington City, April 22, 1856, *Letters Received by the Secretary of the Treasury.* For an excellent examination of the U.S. Army's role in borderland economics, see Thomas T. Smith, *The U.S. Army and the Texas Frontier Economy, 1845–1900* (College Station: Texas A&M University Press, 1999), 71–77.

56. Reg. Qr. Master J. G. Pitcher to Collector of Customs Caleb Sherman, Franklin, Texas, February 8, 1856, *Letters Received by the Secretary of the Treasury.*

57. Collector Caleb Sherman to Hon. James Guthrie, July 3, 1856, *Letters Received by the Secretary of the Treasury.*

58. Caleb Sherman, Custom Collector, District Paso del Norte, to James Guthrie, Secretary of the Treasury, January 1, 1856, *Letters Received by the Secretary of the Treasury.*

59. Collector Caleb Sherman to Hon. James Guthrie, Secretary of the Treasury, Washington City, January 8, 1856, *Letters Received by the Secretary of the Treasury.*

60. William H. Emory, *Report on the United States and Mexican Boundary Survey, Made under the Direction of the Secretary of the Interior,* vol. 1 (Washington D.C.: Cornelius Wendell, 1857), 62.

61. Ibid, 64. For more information on interethnic cooperation in tariff evasion, see "The Problem of Identity in a Changing Culture," in Paredes, *Folklore and Culture,* 23.

62. James H. Durst to Hon. James Guthrie, February 15, 1856, *Letters Received by the Secretary of the Treasury.*

63. Ibid.

64. *Fronterizos* of the lower Rio Grande borderlands valued wealth in terms of ownership of land and domesticated animals. Moreover, livestock served as a means of exchange in a sometimes cashless barter economy. J. Frank Dobie, *The Longhorns* (New York: Little, Brown, 1941), 36–37.

65. U.S. Commercial Agent James Haynes to Second Assistant Sec. of State William Hunter, November 24, 1875, *Despatches from U.S. Consuls in Nuevo Laredo.* The U.S. consular despatches, sometimes spelled dispatches in the original documents, consulted throughout this book are available on microfilm. For information on King's actions against ethnic Mexicans, see Andrés Tijerina, *Tejano Empire: Life on the South Texas Ranchos* (College Station: Texas A&M University Press, 1998), 124–125.

66. U.S. Commercial Agent James Haynes to Second Assistant Sec. of State William Hunter, November 24, 1875, *Despatches from U.S. Consuls in Nuevo Laredo.*

67. Tijerina, *Tejano Empire*, 45–48, 123–125.

68. Deputy Collector and Inspector Edmund Reed Wallace to Collector of Customs, La Salle, February 1, 1855, *Letters Received by the Secretary of the Treasury*.

69. Barbara A. Tenenbaum, *The Politics of Penury: Debts and Taxes in Mexico, 1821–1856* (Albuquerque: University of New Mexico Press, 1986), 13.

70. Ibid., 24.

71. Ibid. Mexico's three customs ports of the time were located in Veracruz, Acapulco, and San Blas. Logistical difficulties also contributed to revenue collection problems. In New Mexico administrators often did not know the proper duty rates for months at a time and under- or overcharged traders. These frustrations caused some officials to attempt novel solutions. From 1839–1844, Governor Manuel Armijo simply charged a flat rate of $500 on each wagonload of imports through New Mexico. See Max L. Moorhead, *New Mexico's Royal Road: Trade and Travel on the Chihuahua Trail* (Norman: University of Oklahoma Press, 1958), 127.

72. Tenenbaum, *The Politics of Penury*, 182. Between 1839 and 1846, Mexico's national deficit averaged 12.7 million pesos annually. See Wilfrid H. Callcott, *Church and State in Mexico, 1822–1857* (Durham: University of North Carolina Press, 1926), 160–161.

73. Tenenbaum, *The Politics of Penury*, 58–59.

74. In his classic work on the Mexican borderlands, David J. Weber discussed the difficulties that tariff enforcement provoked on the eve of the Texas Revolution. *The Mexican Frontier, 1821–1846: The American Southwest Under Mexico* (Albuquerque: University of New Mexico Press, 1982), 155; for more on tensions at Anáhuac see Randolph B. Campbell, *Gone to Texas: A History of the Lone Star State* (New York: Oxford University Press, 2003), 117–122.

75. It is worth noting that many of the events surrounding the American Revolution concerned the right to trade freely. For instance, the Boston Massacre originated as a confrontation between colonists and British Customs officials who called in the army when the crowd became unruly. In June of 1772 as many as sixty colonists set fire to the HMS *Gaspee* after it ran aground pursuing smugglers in Narragansett Bay. Locals commemorate the smuggler-patriots' victory every year during Gaspee Days. On a more negative note, Mexico's abolition of slavery in 1829 prompted some Anglos to smuggle slaves into Texas. For more information on smugglers' role in the American Revolution, see John W. Tyler, *Smugglers and Patriots: Boston Merchants and the Advent of the American Revolution* (Boston, M.A.: Northeastern University Press, 1986). For more on the smuggling of slaves into Mexican Texas, see Paul D. Lack, "Slavery and the Texas Revolution," *Southwestern Historical Quarterly* 89, no. 2 (October 1985): 181–202.

76. Tenenbaum, *The Politics of Penury*, 88, 98, 182.

77. Ibid., 92.

78. Ibid., 169.

79. Mora-Torres, *The Making of the Mexican Border*, 29.

80. Tenenbaum, *The Politics of Penury*, 26.

81. Tenenbaum, *The Politics of Penury*, 29; and Michael C. Meyer, William Sher-

man, and Susan Deeds, *The Course of Mexican History*, 6th ed. (New York: Oxford University Press, 1999), 373.

82. *Reglamento para el contra-resguardo de Nuevo León y Tamaulipas* (Mexico: Imprenta de las Escalerillas n. 7, 1850), available at the DeGolyer Library Special Collections, Southern Methodist University.

83. *Reglamento para el contra-resguardo*, 7.

84. *Reglamento para el contra-resguardo*, 10.

85. Carlos J. Sierra and Rogelio Martínez Vera, *El resguardo aduanal y la gendarmería fiscal, 1850–1925* (Mexico City: Secretaría de Hacienda y Crédito Público, 1971), 13–14; and *Reglamento para el contra-resguardo*, 4–8.

86. *Reglamento para el contra-resguardo*, 10.

87. Jorge A. Hernandez, "Trading Across the Border: National Customs Guards in Nuevo León," *Southwestern Historical Quarterly* 100, no. 4 (1997): 442–443.

88. Alex M. Saragoza, *The Monterrey Elite and the Mexican State, 1880–1940* (Austin: University of Texas Press, 1988), 20; and Hernandez, "Trading Across the Border," 444. Not all merchants hated the Contraresguardo. Merchants closer to the interior of the country who did not receive contraband goods found it difficult to compete against the cheaper smuggled products their competitors sold. For more information on interior merchants' interests in the Mexican Customs Service, see Sierra and Vera, *El resguardo aduanal*, 18.

89. *Reglamento para el contra-resguardo*, 13.

90. *Reglamento para el contra-resguardo*, 6, 7.

91. Administrador de Aduana Francisco Jiménez al Contaduría de la Aduana Manuel Berrea, December 30, 1854, Justicia, Vol. 506, Exp. 11, Archivo General de la Nación, Mexico City (hereafter AGN).

92. Peter J. Bakewell, *Silver Mining and Society in Colonial Mexico: Zacatecas, 1546–1700* (Cambridge: Cambridge University Press, 1971), 182–183.

93. Richard J. Salvucci, "The Origins and Progress of U.S.-Mexican Trade, 1825–1884: 'Hoc opus, hic labor est,'" *Hispanic American Historical Review* 71, no. 4 (November 1991): 706.

94. Mexican national export duties on silver often ran as high as 12 percent. Mint duties pushed the price of lawful exportation up to 17 percent. Other taxes and duties could increase the price of lawful silver exports even higher. Romero, *Mexico and the United States*, 28, 187; Salvucci, "Origins and Progress," 706; for an excellent examination of silver smuggling out of Mexico in the nineteenth century, see John Mayo, "Consuls and Silver Contraband on Mexico's West Coast in the Era of Santa Anna," *Journal of Latin American Studies* 19, no. 2 (November 1987).

95. Administrador de Aduana Francisco Jiménez al Contaduría de la Aduana Manuel Berrea, December 30, 1854, Justicia, Vol. 506, Exp. 11, AGN.

96. J. S. Rhea to W. M. Meredith, November 7, 1849, Treasury, quoted in Graf, "The Economic History," 309–310.

97. Ernest C. Shearer, "The Carvajal Disturbances," *Southwestern Historical Quarterly* 55, no. 2 (October 1951): 208.

98. Ibid., 204.

99. See Shearer, "The Carvajal Disturbances," 208.

100. The Plan de la Loba limited customs duties to 40 percent ad valorem. Joseph E. Chance, *José María de Jesús Carvajal: The Life and Times of a Mexican Revolutionary* (San Antonio, T.X.: Trinity University Press, 2006), 105.

101. Ibid.

102. Ibid., 104–105.

103. Shearer, "The Carvajal Disturbances," 209.

104. Ibid., 219.

105. Chance, *José María de Jesús Carvajal*, 205.

106. Adams, *Conflict and Commerce*, 84–86; Chance, *José María de Jesús Carvajal*, 204–205; and Shearer, "The Carvajal Disturbances," 218–219.

107. Samuel E. Bell and James M. Smallwood, *The Zona Libre, 1858–1905: A Problem in American Diplomacy* (El Paso: Texas Western Press, 1982), 4; and Octavio H. Pérez, *La Zona Libre: Excepción fiscal y conformación histórica de la frontera norte de México* (Mexico City: Dirección General Del Acervo Histórico Diplomático, 2004).

108. Sandra Kuntz Ficker, "Institutional Change and Foreign Trade in Mexico, 1870–1911," in *The Mexican Economy, 1870–1930: Essays on The Economic History of Institutions, Revolution, and Growth*, ed. Jeffery L. Bortz and Stephen Haber (Stanford, C.A.: Stanford University Press, 2002), 164.

109. Bell and Smallwood, *The Zona Libre*, 10.

110. Tenenbaum, *The Politics of Penury*, 13.

111. Tariffs slowly crept into the Zona Libre over the course of its existence. During the 1880s goods could be introduced at 3 percent of their actual rate. This increased to 10 percent of their regular rate in the 1890s. For more information on the Zona Libre see Herrera Pérez, *La Zona Libre*.

112. Matías Romero, "The Free Zone in Mexico," *North American Review* 154, no. 425 (April 1892): 464.

113. See Meyer, Sherman, and Deeds, *The Course of Mexican History*, 374–375; and Robert R. Miller, "Arms Across the Border: United States Aid to Juárez during the French Intervention in Mexico," *Transactions of the American Philosophical Society* 63, no. 6 (December 1973): 11.

114. Robert W. Delaney, "Matamoros, Port for Texas during the Civil War," *Southwestern Historical Quarterly* 58, no. 4 (April 1955): 473; Milo Kearney and Anthony Knopp, *Boom and Bust: The Historical Cycles of Matamoros and Brownsville* (Austin, T.X.: Eakin Press, 1991), 105; and Ronnie C. Tyler, *Santiago Vidaurri and the Southern Confederacy* (Austin: Texas State Historical Association, 1973), 104–105.

115. Miller, "Arms Across the Border," 19; and Romero, *Mexico and the United States*, 450–451.

116. Thompson, *Laredo: A Pictorial History*, 160.

117. Don Graham, *Kings of Texas: The 150-Year Saga of an American Ranching Empire* (Hoboken, N.J.: John Wiley, 2003), 96–97; and Tyler, *Santiago Vidaurri*, 151–152.

118. Aside from his dealings with the Confederacy, Vidaurri's agents gathered as

much as $175,000 in customs revenue from the ports of Piedras Negras and Nuevo Laredo. See Adams, *Conflict and Commerce*, 93; and Tyler, *Santiago Vidaurri*, 51–52, 136–137.

119. Milmo also used his money to build a gathering hall in Laredo. In later years Milmo's name was attached to a company of volunteers who guarded the town during the Mexican Revolution, a local baseball team active in the 1910s and '20s, and a street. Such immersion into local culture helped cement Milmo's elite status despite his involvement in illicit trade. See Adams, *Conflict and Commerce*, 92–93; and Jerry Thompson, *Warm Weather and Bad Whiskey: The 1886 Laredo Election Riot* (El Paso: Texas Western Press, 1991), 51.

120. Jerry Thompson, *Vaqueros in Blue and Gray* (Austin: State House Press, 2000), 107.

121. Four members of the Benavides family served as mayors of Laredo between 1848 and 1881. Thompson, *Warm Weather and Bad Whiskey*, 54, 200–201.

122. Evidence that the Benavides brothers paid American tariffs appears throughout U.S. impost books for Laredo. For example, on April 28, 1871, the brothers paid $3.10 to import nine rawhides valued at $30.36. Impost Books for Laredo, NARA–Fort Worth, Texas.

123. Thomas Gilgan to Mr. Hunter, Commercial Agency of the United States of America, Nuevo Laredo, Tamaulipas, February 26, 1872, *Despatches from U.S. Consuls in Nuevo Laredo*. For more information on hide smuggling see Adams, *Conflict and Commerce*, 100.

124. Julián Cerda, Aduana Fronteriza del Bravo, Monterey Laredo, to U.S. Vice Consul en este Villa, February 22, 1872, *Despatches from U.S. Consuls in Nuevo Laredo*.

125. Santos and Cristóbal Benavides to U.S. Consul in Monterey Laredo, Mexico, February 21, 1872, *Despatches from U.S. Consuls in Nuevo Laredo*.

126. Thomas Gilgan to Mr. Hunter, Commercial Agency of the United States of America, Nuevo Laredo, Tamaulipas, February 26, 1872, *Despatches from U.S. Consuls in Nuevo Laredo*.

127. U.S. Commercial Agent Thomas Gilgan to Hon. William Hunter, June 22, 1872, *Despatches from U.S. Consuls in Nuevo Laredo*; Thomas Gilgan to Hon. William Hunter, July 12, 1872, *Despatches from U.S. Consuls in Nuevo Laredo*; and Thomas Gilgan to Hon. William Hunter, September 2, 1872, *Despatches from U.S. Consuls in Nuevo Laredo*.

128. Julián Cerda, Aduana Fronteriza del Bravo, Monterey Laredo, to U.S. Vice Consul en este Villa, February 22, 1872, *Despatches from U.S. Consuls in Nuevo Laredo*.

129. "The Benavides Brothers," Texas Historical Commission plaque, Laredo, Texas, 1976.

130. "Ready or Not: School Begins!," *Laredo Morning Times*, August 16, 2005.

131. Emory, *Report on the United States and Mexican Survey*, 64.

132. Martínez, *Border People*, 313.

133. Commissioner N. Sargent to Robert A. Crawford, Brownsville, Texas, December 26, 1868, *Letters Sent by the Commissioner of Customs Relating to Smuggling*.

134. In his study of borderland economic development, Alex Saragoza stated, "Many traders doubled as smugglers in their attempts to avoid payment of customs fees." Although Saragoza's statement regards smugglers entering goods into Mexico rather than the United States, his point is valid to those carrying contraband north across the border. Saragoza, *The Monterrey Elite*, 24; see also Mora-Torres, *The Making of the Mexican Border*, 36.

135. For an interesting, yet anecdotal, examination of Tejano perceptions of smuggling in this period see "The Problem of Identity in a Changing Culture," in Paredes, *Folklore and Culture*, 23–26.

136. U.S. authorities stated that this "consumption is limited chiefly to the Mexican population." U.S. Commercial Agent James J. Haynes to Hon. William Hunter, September 28, 1879, *Despatches from U.S. Consuls in Nuevo Laredo*.

137. Request for the Release of Seized Goods for the Port of Laredo, 1875–1894, LR 2, A–32–48–4, Records of the U.S. Customs Service, Record Group 36, NARA–Fort Worth, Texas.

138. Ibid.

139. Ibid.

140. Ficker, "Institutional Change and Foreign Trade," 178.

141. Henry M. Stille to William Hunter, Guerrero, Tamaulipas, December 31, 1878, *Despatches from U.S. Consuls in Guerrero*.

142. Ibid.

143. U.S. Vice Consul John Seene to William Hunter, Nuevo Laredo, Tamaulipas, September 4, 1880, *Despatches from U.S. Consuls in Nuevo Laredo*.

144. Henry M. Stille to William Hunter, Guerrero, Tamaulipas, December 31, 1878, *Despatches from U.S. Consuls in Guerrero*.

145. Finding documented instances of state agents turning a blind eye to low-level smuggling is exceedingly difficult. However, noted scholar Oscar Martínez mentions that borderlanders "expect officials to be flexible and tolerant, allowing a certain amount of illegal traffic to go on." Martínez, *Border People*, 53.

146. Paredes, *Folklore and Culture*, 26; Henry M. Stille to William Hunter, Guerrero, Tamaulipas, December 31, 1878, *Despatches from U.S. Consuls in Guerrero*; and Charles Winslow to Secretary of State, Guerrero, Mexico, October 1, 1881, *Despatches from U.S. Consuls in Nuevo Laredo*.

147. Charles Winslow to Secretary of State, Guerrero, Mexico, October 2, 1881, *Despatches from U.S. Consuls in Nuevo Laredo*. For more information on hide smuggling, see Henry M. Stille to William Hunter, Guerrero, Tamaulipas, December 31, 1878, *Despatches from U.S. Consuls in Guerrero*.

148. Charles Winslow to Secretary of State, Guerrero, Mexico, October 2, 1881, *Despatches from U.S. Consuls in Nuevo Laredo*.

149. Andreas, *Smuggler Nation*, 178.

150. Charles Winslow to Secretary of State, Guerrero, Mexico, October 2, 1881, *Despatches from U.S. Consuls in Nuevo Laredo*; See also Henry M. Stille to William

Hunter, Guerrero, Tamaulipas, December 31, 1878, *Despatches from U.S. Consuls in Guerrero.*

151. Charles Winslow to Secretary of State, Guerrero, Mexico, October 2, 1881, *Despatches from U.S. Consuls in Nuevo Laredo.*

152. Ibid.

153. Ibid.

CHAPTER 2

1. M. Romero to Thomas Bayard, Washington, D.C., April 26, 1887, in "Incursiones a México por el contrabandista Mariano Reséndez, en la frontera con los estados de Tamaulipas y Coahuila," Archivo Histórico de la Secretaría de Relaciones Exteriores, Mexico City (hereafter SRE).

2. The document uses the word *malhechor.* Ibid.

3. Ibid.

4. James A. Garza, "On the Edge of a Storm: Laredo and the Mexican Revolution, 1910–1917" (master's thesis, Texas A&M International University, 1996), 15.

5. Matías Romero and John Bigelow, *Railways in Mexico* (Washington, D.C.: W. H. Moore, 1882), 15.

6. Adams, *Conflict and Commerce,* 129.

7. Ibid.

8. U.S. federal district court records for Laredo begin in 1899, and smuggling cases can be found in almost every box of the records. Of the many boxes examined, however, not a single case of smugglers using the railroad to ship their contraband cargo has been discovered in this period. Criminal Case Files for Laredo, Texas, Records of the U.S. District Courts for the Southern District of Texas, Record Group 21, NARA–Fort Worth, Texas.

9. Consul General R. B. Mahone to Assistant Secretary of State David J. Hill, Nuevo Laredo, Mexico, April 21, 1899, *Despatches from U.S. Consuls in Nuevo Laredo.*

10. For more information on corruption in South Texas, particularly in regard to federal patronage of Customs Service jobs, see Evan Anders, *Boss Rule in South Texas: The Progressive Era* (Austin: University of Texas Press, 1982), 26–43; for more information on the U.S. Customs Service's activities at this time, see Laurence F. Schmeckebier, *The Customs Service: Its History, Activities and Organization* (Baltimore, M.D.: Johns Hopkins Press, 1924), 32–34.

11. Consul General R. B. Mahone to Assistant Secretary of State David J. Hill, Nuevo Laredo, Mexico, June 27, 1898, *Despatches from U.S. Consuls in Nuevo Laredo.*

12. Commercial Agent Marcus J. Milona to Second Assistant Secretary of State William Hunter, July 16, 1874, *Despatches from U.S. Consuls in Nuevo Laredo;* and Commercial Agent James Haynes to Second Assistant Secretary of State William Hunter, Nuevo Laredo, Mexico, July 3, 1875, *Despatches from U.S. Consuls in Nuevo Laredo.*

13. Consul General R. B. Mahone to Assistant Secretary of State David J. Hill, Nuevo Laredo, Mexico, January 11, 1899, *Despatches from U.S. Consuls in Nuevo Laredo*.

14. Ibid.

15. Aduana Fronteriza de Laredo, Tamaulipas, Exp. No. 16 de December 1, 1899, Por J. Archibald, Hacienda Pública, C 1230, AGN; Aduana Fronteriza de Laredo, Tamaulipas, Exp. No. 360 de December 8, 1899, Por J. Archibald, Hacienda Pública, C 1230, AGN; Aduana Fronteriza de Laredo, Tamaulipas, Exp. No. 335 de December 5, 1899, Por la Agencia Aduanal, Hacienda Pública, C 1230, AGN; and Aduana Fronteriza de Laredo, Tamaulipas, Exp. No. 391 de December 22, 1899, Por J. Archibald, Hacienda Pública, C 1230, AGN.

16. Aduana Fronteriza de Laredo, Tamaulipas, Exp. No. 324 de November 27, 1899, Por la Agencia Aduanal, Hacienda Pública, C 1230, AGN.

17. Ibid.

18. Aduana Fronteriza de Laredo, Tamaulipas, Exp. No. 360 de December 8, 1899, Por J. Archibald, Hacienda Pública, C 1230, AGN.

19. Aduana Fronteriza de Laredo, Tamaulipas, Exp. No. 335 de December 5, 1899, Por la Agencia Aduanal, Hacienda Pública, C 1230, AGN.

20. Florsheim Company, Chicago, Illinois, to U.S. Consul R. B. Mahone, Nuevo Laredo, Mexico, October 8, 1899, *Despatches from U.S. Consuls in Nuevo Laredo*.

21. Florsheim Company, Chicago, Illinois, to U.S. Consul R. B. Mahone, Nuevo Laredo, Mexico, October 8, 1899, *Despatches from U.S. Consuls in Nuevo Laredo*; Consul General R. B. Mahone to Assistant Secretary of State David J. Hill, Nuevo Laredo, Mexico, June 27, 1898, *Despatches from U.S. Consuls in Nuevo Laredo*; and Aduana Fronteriza de Laredo, Tamaulipas, Exp. No. 360 de December 8, 1899, Por J. Archibald, Hacienda Pública, C 1230, AGN.

22. Hinojosa, *A Borderlands Town*, 98.

23. Oscar J. Martínez, *Border Boom Town: Ciudad Juárez since 1848* (Austin: University of Texas Press, 1978), 161.

24. Young, "Deconstructing *La Raza*," 228.

25. Laredo would not be spared the raiding of the Mexican Revolution, but it did escape the genocidal violence that occurred in the Lower Rio Grande Valley. Moreover, the *gente decente* did not allow the Ku Klux Klan to march in Laredo in 1922. See Garza, "On the Edge of a Storm," 40; and Thompson, *Laredo: A Pictorial History*, 26.

26. Thompson, *Warm Weather and Bad Whiskey*, 200–201.

27. Hinojosa, *A Borderlands Town*, 71.

28. Laredo's experience balances the perception of the Texas-Mexican borderlands as a place of ethnoracial conflict between Anglos and ethnic Mexicans. While scholars have rightfully asserted that Anglo/ethnic Mexican tensions in the region were racialized, few scholars have examined mutual cooperation in the area. For good reason, Chicano scholars like David Montejano, Arnoldo De León, and Américo Paredes have examined how racial tensions adversely affected Anglo/ethnic Mexican relations. Comparatively few scholars consider how Anglos and ethnic Mexicans

cooperated in the making of a common border society. My research has unearthed many instances of Anglos and ethnic Mexicans cooperating to evade U.S. and Mexican national tariffs. Moreover, Anglo/ethnic Mexican interactions in Laredo were such as to make the state/local violent conflicts that did break out less race based and more to do with the weakness of state forces on the border or simple happenstance. See David Montejano, *Anglos and Mexicans in the Making of Texas, 1836–1986* (Austin: University of Texas Press, 1987); Arnoldo De León, *They Called them Greasers: Anglo Attitudes toward Mexicans in Texas, 1821–1900* (Austin: University of Texas Press, 1983); Américo Paredes, *With His Pistol in His Hand: A Border Ballad and Its Hero* (Austin: University of Texas Press, 1958); Paredes, *Folklore and Culture*; and Miguel Ángel González de Quiroga, "Conflict and Cooperation in the Making of Texas-Mexico Border Society, 1840–1880," in *Bridging National Borders in North America: Transnational and Comparative Histories*, ed. Andrew Graybill and Benjamin Johnson (Durham, N.C.: Duke University Press, 2010).

29. Young, "Red Men, Princess Pocahontas, and George Washington," 53.

30. Hinojosa, *A Borderlands Town*, 70–71; and Adams, *Conflict and Commerce*, 78–79.

31. Young, "Red Men, Princess Pocahontas, and George Washington," 80.

32. Thompson, *Laredo: A Pictorial History*, 204–209.

33. John F. Senne, U.S. Vice Consul, Nuevo Laredo, Tamaulipas, to William Hunter, Second Assistant Secretary of State, Washington, D.C., February 11, 1881, *Despatches from U.S. Consuls in Nuevo Laredo*.

34. The smuggling of American goods was so blatant that the *Laredo Times* reported that the Zona Libre had opened the way to a "vast deal of smuggling, which the people . . . do not hesitate to avail themselves of." "Laredo: Its Railroad Connections — The Texas and Mexican Narrow Gauge International and Great Northern Railroad," *Laredo Times*, August 24, 1881. C. E. Hodson, an American journalist touring Mexico, went so far as to report that in Laredo "several large houses . . . [are] largely engaged in smuggling." C. E. Hodson, "Saltillo," *The Catholic World* 46 (January 1888): 448–449.

35. John F. Senne, U.S. Vice Consul, Nuevo Laredo, Tamaulipas, to William Hunter, Second Assistant Secretary of State, Washington, D.C., February 12, 1881, *Despatches from U.S. Consuls in Nuevo Laredo*.

36. Ibid.

37. "Laredo: Its Railroad Connections," *Laredo Times*, August 24, 1881.

38. Paredes points out in his essay "The Problem of Identity in a Changing Culture" that when visiting family or friends across the river, borderlanders crossed at the most convenient spots, and the gifts they took were technically "contraband." Paredes, *Folklore and Culture*, 26.

39. Lt. Stephen O'Connor to Assistant Adjutant General Department of Texas, Carrizo, Texas, July 14, 1893, *The Garza Revolution, 1891–1893: Records of the U.S. Army Continental Commands, Department of Texas* (Bethesda, M.D.: LexisNexis, 2008), microfilm.

40. Ficker, "Institutional Change and Foreign Trade," 165.

41. Romero, *Mexico and the United States*, 143; and Ficker, "Institutional Change and Foreign Trade," 172.

42. Romero, *Mexico and the United States*, 221.

43. Young, *Catarino Garza's Revolution*, 58–59.

44. John F. Senne, U.S. Vice Consul, Nuevo Laredo, Tamaulipas, to William Hunter, Second Assistant Secretary of State, Washington, D.C., February 12, 1881, *Despatches from U.S. Consuls in Nuevo Laredo*.

45. M. Romero to Thomas Bayard, Washington, D.C., April 26, 1887, in "Incursiones a México por el contrabandista Mariano Reséndez, en la frontera con los estados de Tamaulipas y Coahuila," SRE.

46. Reséndez had public support as evinced by folk songs that depict him as a hero and as an exemplar of masculine honor. Paredes, *A Texas-Mexican Cancionero*, 96–100.

47. "Laredo Locals," *Corpus Christi Weekly Caller*, July 27, 1884.

48. Paredes, *Folklore and Culture*, 24.

49. Paredes informs that the ballad "Mariano Reséndez" dates from the late nineteenth century and arose from the lower border area, which includes los dos Laredos. Versions of the corrido state that Mexican forces executed Reséndez near the turn of the century. Paredes, *A Texas-Mexican Cancionero*, 41–42, 98.

50. Aduana Fronteriza de Laredo de Tamaulipas, Hacienda Pública, Exp. No. 335, December 5, 1899, AGN.

51. Ibid.

52. Ficker, "Institutional Change and Foreign Trade," 186.

53. Pedro Argüelles, *La Zona Libre* (Nuevo Laredo, Tamaulipas: Tipografia de A. Cueva y Hno., 1890), 17. Available in *Despatches from U.S. Consuls in Nuevo Laredo*.

54. Paredes, *A Texas-Mexican Cancionero*, 98. U.S. consular despatches verify Mexican officials' corruption and complicity with smugglers; for instance Consul Joseph Donnelly complained that "smuggling . . . is an organized business . . . carried on with the cognizance if not with the concealed co-operation of the local [Mexican] authorities." Joseph G. Donnelly, Consulate General of the United States, Nuevo Laredo, Mexico, May 20, 1897, *Despatches from U.S. Consuls in Nuevo Laredo*.

55. Hodson, "Saltillo," 448.

56. Ibid. Despite these shortcomings, some U.S. officials regarded Mexican customs enforcement as superior to American. In 1881 Charles Winslow, the American consul in Guerrero, Tamaulipas, wrote the U.S. secretary of state that the "Mexicans manage this [customs enforcement] better than we do." Aside from a "small well equipped body of guards," Mexican Customs forces were assisted by cavalry units stationed at each town along the frontier. Moreover, Winslow commented on the aggressiveness of Contraresguardo agents, who "scour the country each day in search of contrabands, and who have orders to shoot the traders . . . if they make the slightest resistance." Charles Winslow to Secretary of State, Guerrero, Mexico, October 1, 1881, *Despatches from U.S. Consuls in Nuevo Laredo*.

57. Hodson, "Saltillo," 445.

58. Ibid.

59. Paredes, *Folklore and Culture*, 23–24.

60. Alonso, *Thread of Blood*, 80; Paredes, *With His Pistol in His Hand*, 144; and A. Aramoni, *Psicoanálisis de la dinámica de un pueblo* (Mexico City: B. Costa-Amic, 1965), 163.

61. Paredes, *A Texas-Mexican Cancionero*, 98.

62. Herrera Pérez, *La Zona Libre*, 226.

63. "Incursiones a México por el contrabandista Mariano Reséndez, en la frontera con los estados de Tamaulipas y Coahuila," SRE.

64. Américo Paredes recorded the corrido "Mariano Reséndez" in the summer of 1954, over sixty years after the smuggler's death. See Paredes, *With His Pistol in His Hand*, 251. Los Alegres de Terán's performance of the song remains a popular classic. See Los Alegres de Terán, *Original Recordings: 1952–1954*, Arhoolie. Originally recorded for Falcon Records, McAllen, Texas.

65. In official correspondence between various branches of the Mexican government and the United States, Mariano Reséndez is again and again referred to as "el contrabandista" or "conocido contrabandista," translated "the smuggler" and "the known smuggler." In the documents found in the Secretaría de Relaciones Exteriores, never is Reséndez referred to as a common smuggler. Similarly, the corrido never refers to Reséndez as simply a smuggler, but as "El Contrabandista" "el hombre contrabandista," or simply "don Mariano" or "Mariano Reséndez." Clearly, both the Mexican government and ballad singers thought of Reséndez as more than just a petty smuggler. Paredes, *A Texas-Mexican Cancionero*, 96–100; and "Incursiones a México por el contrabandista Mariano Reséndez, en la frontera con los estados de Tamaulipas y Coahuila," SRE.

66. Paredes, *A Texas-Mexican Cancionero*, 98–100.

67. "Detalles sobre el combate de los contrabandistas," *El Correo de Laredo*, July 29, 1891.

68. "Otro encuentro entre guardas y contrabandistas," *El Correo de Laredo*, August 8, 1891.

69. Pedro Argüelles, *La Zona Libre* (Nuevo Laredo: Tipografía de A. Cueva y Hno., 1890), 22.

70. "Pues mientras haya impuestos elevados, habrá ambiciosos que expongan la vida por lucrar con el contrabando." "El Contrabando en la frontera," *El Correo de Laredo*, August 7, 1891.

71. "Contrabanditos," *El Correo de Laredo*, August 7, 1891.

72. Mora-Torres, *The Making of the Mexican Border*, 89.

73. Customs House, Collector's Office, Laredo, Texas, February 23, 1895, in Romero, *Mexico and the United States*, 489.

74. In 1881 U.S. Vice Consul John Senne estimated that three-fourths of the native population of Laredo and Nuevo Laredo engaged in smuggling of some sort. John F. Senne, U.S. Vice Consul, Nuevo Laredo, Tamaulipas, to William Hunter, Second As-

sistant Secretary of State, Washington, D.C., February 11, 1881, *Despatches from U.S. Consuls in Nuevo Laredo.*

75. Customs House, Collector's Office, Laredo, Texas, February 23, 1895, in Romero, *Mexico and the United States,* 489.

76. Alfred E. Eckes Jr., *Opening America's Market: U.S. Foreign Trade Policy Since 1776* (Chapel Hill: University of North Carolina Press, 1995), 28.

77. A. Alvarez, Request for the Release of Seized Goods for the Port of Laredo, 1875–1894, LR 2, A–32–48–4, Records of the United States Customs Service, Record Group 36, NARA–Fort Worth, Texas.

78. Ibid.

79. F. W. Taussig, *The Tariff History of the United States,* 7th ed. (New York: G. P. Putnam's Sons, 1923), 527.

80. Paredes stated that "ordinary people . . . regularly engaged in smuggling" along the lower Rio Grande. Paredes, *Folklore and Culture,* 23.

81. Request for the Release of Seized Goods for the Port of Laredo, NARA–Fort Worth, Texas; and "The Charges of Smuggling along the Rio Grande," *Times Democrat,* May 17, 1887, in "Incursiones a México por el contrabandista Mariano Reséndez, en la frontera con los estados de Tamaulipas y Coahuila," SRE.

82. "Contrabanditos," *El Correo de Laredo,* August 7, 1891; and *United States v. Antonio Jacour* (1899), Criminal Case Files for Laredo, A–20–51–2, NARA–Fort Worth, Texas.

83. Lt. Stephen O'Connor to Assistant Adjutant General Department of Texas, Carrizo, Texas, September 9, 1893, *The Garza Revolution, 1891–1893.*

84. Ibid. For more information on the Garza Revolution see Young, *Catarino Garza's Revolution.*

85. M. Romero to Thomas Bayard, Washington, D.C., April 26, 1887, in "Incursiones a México por el contrabandista Mariano Reséndez, en la frontera con los estados de Tamaulipas y Coahuila," SRE.

86. *United States v. Antonio Pena* (1899), Criminal Case Files for Laredo, NARA–Fort Worth, Texas.

87. "Brutally Murdered," *Laredo Daily Times,* October 31, 1891.

88. *United States v. Felipa Delesa* (1899), Criminal Case Files for Laredo, NARA–Fort Worth, Texas.

89. Jesse Perez, "The Memoirs of Jesse Perez, 1870–1927" (unpublished typed manuscript), Center for American History (hereafter CAH), University of Texas at Austin, 55.

90. "Brutally Murdered," *Laredo Daily Times,* October 31, 1891.

91. Ibid.

92. "Detalles sobre el combate de los contrabandistas," *El Correo de Laredo,* July 29, 1891; "Contrabanditos," *El Correo de Laredo,* August 7, 1891; and "Otro encuentro entre guardas y contrabandistas," *El Correo de Laredo,* August 8, 1891.

93. "Brutally Murdered," *Laredo Daily Times,* October 31, 1891.

94. Ibid.

95. Almost all of the Laredo cases before the Southern District Court of Texas for the December 1899 docket, the earliest docket available, deal with the smuggling of mescal. See Criminal Case Files for Laredo, NARA-Fort Worth, Texas.

96. "Brutally Murdered," *Laredo Daily Times*, October 31, 1891.

97. Ibid. Although Francisco Flores's fate is uncertain, the contrabandista community did not protect those who transgressed the moral economy and prompted greater state intrusion. In his memoir Jesse Perez recorded two instances of murderers who escaped trial only to meet justice of another sort. Matías Martinez, a liquor smuggler who allegedly murdered rancher Greg Gibson on June 28, 1923, met his end when he was betrayed by a fellow liquor smuggler who no longer wished to be associated with the pariah. Prior to Martinez's murder, Perez felt certain about the matter, writing, "There was no hurry[;] every one knew in the border country that Martinez was doomed[.] Little was said but much was done." Jesse Perez, "Memoirs," CAH, 112. Refugio Eschavarrete, one of the bootleggers involved in the murder of mounted Customs inspector Robert Rumsey in August of 1922, was killed just across the Mexican border in 1925. Of Eschavarrete's death Perez wrote simply, "37 buck shots in his boddy [*sic*] . . . well one less." Jesse Perez, "Memoirs," CAH, 123.

98. *Corpus Christi Caller*, July 27, 1884.

99. For more information on ethnic Mexican borderlanders' attitudes regarding women see Alonso, *Thread of Blood*, 96; for more information on nineteenth-century Anglo views on women see Barbara Welter, "The Cult of True Womanhood: 1820-1860," *American Quarterly* 18, no. 2, part 1 (Summer 1966).

100. *United States v. Felipa Delesa* (1899), Criminal Case Files for Laredo, NARA-Fort Worth, Texas.

101. *United States v. Brigida Hidalgo* (1899); and *United States v. Dolores Juarez* (1899), Criminal Case Files for Laredo, NARA-Fort Worth, Texas.

102. *United States v. Dolores Juarez* (1899), Criminal Case Files for Laredo, NARA-Fort Worth, Texas.

103. Ibid.

104. Ibid.

105. *United States v. Brigida Hidalgo* (1899), Criminal Case Files for Laredo, NARA-Fort Worth, Texas.

106. *United States v. Thomas Bishop* (1900), Criminal Case Files for Laredo, NARA-Fort Worth, Texas.

107. Ibid.

108. *United States v. Thomas Bishop* (1900), Criminal Case Files for Laredo, NARA-Fort Worth, Texas.

109. Clifford Alan Perkins, *Border Patrol: With the U.S. Immigration Service on the Mexican Boundary, 1910-1954* (El Paso: Texas Western Press, 1978), 56-58, 62-63. Clifford Alan Perkins served with the U.S. Immigration Service and the Border Patrol during the early decades of the twentieth century. In his classic book *Border Patrol* he mentions several occasions in which smugglers approached him to converse or threaten him. Although Perkins does not discuss American law enforcement agents'

recognition of smugglers explicitly, we can imagine that observant officers living in small borderland communities became aware of professional smugglers' identities. Maude T. Gilliland recorded her husband's experience as a Texas Ranger in her book *Horsebackers of the Brush Country*. In it she explicitly mentions that many law enforcement officers in the region "knew the border . . . and some of the smugglers themselves." Gilliland, *Horsebackers of the Brush Country: A Story of the Texas Rangers and Mexican Liquor Smugglers* (Alpine, T.X.: Library of Sul Ross State University, 1968), 32. For a further examination of this issue see Clifford Geertz's chapter "Common Sense" in his book *Local Knowledge: Further Essays in Interpretive Anthropology* (New York: Basic Books, 1983).

110. *United States v. Cipriano Rosales* (1899), Criminal Case Files for Laredo, NARA–Fort Worth, Texas.

111. For cases involving informants, see *United States v. Victoriana Rodriguez* (1899); and *United States v. Genevava Contreras* (1900), Criminal Case Files for Laredo, NARA–Fort Worth, Texas.

112. *United States v. Victoriana Rodriguez* (1899), Criminal Case Files for Laredo, NARA–Fort Worth, Texas.

113. *United States v. Genevava Contreras* (1900), Criminal Case Files for Laredo, NARA–Fort Worth, Texas.

114. Virgil N. Lott and Mercurio Martinez, *The Kingdom of Zapata* (San Antonio, T.X.: Naylor, 1953), 186.

115. None of the persons charged with smuggling foodstuffs or household items in the Laredo area had locals testify against them. Criminal Case Files for Laredo, NARA–Fort Worth, Texas. For more information on the prevalence of smuggling, see Charles Winslow to Secretary of State, Guerrero, Mexico, October 1, 1881, *Despatches from U.S. Consuls in Nuevo Laredo*.

116. "Brutally Murdered," *Laredo Daily Times*, October 31, 1891; *United States v. Victoriana Rodriguez* and *United States v. Genevava Contreras*, Criminal Case Files for Laredo, NARA–Fort Worth, Texas.

117. *United States v. Thomas Bishop* (1900), Criminal Case Files for Laredo, NARA–Fort Worth, Texas.

118. Hodson, "Saltillo," 448.

119. M. Romero to Thomas Bayard, Washington, D.C., April 26, 1887, in "Incursiones a México por el contrabandista Mariano Reséndez, en la frontera con los estados de Tamaulipas y Coahuila," SRE; Paredes, *A Texas-Mexican Cancionero*, 98. For information on U.S.-Mexican commercial relations see Alexis McCrossen, ed., *Land of Necessity: Consumer Culture in the United States–Mexico Borderlands* (Durham, N.C.: Duke University Press, 2009).

120. T. J. Bayard to Sr. Don Matías Romero, Washington, D.C., May 9, 1887, in "Incursiones a México por el contrabandista Mariano Reséndez, en la frontera con los estados de Tamaulipas y Coahuila," SRE.

121. "The Charges of Smuggling along the Rio Grande," *Times Democrat*, May 17,

1887, in "Incursiones a México por el contrabandista Mariano Reséndez, en la frontera con los estados de Tamaulipas y Coahuila," SRE.

122. Ibid.

123. Bell, *The Zona Libre*, 12-13; Herrera Pérez, *La Zona Libre*, 260.

124. U.S Commercial Agent James J. Haynes to Hon. William Hunter, September 28, 1879, *Despatches from U.S. Consuls in Nuevo Laredo.*

125. Romero, *Mexico and the United States*, 449.

126. Colonel W. H. Thompson, special collector of customs, stated, "there is no smuggling from the Mexican *zona libre* to the United States, or from the United States to Mexico, except in petty amounts for consumption on the border alone and by the poorer class of the Mexican population." "Mexican Smuggling," *Globe Democrat*, May 17, 1887; and "The Charges of Smuggling along the Rio Grande," *Times Democrat*, May 17, 1887, in "Incursiones a México por el contrabandista Mariano Reséndez, en la frontera con los estados de Tamaulipas y Coahuila," SRE.

127. "The Charges of Smuggling along the Rio Grande," *Times Democrat*, May 17, 1887, in "Incursiones a México por el contrabandista Mariano Reséndez, en la frontera con los estados de Tamaulipas y Coahuila," SRE.

128. Commercial Agent Lewis Avery to Second Assistant Sec. of State William Hunter, September 2, 1878, *Despatches from U.S. Consuls in Camargo, Mexico, 1870-1880* (Washington, D.C.: National Archives Microfilm Publcations, 1964), microfilm, M288.

129. Bell, *The Zona Libre*, 57-59; Herrera Pérez, *La Zona Libre*, 304-307; and Romero, *Mexico and the United States*, 450-452.

130. Adelman and Aron, "From Borderlands to Borders," 816.

131. Hobsbawm, *Primitive Rebels.*

132. M. Romero to Thomas Bayard, Washington, D.C., April 26, 1887, in "Incursiones a México por el contrabandista Mariano Reséndez, en la frontera con los estados de Tamaulipas y Coahuila," SRE.

133. "Local News," *Borderland*, May 19, 1906.

134. "Importación Ilegal de Armas," 1909, SRE.

CHAPTER 3

1. Portions of this chapter are drawn from my essay "Smugglers in Dangerous Times: Revolution and Communities in the Tejano Borderlands," in *War Along the Border: The Mexican Revolution and Tejano Communities*, ed. Arnoldo De León (College Station: Texas A&M University Press, 2012). Collector R. W. Dowe to American Consul Luther T. Ellsworth, Eagle Pass, Texas, December 24, 1910, *Records of the Department of State Relating to the Internal Affairs of Mexico, 1910-1929* (Washington, D.C.: National Archives Microfilm Publications, 1961), microfilm, M274.

2. Adams, *Conflict and Commerce*, 195.

3. Garza, "On the Edge of a Storm," 16–24; and Young, "Red Men, Princess Pocahontas, and George Washington," 52–53.

4. *United States v. María Martínez* (1910), Criminal Case Files for Laredo, NARA–Fort Worth, Texas.

5. *Corpus Christi Caller,* July 27, 1884.

6. *United States v. Felipe González* (1911), Criminal Case Files for Laredo, NARA–Fort Worth, Texas.

7. For more on *norteños'* views toward women, see Alonso, *Thread of Blood,* 85–87.

8. In 1866 the U.S. Customs Service authorized the employment of female inspectors "for the examination and search of persons of their own sex." Despite this authorization, no female Customs agents are known to have served along the border until the 1910s. *A History of Enforcement in the United States Customs Service, 1789–1875* (Washington, D.C.: Department of the Treasury, 1986), 143; N. Sargent Commissioner to My Dear Madam, March 12, 1866, *Letters Sent by the Commissioner of Customs Relating to Smuggling;* and "Notice of Sale," *Laredo Weekly Times,* November 9, 1913.

9. *United States v. Juana Pequeño* (1913), Criminal Case Files for Laredo, NARA–Fort Worth, Texas.

10. *United States v. Romana Garza* (1913), Criminal Case Files for Laredo, NARA–Fort Worth, Texas.

11. *United States v. Miguel Castro* (1915), Criminal Case Files for Laredo, NARA–Fort Worth, Texas.

12. Deputy Collector Luke Dowe to the Collector of Customs, Eagle Pass, Texas, June 15, 1910, *Letters Sent by the Collector of Customs at Del Rio, Texas, to the Collector of Customs at Eagle Pass, 1909–1913* (Washington, D.C.: National Archives Microfilm Publications, 2001), microfilm, P2159.

13. Deputy Collector Luke Dowe to the Collector of Customs, Eagle Pass, Texas, June 22, 1910, *Letters Sent by the Collector of Customs.*

14. Criminal Case Files for Laredo, NARA–Fort Worth, Texas.

15. *United States v. Felipe González* (1911), Criminal Case Files for Laredo, NARA–Fort Worth, Texas.

16. *United States v. Macedonio Martínez* (1917), Criminal Case Files for Laredo, NARA–Fort Worth, Texas.

17. *United States v. Faustino González* (1917); and *United States v. Manuel Alvarez* (1912), Criminal Case Files for Laredo, NARA–Fort Worth, Texas.

18. Deputy Collector of Customs Luke Dowe to The U.S. District Attorney, W. D. T., Del Rio, Texas, June 20, 1911, *Letters Sent to the Collector of Customs at Eagle Pass,* DL 1, A–32–8–6, NARA–Fort Worth, Texas.

19. *United States v. Ursulo Guzman* (1913), Criminal Case Files for Laredo, NARA–Fort Worth, Texas.

20. Charles L. Zelden, *Justice Lies in the District: The U.S. District Court, Southern District of Texas, 1902–1960* (College Station: Texas A&M University Press, 1993), 51; for more on police intimidation of ethnic Mexicans, see Arturo F. Rosales, *¡Pobre Raza!*

Violence, Justice, and Mobilization among México Lindo Immigrants, 1900–1936 (Austin: University of Texas Press, 1999), 85–86.

21. W. Elliott Brownlee, *Federal Taxation in America: A Short History*, 2nd ed. (Cambridge: Cambridge University Press, 2004), 57; Magness, "From Tariffs to the Income Tax," 266; and Albert W. Niemi Jr., *U.S. Economic History: A Survey of the Major Issues* (Chicago: Rand McNally, 1975), 120. For a concise examination of increasing demands on the U.S. Customs Service during World War I, see Prince and Keller, *The U.S. Customs Service*, 278–286.

22. Deputy Collector Luke Dowe to The Collector of Customs at Eagle Pass, Texas, March 7, 1911, *Letters Sent to the Collector of Customs at Eagle Pass*, DL 1, A-32-8-6, NARA–Fort Worth, Texas.

23. Deputy Collector Luke Dowe to The Collector of Customs at Eagle Pass, Texas, January 16, 1911, *Records of the Department of State relating to Internal Affairs of Mexico, 1910–1929*.

24. "New Tariff Law Will Make Many Rate Reductions," *Laredo Weekly Times*, October 12, 1913.

25. "New Tariff Law," *Laredo Weekly Times*, October 12, 1913.

26. Of the 122 cases examined from between 1910 and 1920, only seventeen concerned tariff evasion on consumer goods. Criminal Case Files for Laredo, NARA–Fort Worth, Texas; and Zelden, *Justice Lies in the District*, 50–51. For more on democratic tariff reform see Eckes, *Opening America's Market*, 85–86.

27. *United States v. Geronimo Villareal and Julia Cardenas* (1914), Criminal Case Files for Laredo, NARA–Fort Worth, Texas.

28. Ibid.

29. *United States v. Naser Ach Hatem* (1916), Criminal Case Files for Laredo, NARA–Fort Worth, Texas.

30. Criminal Case Files for Laredo, NARA–Fort Worth, Texas. For more on the federal court's attitudes about petty smuggling, see Zelden, *Justice Lies in the District*, 51–53.

31. Garza, "On the Edge of a Storm," 29.

32. Garza, "On the Edge of a Storm," 35–36; Charles Harris III and Louis Sadler, "The 1911 Reyes Conspiracy: The Texas Side," *Southwestern Historical Quarterly* 83, no. 4 (April 1980); and "Startling Developments Follow Indictments by the Grand Jury," *Laredo Weekly Times*, November 26, 1911.

33. Deputy Collector Luke Dowe to The Collector of Customs, Eagle Pass, Texas, December 27, 1910, *Letters Sent by the Collector of Customs*.

34. "Startling Developments Follow Indictments by the Grand Jury," *Laredo Weekly Times*, November 26, 1911. Perhaps because he married a local ethnic Mexican woman and started a family in Laredo, Customs Inspector Rumsey proved particularly adept at securing informants against alleged neutrality violators. Late in December 1917, an informant tipped Rumsey off to thirty individuals organizing to invade Mexico from the United States. J. J. Lawrence, "Prudencio Miranda, General Cuellar,

and Col. Braniff Alleged Vio. Neutrality Laws," December 25, 1917, *Investigative Case Files of the Bureau of Investigation, 1908–1922,* Investigative Records Relating to Mexican Neutrality Violations ("Mexican Files"), 1909–1921 (Washington, D.C.: National Archives Microfilm Publications, 1983), microfilm, M1085. For another example of locals tipping off Customs agents, see J. J. Lawrence, "In re: Smuggling Ammunition to Mexico," January 18, 1919, *Investigative Case Files,* "Mexican Files."

35. For more on Sánchez's connections with Reyes see Harris and Sadler, "The 1911 Reyes Conspiracy," 331.

36. Garza, "On the Edge of a Storm," 35; and Harris and Sadler, "The 1911 Reyes Conspiracy," 331.

37. De la Garza, *A Law for the Lion,* 71–72; and Harris and Sadler, "The 1911 Reyes Conspiracy," 338.

38. Harris and Sadler, "The 1911 Reyes Conspiracy," 341; and Movimientos Revolucionarios en Tejas y Otros Puntos Contra el Gobierno de la Republica, LE 719, Leg 3, SRE.

39. *United States v. Pedro Villarreal* (1913), Criminal Case Files for Laredo, NARA–Fort Worth, Texas; Luz María Hernández Sáenz, "Smuggling for the Revolution: Illegal Trafficking of Arms on the Arizona-Sonora Border, 1912–1914," *Arizona and the West* 28, no. 4 (Winter 1986): 358; and Meyer, Sherman, and Deeds, *The Course of Mexican History,* 496–497.

40. *United States v. Pedro Villarreal* (1913), Criminal Case Files for Laredo, NARA–Fort Worth, Texas.

41. On October 15, 1910, Luther Ellsworth, U.S. consul for Ciudad Porfirio Díaz (Piedras Negras), noted in his despatches that "merchants in Texas . . . have been doing quite a business in .30-.30 Winchester Rifles and Cartridges." Luther Ellsworth to The Honorable Secretary of State, Ciudad Porfirio Díaz, October 15, 1910, *Records of the Department of State relating to Internal Affairs of Mexico, 1910–1929.* Customs Collector Robert Dowe complained that Anglo and Mexican American merchants made it a "practice to supply all comers with arms and cartridges even when aware they were used for revolutionary purposes." Luther Ellsworth to The Honorable Secretary of State, Ciudad Porfirio Díaz, December 5, 1910, *Records of the Department of State relating to Internal Affairs of Mexico, 1910–1929.*

42. The song proclaims, ".30-30 carbine that the rebels carried . . . with my .30-30 I go marching, to join the ranks of the rebellion." "Carabina .30-30," Mexican traditional.

43. Collector R. W. Dowe to Honorable Luther T. Ellsworth, Ciudad Porfirio Díaz, October 15, 1910, *Records of the Department of State relating to Internal Affairs of Mexico, 1910–1929;* and Luther Ellsworth to The Honorable Secretary of State, Ciudad Porfirio Díaz, October 15, 1910, *Records of the Department of State relating to Internal Affairs of Mexico, 1910–1929.*

44. Dorothy Pierson Kerig, *Luther T. Ellsworth: U.S. Consul on the Border During the Mexican Revolution* (El Paso: Texas Western Press, 1975), 36. For an excellent examination of U.S. security forces' efforts to investigate neutrality violations see José A.

Ramírez, *To the Line of Fire! Mexican Texans and World War I* (College Station: Texas A&M University Press, 2009).

45. Mendoza y Vizcaíno, Servicio Consular Mexicano, September 25, 1912, Movimiento Revolucionario, LE 830, Leg 30, SRE.

46. Ibid.

47. Luther Ellsworth to The Honorable Secretary of State, Ciudad Porfirio Díaz, September 20, 1910, *Records of the Department of State relating to Internal Affairs of Mexico, 1910-1929*.

48. "An Attractive Display," *Laredo Weekly Times*, November 23, 1913.

49. Garza, "On the Edge of a Storm," 48-49.

50. Netzer emigrated from Germany as a young man and served in the U.S. Army during its Indian wars before starting a life in Laredo. For more information on Joseph Netzer and other businessmen and women on the border, see Alicia M. Dewey, *Pesos and Dollars: Entrepreneurs in the Texas-Mexico Borderlands, 1880-1940* (College Station: Texas A&M University Press, 2014); and Young, "Red Men, Princess Pocahontas, and George Washington," 57.

51. Garza, "On the Edge of a Storm," 48-49; and Green, *The Story of Laredo*, 395.

52. Stanley C. Green, *A History of the Washington Birthday Celebration* (Laredo: Border Studies, 1999), 152. For more on the George Washington's Birthday celebration, see Young, "Red Men, Princess Pocahontas, and George Washington."

53. J. J. Lawrence, January 18, 1919, Smuggled Ammunition, *Investigative Case Files*, "Mexican Files"; and Green, *A History of the Washington Birthday Celebration*, 152.

54. Green, *A History of the Washington Birthday Celebration*, 152.

55. Local elites dealt illicit arms along the length of the U.S.-Mexico border. Adolph Krakauer knowingly sold untold quantities of arms to revolutionaries yet served as the president of the El Paso Chamber of Commerce. Charles Harris III and Louis Sadler, *The Secret War in El Paso: Mexican Revolutionary Intrigue, 1906-1920* (Albuquerque: University of New Mexico Press, 2009), 87. The Mexican government also complained of locals' complicity in arms sales. In the summer of 1913 A. M. Lozano, a Mexican consul inspector monitoring arms sales on the border, complained that authorities in Laredo did not cooperate in investigations because they "sympathize notoriously with the Carranza movement." Revolución Mexicana, LE 718, Leg 1, SRE.

56. "Leader in Many Fields Dies at 74," *Laredo Times*, July 30, 1937.

57. Martínez, *U.S.-Mexico Borderlands*, 139-141.

58. Estimates for the numbers of victims range from 300 to 5,000 killed. Trinidad Gonzales, whose detailed research provides the most current figures, places the number of victims at 106. See Gonzales, "The Mexican Revolution, *Revolución de Texas*, and *Matanza de 1915*," in *War Along the Border: The Mexican Revolution and Tejano Communities*, ed. Arnoldo De León (College Station: Texas A&M University Press, 2012), 121; Benjamin H. Johnson, *Revolution in Texas: How a Forgotten Rebellion and Its Bloody Suppression Turned Mexicans into Americans* (New Haven, C.T.: Yale Univer-

sity Press, 2003), 3. See also James A. Sandos, *Rebellion in the Borderlands: Anarchism and the Plan of San Diego, 1904–1923* (Norman: University of Oklahoma Press, 1992).

59. Laredo's resistance to Anglo racism is evident in locals' reaction against attempts by the Ku Klux Klan to march in town in 1922. Rather than allow the outsiders to parade, local elites called city and county law enforcement agents to watch for signs of the KKK's arrival. Local World War I veterans, many of them Tejano, also took up arms and maintained vigilance. Not surprisingly, the KKK's planned march never materialized. Thompson, *Laredo: A Pictorial History*, 280; and Young, "Red Men, Princess Pocahontas, and George Washington," 77.

60. José E. Limón, "El Primer Congreso Mexicanista de 1911: A Precursor to Contemporary Chicanismo," *Aztlán* 5, nos. 1–2 (Spring/Fall 1974): 96.

61. Linda B. Hall and Don M. Coerver, *Revolution on the Border: The United States and Mexico, 1910–1920* (Albuquerque: University of New Mexico Press, 1988), 142–143.

62. "Can Not Bring in Aigrettes," *Laredo Weekly Times*, November 30, 1913.

63. Ibid.

64. *United States v. Charles J. Levy and Harry Ahrens* (1917), Criminal Case Files for Laredo, NARA–Fort Worth, Texas.

65. Thompson, *Laredo: A Pictorial History*, 116.

66. *United States v. John Nottonson, John Bruni, and Alex Luban* (1917), Criminal Case Files for Laredo, NARA–Fort Worth, Texas.

67. For more on Laredo's businessmen see Alicia M. Dewey, *Pesos and Dollars*.

68. For a concise theoretical explanation of elites' social power in their communities see Rhys Isaac, *The Transformation of Virginia, 1740–1790* (Chapel Hill: University of North Carolina Press, 1982), 338–339.

69. *United States v. Juana Velendes* (1916), Criminal Case Files for Laredo, NARA–Fort Worth, Texas.

70. Ibid.

71. *United States v. Benito Salinas* (1916), Criminal Case Files for Laredo, NARA–Fort Worth, Texas.

72. *United States v. Basilio Hinojosa* (1917), Criminal Case Files for Laredo, NARA–Fort Worth, Texas.

73. For more on the U.S. federal court in South Texas and its attitudes on crime see Zelden, *Justice Lies in the District*, 52–53.

74. "In re Conditions in Monterrey, Mexico," M. E. Parker, Brownsville, Texas, December 20, 1917, *Investigative Case Files*, "Mexican Files."

75. Ibid.

76. "Evading Export Laws," *Laredo Weekly Times*, January 13, 1918.

77. Established by Woodrow Wilson in October 1917, the War Trade Board was the principal agency charged with regulating U.S. international commerce during the First World War. For more on the War Trade Board see David M. Kennedy, *Over Here: The First World War and American Society* (New York: Oxford University Press, 1980), 314–315.

78. *United States v. Mauricio Carreno* (1918), Criminal Case Files for Laredo, NARA-Fort Worth, Texas.

79. *United States v. Juan Lozano and Jacinto Esquamia* (1917), Criminal Case Files for Laredo, NARA-Fort Worth, Texas.

80. "Clever Smuggling Stunt Unearthed by Inspector," *Laredo Weekly Times*, February 3, 1918.

81. "Garcia Case Law Evasion is One of the Most Typical," *Laredo Weekly Times*, January 13, 1918. For more on low-level "ant" or "armpit" smugglers see Nugent, *Smugglers, Secessionists & Loyal Citizens*; Silvia Rivera Cusicanqui, "'Here, Even the Legislators Chew Them': Coca Leaves and Identity Politics in Northern Argentina," in van Schendel and Abraham, *Illicit Flows and Criminal Things*; and Melissa Gauthier, "Fayuca Hormiga: The Cross-border Trade of Used Clothing between the United States and Mexico," in *Borderlands: Comparing Border Security in North America and Europe*, ed. Emmanuel Brunet-Jailly (Ottawa: University of Ottawa Press, 2007), 95.

82. *United States v. Antonio Rojano and Anslemo Chapa* (1918), Criminal Case Files for Laredo, NARA-Fort Worth, Texas.

83. *United States v. Jose Guerra* (1917), Criminal Case Files for Laredo, NARA-Fort Worth, Texas.

84. *United States v. Antonio Rojano and Anslemo Chapa* (1918), Criminal Case Files for Laredo, NARA-Fort Worth, Texas. Of the numerous cases examined from during the war years, no suspects were charged for trafficking rationed items in prohibited amounts. For more information on the federal court's operation see Zelden, *Justice Lies in the District*, 65.

85. *United States v. Pedro Benavides et al.* (1918), Criminal Case Files for Laredo, NARA-Fort Worth, Texas; and "Trio Mexicans Arrested Charged With Smuggling," *Laredo Weekly Times*, February 10, 1918.

86. *United States v. Modesto Gutierrez et al.* (1917), Criminal Case Files for Laredo, NARA-Fort Worth, Texas.

87. *United States v. Mariano Lozano* (1918), Criminal Case Files for Laredo, NARA-Fort Worth, Texas.

88. *United States v. Edmondo Rodiles* (1918), Criminal Case Files for Laredo, NARA-Fort Worth, Texas.

89. "Travelers Duly Advised to Get Posted on the Law," *Laredo Weekly Times*, January 20, 1918.

90. *United States v. Arcadio García* (1918), Criminal Case Files for Laredo, NARA-Fort Worth, Texas.

91. *United States v. Rebecca Prado* (1918), Criminal Case Files for Laredo, NARA-Fort Worth, Texas.

92. *United States v. Maximo Martínez et al.* (1911), Criminal Case Files for Laredo, NARA-Fort Worth, Texas.

93. The lack of bloodshed in the encounter runs contrary to many corridos, which document violent confrontations between ethnic Mexican smugglers and "rinche" law

enforcement. See for example "Laredo," "Los Tequileros," and "Dionisio Maldonado" in Paredes, *A Texas-Mexican Cancionero*, 100–103.

94. "D. Guerrero VDA de Falcón v. United States," *American Journal of International Law* 21, no. 3 (July 1927): 566–568.

95. "Teodoro García and M. A. Garza v. United States," *American Journal of International Law* 21, no. 3 (July 1927): 581–586.

96. "In Pitched Battle With Smugglers Three of the Smugglers Are Killed," *Laredo Weekly Times*, April 4, 1920.

97. "Lo que siento es a mi Chucha que dejé pedida y dada," from "Texas Cactus Council Members Visit Benavides Cemetery: The Story Behind *El Corrido de Oliveira*," newsletter courtesy of José C. Martínez.

98. "In Pitched Battle With Smugglers Three of the Smugglers Are Killed," *Laredo Weekly Times*, April 4, 1920. Rita Utley, a local, recalled that loved ones of the deceased took the bodies to the town of Benavides, Texas, for proper burial and that this was done under cover of darkness to avoid further conflict with law enforcement. Joe Martínez, e-mail communication with author, December 20, 2010.

CHAPTER 4

1. "El corrido de 'El Contrabandista' Pt. I," accessed May 24, 2013, http://www .laits.utexas.edu/jaime/cwp5/lpg/contrabandista1.html.

2. Ibid.

3. Ibid.

4. "El corrido de 'El Contrabandista' Pt. II," accessed May 24, 2013, http://www .laits.utexas.edu/jaime/cwp5/lpg/contrabandista2.html.

5. David F. Musto, *The American Disease: Origins of Narcotic Control*, 3rd ed. (New York: Oxford University Press, 1999), 5.

6. *United States v. Minnie Bishop* (1915), Criminal Case Files for Laredo, NARA–Fort Worth, Texas.

7. Chinese opium peddlers were some of the earliest suppliers of illegal drugs on the border. For more on Chinese opium dealers see Perkins, *Border Patrol*, 50–53; Recio, "Drugs and Alcohol," 23–25; and Romero, *The Chinese in Mexico*, 136–138.

8. *United States v. Allen English* (1916), Criminal Case Files for Laredo, NARA–Fort Worth, Texas.

9. *United States v. Charlie Williams* (1917), Criminal Case Files for Laredo, NARA–Fort Worth, Texas.

10. *United States v. Vicente Calero & Eneas Levi* (1917), Criminal Case Files for Laredo, NARA–Fort Worth, Texas.

11. David Courtwright, *Dark Paradise: A History of Opiate Addiction in America* (Cambridge, M.A.: Harvard University Press, 2001), 28; and Musto, *The American Disease*, 5.

12. Adams, *Conflict and Commerce*, 195.

13. *United States v. John Nixon et al.* (1918), Criminal Case Files for Laredo, NARA–Fort Worth, Texas.

14. Ibid.

15. Ibid.

16. The Nixon case provides an excellent example of how professional smugglers at times used state forces against their rivals. Dan L. Steakley, who received his information from active Texas Rangers, U.S. Customs agents, and members of the U.S. Border Patrol for his research, wrote that law enforcement gained information from two types of informants: professional informants who "make this a business and live handsomely off the proceeds" and the "spite informer." Spite informers reported their rivals. These tips should not be seen as local efforts to enforce the moral economy of illicit trade, but rather as traffickers' use of the state toward their own ends. Another noteworthy detail Steakley records is that officers made most of their apprehensions through tips. Howard Campbell finds evidence of this continuing practice on the border in an interview with a retired Customs agent who stated that "dopers take out other dopers to eliminate competition. . . . [P]eople are mad at someone else and they turn them in." Campbell, *Drug War Zone*, 262; Dan L. Steakley, "The Border Patrol of the San Antonio Collection District" (master's thesis, University of Texas at Austin, 1936), 64; and *United States v. John Nixon et al.* (1918), Criminal Case Files for Laredo, NARA–Fort Worth, Texas.

17. *United States v. John Nixon et al.* (1918), Criminal Case Files for Laredo, NARA–Fort Worth, Texas.

18. Ibid.

19. For a fascinating examination of Mexican public health debates regarding narcotics control see Isaac Campos, *Home Grown: Marijuana and the Origins of Mexico's War on Drugs* (Chapel Hill: University of North Carolina Press, 2012).

20. William O. Walker III, *Drug Control in the Americas*, revised ed. (Albuquerque: University of New Mexico Press, 1989), 22.

21. Sandos, "Northern Separatism During the Mexican Revolution," 191.

22. With the exception of Daniel Okrent's recent book, *Last Call: The Rise and Fall of Prohibition*, most of the historiography on Prohibition is older or popular in nature. Charles Merz's *The Dry Decade*, although an excellent work, was first published in 1930, while Prohibition was still ongoing. Daniel Okrent, *Last Call: The Rise and Fall of Prohibition* (New York: Scribner, 2010); Charles Merz, *The Dry Decade*, 2nd ed. (Seattle: University of Washington Press, 1970); and Edward Behr, *Prohibition: Thirteen Years that Changed America* (New York: Arcade, 1996).

23. Portions of the following section are drawn upon my essay, "Twilight of the Tequileros: Prohibition-Era Smuggling in the South Texas Borderlands, 1919–1933," in *Smugglers, Brothels, and Twine: Historical Perspectives on Contraband and Vice in North America's Borderlands*, ed. Elaine Carey and Andrae M. Marak (Tucson: University of Arizona Press, 2011). Reprinted by permission of University of Arizona Press.

24. Lewis L. Gould, *Progressives and Prohibitionists: Texas Democrats in the Wilson Era* (Austin: Texas State Historical Association, 1992), 36–37.

25. "Local News," *Laredo Weekly Times*, January 5, 1919.

26. "In Battle with Smugglers Charles Hopkins Killed," *Laredo Weekly Times*, May 11, 1919; "Grim Reaper Wins Battle Fought by Brave Officer," *Laredo Weekly Times*, June 8, 1919; and "Fourth Smuggler is Dead Having Died Yesterday," *Laredo Weekly Times*, May 11, 1919.

27. *Biennial Report of the Adjutant General of Texas from January 1, 1917, to December 31, 1918* (Austin: Von Boeckmann—Jones, 1919), 44; "Smugglers Get Surprise and Eight are Prisoners," *Laredo Weekly Times*, September 26, 1920; James Randolph Ward, "The Texas Rangers, 1919–1935: A Study in Law Enforcement" (Ph.D. diss., Texas Christian University, 1972), 35; "Two Smugglers are Slain and Quantity Booze Taken," *Laredo Weekly Times*, January 9, 1921; "In Pitched Battle With Smugglers Three of the Smugglers Are Killed," *Laredo Weekly Times*, April 4, 1920; "Kill the Chief and Bag the Others," *Laredo Weekly Times*, September 18, 1921; "Two Smugglers are Wounded and Captured by Officers," *Laredo Weekly Times*, November 20, 1921; and "Customs Officers Fled From Gang of Bootleggers," *Laredo Weekly Times*, October 1, 1922.

28. Gilliland, *Horsebackers of the Brush Country*, 16; and William Warren Sterling, *Trails and Trials of a Texas Ranger* (Norman: University of Oklahoma Press, 1979), 86.

29. "Kill the Chief and Bag the Others," *Laredo Weekly Times*, September 18, 1921.

30. Alonzo H. Alvarez, "Los Tequileros" (unpublished paper, August 13, 1974, courtesy of Manuel Guerra); Gilliland, *Horsebackers*, 33; and Perez, "Memoirs," 80.

31. Gilliland, *Horsebackers*, 33–39; and Walter Prescott Webb, *The Texas Rangers: A Century of Frontier Defense* (Austin: University of Texas Press, 1965), 556.

32. Perez, "Memoirs," 109.

33. Ibid., 110.

34. Much of the information on mules and their many talents comes from scattered sources. In *Horsebackers* Maude T. Gilliland goes into some depth about the adeptness of mules. Although she also mentions American law enforcement's use of mules, we can assume that tequileros, most of whom came from ranching backgrounds, had equally if not better-trained animals. For more information on the ability of pack animals see Emmett M. Essin III, "Mules, Packs, and Packtrains," *Southwestern Historical Quarterly* 74, no. 1 (July 1970); Gilliland, *Horsebackers*, 51–55; and Perez, "Memoirs," 110.

35. "Kill the Chief and Bag the Others," *Laredo Weekly Times*, September 18, 1921.

36. Results based on calculations done through "Seven Ways to Compute the Relative Value of a U.S. Dollar Amount—1774 to Present," *Measuring Worth*, accessed May 24, 2013, http://www.measuringworth.com/uscompare/?redirurl=calculators /uscompare/.

37. Sterling, *Trails and Trials*, 84.

38. Gilliland, *Horsebackers*, 16.

39. Gilliland, *Horsebackers*, 16; and Sterling, *Trails and Trials*, 84.

40. Paredes, *A Texas-Mexican Cancionero*, 81.

41. Ramírez, *To the Line of Fire!*; and Paredes, *A Texas-Mexican Cancionero*, 81.

Paredes cites Norman Laird McNeil's "*Corridos de Asuntos Vulgares*: Corresponding to the *Romances Vulgares* of the Spanish" (master's thesis, University of Texas, 1944).

42. According to his baptismal record, Leandro Villarreal was born February 27, 1895, making him twenty-seven years old at the time of his death. Certificate of Baptism, Our Lady of Refuge Catholic Church, Roma, Texas.

43. *Rinche* is a highly derogatory term for an American law enforcement agent. For more on *rinches* see Paredes, *With His Pistol in His Hand*, 24.

44. Paredes, *A Texas-Mexican Cancionero*, 81.

45. Paredes, *Folklore and Culture*, 27.

46. "Memorial Mass," *Zapata County News*, November 2, 2000.

47. Gilliland, *Horsebackers*, 17.

48. Webb, *The Texas Rangers*, 556.

49. Gilliland, *Horsebackers*, 17.

50. Period newspapers occasionally mention that American law enforcement recovered quantities of consumer goods from traffickers, but stronger evidence of smugglers bearing holiday gifts is lacking. Still, today untold numbers of gifts are smuggled into Mexico each holiday season, and reports of tequileros' Christmas contraband-running fit this pattern.

51. "Office of the Deputy Collector," *Laredo Times*, December 15, 1925.

52. "Rodríguez, Jorge. Informe el Consulado que este individuo se dedica al contrabando," 1929, IV-225-54, SRE.

53. "Kill the Chief and Bag the Others," *Laredo Weekly Times*, September 18, 1921.

54. Hobsbawm, *Primitive Rebels*.

55. Although Anglo/ethnic Mexican conflicts of the era led to a great degree of "social banditry," these occurrences came mostly out of Anglo racism and conflicts over land. Tequileros, however, did not resist Anglo oppression as much as they circumvented federal laws for personal gain. For examples of ethnic Mexicans as "social bandits" see Robert J. Rosenbaum, *Mexicano Resistance in the Southwest: "The Sacred Right of Self-Preservation"* (Austin: University of Texas Press, 1981); and Jerry Thompson, *Cortina: Defending the Mexican Name in Texas* (College Station: Texas A&M University Press, 2007).

56. Sterling, *Trails and Trials*, 84.

57. Gilliland, *Horsebackers*, 17.

58. Gilliland, *Horsebackers*, 17; John R. Peavey, *Echoes from the Rio Grande* (Brownsville, T.X.: Springman-King, 1963), 228; and Sterling, *Trails and Trials*, 84–85.

59. Webb, *The Texas Rangers*, 556.

60. Ibid.

61. Ibid., 551.

62. Ibid., 557.

63. "Three Smugglers Killed Just East of Mirando City," *Laredo Weekly Times*, December 24, 1922.

64. Ibid.

65. "3 Rum-Runners Slain: Customs Men Win in Fight with Gang," *San Antonio Express*, December 19, 1922.

66. "Funeral of Bob Rumsey Held Sunday and Largely Attended," *Laredo Weekly Times*, August 27, 1922; "This Horse Riderless Because Bootleggers Killed Its Owner," *San Antonio Express*, September 24, 1922; "Fearless Custom Inspector's Murder in 1922 is Recalled," *The Laredo Times*, August 29, 1972; and *State of Texas v. Santos Salinas* (1922), Webb County Court, Criminal Case Files, Texas A&M International University Special Collections.

67. "This Horse Riderless Because Bootleggers Killed Its Owner," *San Antonio Express*, September 24, 1922.

68. Rumsey was one of only sixty-eight mounted inspectors serving in the U.S. Customs Service in 1922. Given the small size of the organization and his connections with other law enforcement agencies, it is very likely that many officers took Rumsey's death as a personal loss. Schmeckebier, *The Customs Service*, 123; and Sterling, *Trails and Trials*, 91.

69. James L. White, letter to Manuel Guerra, May 19, 1994; "Man Indicted of Killing Rumsey Arrested Saturday," *Laredo Weekly*, August 31, 1928.

70. George T. Díaz, "When the River Ran Red: Tequileros, Texas Rangers, and Violence on the Central South Texas Border during Prohibition, 1919–1933" (master's thesis, Texas A&M International University, 2004), appendix B.

71. Guillermo E. Hernández, ed., *Corridos Sin Fronteras/Ballads Without Borders: Cancionero/Song Book* (Washington, D.C.: Smithsonian Institution, 2002), 21; and Elijah Wald, *Narcocorrido: A Journey into the Music of Drugs, Guns, and Guerrillas* (New York: Rayo, 2001), 186–187.

72. Hernández, *Corridos Sin Fronteras*, 21.

73. Not all the smugglers listed in "Pistoleros Famosos" are Prohibition-era tequileros. Some were smugglers killed in earlier and later eras that the ballad's composer includes in his general homage to the contrabandista community's smuggler heroes. Ibid.

74. "Customs Officers Fled From Gang of Bootleggers," *Laredo Weekly Times*, October 1, 1922.

75. "Need for Action," *Laredo Weekly Times*, October 1, 1922.

76. "Are now Prepared to Meet the Droves of Bootleggers," *Laredo Weekly Times*, January 12, 1924.

77. "Officers Make Big Seizure," *Laredo Weekly Times*, January 7, 1924.

78. Sterling, *Trails and Trials*, 85.

79. Perkins, *Border Patrol*, 110–111.

80. Many corridos describe American law enforcement officers as cowards. See "Gregorio Cortez," "Pistoleros Famosos," "Los Tequileros," and "Dionisio Maldonado" in Paredes's *A Texas-Mexican Cancionero* and Hernández's *Corridos Sin Fronteras*.

81. "Two Smugglers are Slain and Quantity of Booze Taken," *Laredo Weekly Times*, January 9, 1921; "Kill the Chief and Bag the Others," *Laredo Weekly Times*, September 18, 1921; Gilliland, *Horsebackers*, 15–17; and Sterling, *Trails and Trials*, 84–86.

82. Paredes, *A Texas-Mexican Cancionero*, 101.

83. Perez, "Memoirs," 82.

84. "Patrol Kills Rum Runner in Jim Hogg Co.," *Laredo Daily Times*, February 5, 1927.

85. Gilliland, *Horsebackers*, 61–62.

86. "Customs Officers Fled From Gang of Bootleggers," *Laredo Weekly Times*, October 1, 1922; and Gilliland, *Horsebackers*, 16.

87. Gilliland, *Horsebackers*, 16.

88. "Pro Guardian Ambushed By 'Leggers," *Laredo Times*, September 25, 1929.

89. Dagoberto Gilb, ed., *Hecho en Tejas: An Anthology of Texas Mexican Literature* (Albuquerque: University of New Mexico Press, 2006), 39.

90. Ibid.

91. "Pro Guardian Ambushed By 'Leggers," *Laredo Times*, September 25, 1929.

92. For more on ranching and its place within the Tejano community see Arnoldo De León, *The Tejano Community, 1836–1900* (Albuquerque: University of New Mexico Press, 1982), 79–82; and Tijerina, *Tejano Empire*, 91–92.

93. Paredes, *A Texas-Mexican Cancionero*, 87. Américo Paredes collected "El Automóvil Gris" and over 350 other ballads between 1941 and 1953. See Paredes, *With His Pistol in His Hand*, 251.

94. Paredes, *A Texas-Mexican Cancionero*, 87.

95. "Dapper Youth Once Held Here Charged in Stevens's Death," September 27, 1929, Roy Wilkinson Aldrich Papers, CAH.

96. Belén was a notorious prison in Mexico City. That the smuggler in "El Automóvil Gris" mentions his business there is further evidence that unlike earlier illicit trades, drug trafficking was practiced by professional criminals, not merchants or contrabandistas within the moral economy.

97. Liquor seizures on the Mexican border were minor compared to the amount of alcohol trafficked across the Canadian border into the United States. The length of the land boundary, the extent of the Great Lakes, and the proximity of Canadian cities to U.S. population centers made liquor smuggling more extensive across the U.S.-Canada line. It is also worth pointing out that Canadian whiskey was more to Anglo palates than Mexican tequila and mescal. Anglo taste for Mexican tequila did not awaken until the 1970s with the invention of the frozen margarita machine, which changed happy hour forever. Laurence F. Schmeckebier, *The Bureau of Prohibition: Its History, Activities and Organization* (Washington, D.C.: Brookings Institution, 1929), 16–17.

98. "Officers Seize $20,000 Smuggled Liquor," *Laredo Daily Times*, February 5, 1927.

99. "Ghost Flier Sought as Border Bootlegger," *Laredo Times*, January 25, 1931.

100. "Customs Officers May Patrol Border Beats in Airplanes," *Dallas Morning News*, November 28, 1922.

101. "Alleged Booze Flier Held For Probe," *Laredo Times*, January 18, 1932; and Romayn Wormuth to Secretary of State, Nuevo Laredo, Mexico, February 2, 1932, *Records*

of the Department of State Relating to Internal Affairs of Mexico, 1930–1939 (Washington, D.C.: National Archives Microfilm Publications, n.d.), microfilm, M1370.

102. "Rum Runners Chased by Planes," *Laredo Times,* July 20, 1932; "War Air Ace Taken With Booze," *Laredo Times,* May 26, 1932; "Air Booze Chasers Praised for Work," *Laredo Weekly Times,* June 13, 1932; and "Anti-Booze Planes Guard Rio Grande About Laredo," *Laredo Times,* November 29, 1932.

103. Campos, *Home Grown,* 181; and Walker, *Drug Control in the Americas,* 48, 58.

104. Courtwright, *Dark Paradise,* 106; for regional figures see Díaz, "When the River Ran Red," 81.

105. "Check on Narcotics Hampered at Border," *New York Times,* February 26, 1928.

106. Ibid.

107. Ibid.

108. Ibid.

109. Wald, *Narcocorrido,* 13–14.

110. Hernández, *Corridos Sin Fronteras,* 64.

111. Campos, *Home Grown,* 162–163.

112. *United States of America v. Miguel Salinas et al.* (1938), Criminal Case Files for Laredo, NARA–Fort Worth, Texas.

113. Musto, *The American Disease,* 221–222.

114. Martin Booth, *Cannabis: A History* (New York: Thomas Dunne Books, 2004), 156.

115. Aside from the Customs Service's role in countering the narcotics trade, other traditionally revenue-based agencies became antidrug warriors as U.S. law grew increasingly prohibitive. The U.S. Treasury Department administered the Harrison Act under its Narcotics Division. Advocates for stricter antidrug policies succeeded in forging the Narcotics Division into the Federal Bureau of Narcotics (FBN) in 1930, but did not prevail in breaking the narcotics unit away from the Treasury Department until 1968, when the FBN was merged with the Department of Health, Education, and Welfare's Bureau of Drug Abuse Control. The new unit, now called the Bureau of Narcotics and Dangerous Drugs (BNDD), worked under the Department of Justice. President Richard Nixon transformed the BNDD into the Drug Enforcement Agency in July of 1973. Musto, *The American Disease,* 183; and "Drug Enforcement Administration, 1970–1975," accessed July 30, 2012, http://www.justice.gov/dea/about/history/1970-1975.pdf.

116. Nicole Mottier, "Drug Gangs and Politics in Ciudad Juárez: 1928–1936," *Mexican Studies/Estudios Mexicanos* 25, no. 1 (Winter 2009): 26.

117. Stewart E. McMillin, American Consul Piedras Negras, to the Honorable Secretary of State, June 23, 1934, *Records of the Department of State Relating to Internal Affairs of Mexico, 1930–1939.*

118. Ibid.

119. H. S. Creighton to Commissioner of Customs, August 13, 1936, *Records of the Department of State Relating to Internal Affairs of Mexico, 1930–1939.*

120. Stewart E. McMillin, American Consul Piedras Negras, to the Honorable Secretary of State, June 23, 1934, *Records of the Department of State Relating to Internal Affairs of Mexico, 1930–1939.*

121. H. S. Creighton to Commissioner of Customs, August 13, 1936, *Records of the Department of State Relating to Internal Affairs of Mexico, 1930–1939.*

122. Romayn Wormuth to Secretary of State, Nuevo Laredo, Mexico, March 18, 1938, *Records of the Department of State Relating to Internal Affairs of Mexico, 1930–1939.*

123. Romayn Wormuth to Secretary of State, Nuevo Laredo, Mexico, March 29, 1938, *Records of the Department of State Relating to Internal Affairs of Mexico, 1930–1939.*

124. Ibid.

125. Ibid.

126. Challenges provoking men were another way women influenced the moral economy of illicit trade. For an excellent example of women's role in enforcing community values see Linda Gordon, *The Great Arizona Orphan Abduction* (Cambridge, M.A.: Harvard University Press, 1999).

127. Romayn Wormuth to Secretary of State, Nuevo Laredo, Mexico, March 29, 1938, *Records of the Department of State Relating to Internal Affairs of Mexico, 1930–1939.*

128. Romayn Wormuth to Secretary of State, Nuevo Laredo, Mexico, August 2, 1940, *Confidential U.S. State Department Central Files: Mexico, 1940–1944, Internal Affairs* (Frederick, M.D.: University Publications of America, 1986), microfilm; "Detective Murdered," *Laredo Times*, March 17, 1938; and "Thought to be Victim of Smugglers," *Laredo Times*, March 18, 1938.

129. A. R. Sellers to the Supervising Customs Agent, Houston, Texas, June 28, 1940, *Confidential U.S. State Department Central Files: Mexico, 1940–1944, Internal Affairs.*

130. W. J Harmon to The Customs Agent in Charge, Laredo, Texas, July 31, 1941, *Confidential U.S. State Department Central Files: Mexico, 1940–1944, Internal Affairs.*

131. "Memorandum," May 20, 1943, *Confidential U.S. State Department Central Files: Mexico, 1940–1944, Internal Affairs.*

132. George S. Messersmith to Secretary of State, May 11, 1943, *Confidential U.S. State Department Central Files: Mexico, 1940–1944, Internal Affairs.*

133. Ibid.

134. Ibid.

CHAPTER 5

1. Asociación de Contrabandistas, En Reynosa, Tamp., Topográfica 17–20–272, SRE.

2. Ibid.

3. Ibid.

4. Ibid.

5. Stephen H. Haber, *Industry and Underdevelopment: The Industrialization of Mexico, 1890–1940* (Stanford, C.A.: Stanford University Press, 1989), 137–139.

6. Héctor Aguilar Camín and Lorenzo Meyer, *In the Shadow of the Mexican Revo-*

lution: Contemporary Mexican History, 1910–1989, trans. Luis Alberto Fierro (Austin: University of Texas Press, 1993), 103.

7. For more on trade and the Mexican economy in this period, see Clark W. Reynolds, *The Mexican Economy: Twentieth-Century Structure and Growth* (New Haven, C.T.: Yale University Press, 1970), 208.

8. Prof. Francisco Pérez, "Contrabando en Reynosa Tamp.," *Topográfica* 18–19–330, SRE.

9. "Contrabandos en la frontera," *Topográfica* 19–20–1, SRE.

10. Ibid.

11. I. M. Vázquez to Lic. Aaron Sáenz Ministro de Relaciones Exteriores, April 23, 1925, in "Contrabandos Descubiertos por el Consulado de Mexico en Laredo, Tex. U.S.A.," *Topográfica* 18–19–332, SRE.

12. "Contrabando de Sedas y Aves de Corral Descubierto," *El Jalisciense Cuadala*, March 16, 1933, in Comercio Internacional Aduanas, 1930–1949, Biblioteca de la Secretaría de Hacienda y Crédito Público "Miguel Lerdo de Tejada," Mexico City (hereafter MLT).

13. "Dos Empleados Aduanales Fueron Muertos por los Contrabandistas," *El Universal*, January 22, 1933, in Comercio Internacional Aduanas, 1930–1949, MLT.

14. "Combatieron Los Fiscales Con Los Contrabandistas," *La Prensa*, February 18, 1934, in Comercio Internacional Aduanas, 1930–1949, MLT.

15. "Contrabando en la Frontera," *El Universal*, April 21, 1932, in Comercio Internacional Aduanas, 1930–1949, MLT.

16. Reynolds, *The Mexican Economy*, 216.

17. "Contrabando en la Frontera," *El Universal*, April 21, 1932, in Comercio Internacional Aduanas, 1930–1949, MLT.

18. Ibid.

19. "Han Sido Descubiertos Números Contrabandos," *El Excélsior*, March 15, 1933, in Comercio Internacional Aduanas, 1930–1949, MLT.

20. Ibid.

21. El Oficial Primero to El Jefe del Departamento de Gobernación, December 14, 1925, Investigaciones Políticas y Sociales (hereafter IPS), AGN.

22. El Oficial Mayor to Secretario de Guerra y Marina, December 17, 1925, IPS, C 2053 A, AGN.

23. El Del. Del Serv. Gral. De Migración, to Secretario de Gobernación, Mexico, D.F., January 20, 1926, IPS, C 2053 A, AGN.

24. El Agente Especial # 2, "Informa sobre varios asuntos relacionados con la comisión que se le confirió en la frontera del Estado de Chihuahua, según citado memorándum," December 3, 1926, IPS, C 2053 A, AGN.

25. El Agente Especial # 2, "Informa sobre actividades de los enemigos del Gobierno refugiados en Estados Unidos," January 9, 1927, IPS, C 2053 A, AGN.

26. Ibid.

27. Vicente Rendón Quijano, "Informe Político Confidencial," August 2, 1926, IPS, C 2053 A, AGN.

28. Ibid.

29. Prof. Francisco Pérez, "Movimiento de sediciosos in la frontera," January 4, 1924, LE 860 Lg 3, SRE; and Prof. Francisco Pérez, "Movimiento de sediciosos in la frontera," January 16, 1924, LE 860 Lg 3, SRE.

30. Prof. Francisco Pérez, "Movimiento sediciosos en la línea fronteriza," January 23, 1924, LE 860 Lg 3, SRE.

31. El Agente No. 21, "Informa sobre la situación actual que prevalece en la región de Piedras Negras, Coah.," September 23, 1926, IPS, C 2053 A, AGN.

32. Ibid.

33. A. P. Carrillo, Cónsul General, Del Rio, Texas, December 3, 1926, IPS, C 2053 A, AGN.

34. Meyer, Sherman, and Deeds, *The Course of Mexican History*, 567. For a good overview see also David C. Bailey, *¡Viva Cristo Rey! The Cristero Rebellion and the Church-State Conflict in Mexico* (Austin: University of Texas Press, 1974).

35. Report to Secretario de Guerra y Marina, December 16, 1926, IPS, C 2053 A, AGN.

36. Actividades del leader Católico René Capistran Garza, February 29, 1927, IPS, C 2053 A, AGN.

37. Report Al C. Secretario de Hacienda y Crédito Público, July 28, 1926, IPS, C 2053 A, AGN.

38. The Guerras were an elite family of Tejanos who dominated the economic and political life of Starr County from the late nineteenth century until the end of the Second World War. As merchants, the Guerras also had ties to illicit trade. For more information on the Guerras, see the case of Manuel Guerra in chapter 3. For further information see Anders, *Boss Rule in South Texas*, 53; and Benjamin H. Johnson, *Bordertown: The Odyssey of an American Place* (New Haven, C.T.: Yale University Press, 2008), 107–108.

39. Inspector PS-5, Reynosa, Tamps., Al C. Jefe de la Oficina de Información Política y Social, September 17, 1938, AGN. For more on the Gold Shirts or Golden Shirts see Aguilar Camín and Meyer, *Shadow of the Mexican Revolution*, 139.

40. "Proyecto de Plan de Trabajo," August 23, 1939, IPS, Exp. 2–1/266.7 (721)/3, p. 54, AGN.

41. Ernesto Hidalgo to C. Secretario de Gobernación, January 3, 1940, IPS, Exp. 2–1/266.7 (721)/2, p. 5, AGN.

42. C. Adolfo de la Huerta, Visitador General de Consulados, Los Angeles, California, June 7, 1940, IPS, Exp. 2–1/266.7 (721.1)/3, p. 17, AGN. Former Zapatista Saturnino Cedillo remained true to the spirit of agrarian reform and took up arms against the Cárdenas government in 1938. Cedillo died fighting for his principles the following year. For more information on Saturnino Cedillo's uprising see Dudley Ankerson, *Agrarian Warlord: Saturnino Cedillo and the Mexican Revolution in San Luis Potosí* (DeKalb: Northern Illinois University Press, 1984).

43. "Contrabando de Parque y Mercancías," Diciembre 1939, IPS, Exp. 2–1/266.7 (73)/1, p. 1, AGN.

44. Ibid., 8.

45. "Contrabando de Parque y Mercancías," Diciembre 1939, IPS, Exp. 2–1/266.7 (73)/1, p. 22, AGN; and Saragoza, *The Monterrey Elite*, 192–193.

46. H. E. Marshburn, "Stability of Government: Reported Entry of Arms into Mexico," undated report, *U.S. Military Intelligence Reports: Mexico, 1919–1941* (Frederick, M.D.: University Publications of America, 1984), microfilm.

47. "Proyecto de Plan de Trabajo," August 23, 1939, IPS, Exp. 2–1/266.7 (721)/3, p. 54, AGN.

48. Inspector [writing illegible, probably Martínez Flores], al C. Jefe de la Oficina de Información Política y Social, México, D.F., Abril 21, 1939, Gobierno, Exp. 2–1/266.7 (721.1)/2, p. 23, AGN.

49. *United Mexican States on behalf of Teodoro García and M. A. Garza v. United States of America* (Docket No. 292), 231 (1926), Collection Relating to the General Claims Commission (Mexico and United States), 1917–1926, Benson Latin American Collection (hereafter BLAC).

50. Martínez Flores, Monterrey, N.L., Junio 19, 1940, Gobierno, Exp. 2–1/266.7 (721.1)/2, p. 31, AGN.

51. Ibid., 36.

52. Martínez Flores to C. Jefe de la Oficina de Información Política y Social, México, D.F., Junio 19, 1940, Gobierno, Exp. 2–1/266.7 (721.1)/2, p. 35, AGN.

53. Import and export duties combined composed 27 percent of Mexico's federal revenue in 1940. Reynolds, *The Mexican Economy*, 274; and Rafael Izquierdo, "Protectionism in Mexico," in *Public Policy and Private Enterprise in Mexico*, ed. Raymond Vernon (Cambridge, M.A.: Harvard University Press, 1964), 250.

54. Martínez Flores, Monterrey, N.L., Junio 19, 1940, Gobierno, Exp. 2–1/266.7 (721.1)/2, p. 31, AGN; and Inspector [name?], al C. Jefe de la Oficina de Información Política y Social, México, D.F., Abril 21, 1939, Gobierno, Exp. 2–1/266.7 (721.1)/2, p. 23, AGN.

55. "Contrabando de Parque y Mercancías," Diciembre 1939, IPS, Exp. 2–1/266.7 (73)/1, p. 31, AGN.

56. Ibid., 32.

57. "Contrabando de Parque y Mercancías," Diciembre 1939, IPS, Exp. 2–1/266.7 (73)/1, p. 32–33, AGN.

58. Romayn Wormuth to the Honorable Secretary of State, Nuevo Laredo, Mexico, January 26, 1940, *Confidential U.S. State Department Central Files: Mexico, 1940–1944, Internal Affairs.*

59. Francisco de Valle Arispe to General and Dr. Francisco Castillo Najera, Laredo, Texas, January 21, 1940, *Confidential U.S. State Department Central Files: Mexico, 1940–1944, Internal Affairs.*

60. Edgar P. Allen to Mr. Green, Department of State Division of Controls, April 22, 1940, *Confidential U.S. State Department Central Files: Mexico, 1940–1944, Internal Affairs.*

61. W. A. Giddens, "Francisco de Valle Arispe, with aliases: Francisco de Valle

Arizpe, Francisco Valle; Gregorio F. Prieto," April 24, 1940, Federal Bureau of Investigations, *Confidential U.S. State Department Central Files: Mexico, 1940–1944, Internal Affairs.*

62. Joseph C. Green to Department of State, Division of Controls, May 6, 1940, *Confidential U.S. State Department Central Files: Mexico, 1940–1944, Internal Affairs.*

63. W. A. Giddens, "Francisco de Valle Arispe, with aliases: Francisco de Valle Arizpe, Francisco Valle; Gregorio F. Prieto," April 24, 1940, *Confidential U.S. State Department Central Files: Mexico, 1940–1944, Internal Affairs.*

64. E. D. Salinas to Secretary of State, Laredo, Texas, April 8, 1940, *Confidential U.S. State Department Central Files: Mexico, 1940–1944, Internal Affairs.*

65. Ibid.

66. "Netzer Line to Change Hands," *Laredo Times*, March 17, 1938.

67. "Netzer Announces Rotary Meetings," *Laredo Times*, January 26, 1940.

68. E. D. Salinas to Secretary of State, Laredo, Texas, April 8, 1940, *Confidential U.S. State Department Central Files: Mexico, 1940–1944, Internal Affairs.*

69. "Hornby Report Shows Big Customs Activity," *Laredo Times*, July 21, 1935; and Kathleen DeCamara, "The History of the City of Laredo" (master's thesis, Texas State College for Women, 1944), 108.

70. Martínez, *Border Boom Town*, 97.

71. Ibid., 161.

72. Ibid., 168–169.

73. "Hornby Report Shows Big Customs Activity," *Laredo Times*, July 21, 1935.

74. Ibid.

75. "Confidential Information on the City of Nuevo Laredo, Tamaulipas," December 23, 1940, *U.S. Military Intelligence Reports: Mexico, 1919–1941.*

76. "Hornby Report Shows Big Customs Activity," *Laredo Times*, July 21, 1935.

77. In addition to Mexican Customs forces, two hundred Mexican troops were garrisoned in Nuevo Laredo. These troops were divided between eight to ten outposts located at road junctions and "important fords of the Rio Grande etc., for the control of arms smuggling." According to U.S. reports, the Pan-American Highway from Nuevo Laredo to Monterrey was the only all-weather road in the region. "Confidential Information on the City of Nuevo Laredo, Tamaulipas," December 23, 1940, *U.S. Military Intelligence Reports: Mexico, 1919–1941.*

78. Inspector PS-5 al C. Jefe de la Oficina de Información Política y Social, May 11, 1940, IPS, Exp. 2–1/266.7 (721.1)/3, AGN.

79. Ibid.

80. "Confidential Information on the City of Nuevo Laredo, Tamaulipas," December 23, 1940, *U.S. Military Intelligence Reports: Mexico, 1919–1941.*

81. Elena to Beatriz R. Clayton, October 27, 1942, Case Files on the Investigations of Espionage and Sabotage, Laredo, Texas, 1942–1944, LR 4, A–32–48–4, Records of the U.S. Customs Service, Record Group 36, NARA–Fort Worth, Texas.

82. L. Goza Ayala to Antonia F. Pérez, November 4, 1942, Case Files on the Investigations of Espionage and Sabotage, NARA–Fort Worth, Texas.

83. Beatriz de Montalvo de Galicia to Azucena Gutierrez, October 31, 1942, Case Files on the Investigations of Espionage and Sabotage, NARA–Fort Worth, Texas. For more on the crossing of gifts illicitly see Paredes, *A Texas-Mexican Cancionero*, 43.

84. Magness, "From Tariffs to the Income Tax," 267.

85. Juan Carlos Molina, "Gold Stars and Ration Cards: A Social, Economic, and Diplomatic Study of Laredo, Texas, During World War II" (master's thesis, Texas A&M International University, 1996), 40.

86. Vernon L. Fluharty to Secretary of State, Nuevo Laredo, Tamaulipas, March 3, 1945, *Confidential U.S. State Department Central Files: Mexico, 1945–1949, Internal Affairs, Part I: Political, Governmental, and National Defense Affairs* (Frederick, M.D.: University Publications of America, 1987), microfilm.

87. Henry G. Krausse to Secretary of State, Reynosa, Tamaulipas, March 10, 1945, *Confidential U.S. State Department Central Files: Mexico, 1945–1949, Internal Affairs*.

88. Frederick D. Hunt to Secretary of State, Nuevo Laredo, Tamaulipas, September 8, 1945, *Confidential U.S. State Department Central Files: Mexico, 1945–1949, Internal Affairs*.

89. Vernon L. Fluharty to Secretary of State, Nuevo Laredo, Tamaulipas, March 3, 1945, *Confidential U.S. State Department Central Files: Mexico, 1945–1949, Internal Affairs*.

90. Rosario de Zambrano to Dr. Francisco Canseco, October 13, 1944, Export Control Misc., 1944, Case Files on the Investigations of Espionage and Sabotage, NARA–Fort Worth, Texas.

91. James R. Offut to the Collector of Customs at Laredo, Texas, February 16, 1944, National Defense Acts Misc., January and February 1944, Case Files on the Investigations of Espionage and Sabotage, NARA–Fort Worth, Texas.

92. Mother to P.F.C. John O. H. Wisner, May 8, 1944, Export Control Misc., May and June 1944, Case Files on the Investigations of Espionage and Sabotage, NARA–Fort Worth, Texas.

93. Ibid.

94. Benjamin White Jr. to The Supervising Customs Agent, June 16, 1944, Export Control Misc., May through June 1944, Case Files on the Investigations of Espionage and Sabotage, NARA–Fort Worth, Texas. The tires themselves were quite valuable. In his July 3, 1945, report for Nuevo Laredo, Vice Consul Frederick D. Hunt informed that tires were one of the most coveted items on the black market, selling for about five hundred pesos each. Frederick D. Hunt to the Honorable Secretary of State, Nuevo Laredo, Tamaulipas, July 3, 1945, *Confidential U.S. State Department Central Files: Mexico, 1945–1949, Internal Affairs*.

95. Ricardo Pérez to Douglas Stockdale, November 1, 1944, Export Control Misc., 1944, Case Files on the Investigations of Espionage and Sabotage, NARA–Fort Worth, Texas.

96. Ibid.

97. Joseph Tanous to Rubén Moreno, November 16, 1943, National Defense Acts,

Misc., November and December 1943, Case Files on the Investigations of Espionage and Sabotage, NARA–Fort Worth, Texas.

98. Gonzalo Pérez to A. Trout, November 24, 1943, National Defense Acts, Misc., November and December 1943, Case Files on the Investigations of Espionage and Sabotage, NARA–Fort Worth, Texas.

99. Ibid.

100. Ibid.

EPILOGUE

1. For more on the political economy of smuggling in regard to states' toleration of tariff evasion see Alan L. Karras, *Smuggling: Contraband and Corruption in World History* (New York: Rowman & Littlefield, 2010), 53.

2. Jack Kerouac, *On the Road* (New York: Penguin Books, 1976; first published 1957), 273.

3. Alicia Dewey, a colleague of mine in the history program at Southern Methodist University, examined businesses in the South Texas borderlands. I have her to thank for shedding light on illicit traders' parallel lives within the legal system. Thanks, Alicia! Dewey, *Pesos and Dollars*.

4. American Consul at Matamoros Cyril L. Thiel to The Honorable Secretary of State, July 16, 1946, *Confidential U.S. State Department Central Files: Mexico, 1945–1949, Internal Affairs.*

5. Applegate informed U.S. authorities that a particular demand existed in "heavy ammunition," meaning .30 caliber and higher, and for revolvers clearly not meant for sport. "Memorandum: Arms & Ammunition," December 26, 1947, *Confidential U.S. State Department Central Files: Mexico, 1945–1949, Internal Affairs.*

6. Beckelhymer's, Laredo, Texas, Inv. Re Pos Smuggling of Arms and Ammo, May 13, 1952, Case Files on Investigations of Neutrality Violations, Laredo, Texas, Records of the U.S. Customs Service, RG 36, NARA–Fort Worth, Texas.

7. Adolfo Martinez Villaliando and Alejandro Organista Romo, Szr. Ammunition, pistols, + 1948 Nasher, Case Files on Investigations of Neutrality Violations, NARA–Fort Worth, Texas.

8. Beckelhymer's, Laredo, Texas, Inv. Re Pos Smuggling of Arms and Ammo, May 13, 1952, Case Files on Investigations of Neutrality Violations, NARA–Fort Worth, Texas.

9. Probation Officer's Pre-Sentence Report, October 2, 1972, *United States of America v. Edward A. Beckelhymer Jr.* (1972), Criminal Case Files for Laredo, NARA–Fort Worth, Texas.

10. Fernández testified that on fourteen occasions Beckelhymer's employees had sent buyers to ask him to sign forms on their behalf. Ibid.

11. Sister Dorothy Salazar, "To Whom it May Concern," August 24, 1972, *United*

States of America v. Edward A. Beckelhymer Jr. (1972), Criminal Case Files for Laredo, NARA–Fort Worth, Texas.

12. J. C. Martin Jr., "Mayor of Laredo, to Honorable Owen D. Cox," August 17, 1972, *United States of America v. Edward A. Beckelhymer Jr.* (1972), Criminal Case Files for Laredo, NARA–Fort Worth, Texas; and Fernando Piñon, *Patron Democracy* (Mexico City: Contraste, 1985), 105.

13. *United States of America v. Edward A. Beckelhymer Jr.* (1972), Criminal Case Files for Laredo, NARA–Fort Worth, Texas.

14. "Exports and Smuggling Fuel Laredo Sales Boom," *New York Times*, January 4, 1982.

15. The term *chiveras* comes from the old practice of exchanging *chivos* (goats) for merchandise. For more information on *chiveras/pasadoras/fayuqueras* see Kathleen A. Staudt, *Free Trade? Informal Economies at the U.S.-Mexico Border* (Philadelphia, P.A.: Temple University Press, 1998), 77–79.

16. Anonymous interview by author, July 8, 2008.

17. Anonymous interview by author, July 8, 2008; see also "Discreets of Laredo" in Tom Miller, *On the Border: Portraits of America's Southwestern Frontier* (New York: Harper & Row, 1981), 48.

18. Anonymous interview by author, July 8, 2008.

19. "Riot Plan Suspected," *Laredo Morning Times*, November 30, 1992.

20. Legends of the use of dead babies to hide drugs may stem from a case late in August 1984 when Nelda Karen Colwell was sentenced to three years' probation for smuggling Mexican infants into the United States for adoption. Still, law enforcement stories may have some basis in fact. In speaking to the McAllen area group supervisor of Immigration and Customs Enforcement (ICE) about this, the officer responded, "Yes, I have seen that," it does not happen often, and the baby is not killed for that purpose but already dead, but it does happen. Although further research is necessary, it is sufficient to say that allegations of this most horrifying type of drug smuggling remain unverified and exist far beyond the bounds of the moral economy. "Woman Gets Probation in Baby Smuggling Case," *New York Times*, August 25, 1984; and Duane Cottrell (group supervisor, Department of Homeland Security, ICE), asked by author, April 8, 2011.

Although contraband-stuffed cadavers are more legend than fact, traffickers have used coffins as a ruse to smuggle items. During the 1910s U.S. federal authorities banned "international funerals" after discovering rifles within coffins being ushered into Mexico. The best-known example of smugglers using coffins to traffic contraband into the United States occurred in the early 1970s when Frank Lucas and others conspired to hide heroin in vessels containing the remains of U.S. soldiers killed in Vietnam. The event was depicted in the 2007 film *American Gangster*. "Eight Seized in Scheme to Bring Heroin into U.S.," *New York Times*, March 19, 1987; and Hall and Coerver, *Revolution on the Border*, 146.

21. Todd Leventhal, "The Child Organ Trafficking Rumor: A Modern Urban

Legend: A Report Submitted to the United Nations Special Rapporteur on the Sale of Children, Child Prostitution, and Child Pornography by the United States Information Agency" (Washington, D.C.: United States Information Agency, December 1994), 11.

22. "Investigan un tráfico ilegal de sangre en la frontera," *El Mundo de Tampico*, April 6, 1974, IPS, C 1091, AGN.

23. Given the very short time that organs remain viable after harvesting and the difficulty of finding matches, let alone of successfully performing the procedure, the feasibility of profiting from stealing organs is dubious. More likely is the complicit, though illegal, sale of blood or organs by people who cross into the United States, or the illegal sale of organs in Mexico to recipients who may "smuggle" the transplanted organ inside them when they leave the country. Patricia Giovine, "Vender la sangre," *Diario de Juárez*, August 21, 1995.

24. The Customs Service has actually been divided into two parallel agencies, Immigration and Customs Enforcement (ICE) and Customs and Border Protection (CBP). Customs duties provided the United States $25.3 billion in revenue in 2010. Although substantial, these figures are dwarfed by income tax receipts, which totaled $898.5 billion that same year. "Federal Receipts," 171, accessed May 25, 2013, http://www.whitehouse.gov/sites/default/files/omb/budget/fy2012/assets/receipts.pdf.

25. James C. McKinley Jr., "With Beheadings and Attacks, Drug Gangs Terrorize Mexico," *New York Times*, October 26, 2006.

26. Randal C. Archibold, "U.S. Adds Drones to Fight Smuggling," *New York Times*, December 7, 2009.

27. Vanessa Grigoriadis and Mary Cuddehe, "An American Drug Lord in Acapulco," *Rolling Stone*, September 2011.

28. Mariano Castillo, "Bodies Hanging from a Bridge in Mexico are a Warning to Social Media Users," *CNN World*, September 15, 2011, accessed May 25, 2013, http://www.cnn.com/2011/WORLD/americas/09/14/mexico.violence/index.html?htp=hp _t2; and Vanessa Grigoriadis and Mary Cuddehe, "An American Drug Lord."

29. The vast majority of the narcotics that illegally enter the United States are quietly trafficked under the noses of American authorities through designated ports of entry. Andreas, *Border Games*, 76.

30. Bruce M. Bagley and William O. Walker III, eds., *Drug Trafficking in the Americas* (Miami, F.L.: North-South Center Press, 1996), 395. Drug smugglers in general seek to avoid the U.S. government meddling in their affairs and would rather not target U.S. citizens. The alleged murder of David Hartley by Mexican "pirates" on the Falcon Reservoir in September 2010, for instance, drew national attention and cries for investigation if not outright intervention against Mexican drug cartels. "Falcon Lake 'Pirate' Murder: Is Beheading 'Message to the Americans'?," *Christian Science Monitor*, October 13, 2010, accessed May 25, 2013, http://www.csmonitor.com/USA/2010/1013 /Falcon-Lake-pirate-murder-Is-beheading-message-to-the-Americans.

APPENDIX

1. This transcription is based on that of Américo Paredes, who did extensive field-work gathering corridos throughout his lifetime. *A Texas-Mexican Cancionero*, 96–98.

2. Paredes, *A Texas-Mexican Cancionero*, 98–100.

3. I collected this corrido while doing fieldwork in South Texas during fall 2010. It differs from the version that Paredes includes in *A Texas-Mexican Cancionero* in that this version focuses more on Crescencio Oliveira and his death before marrying his beloved Chucha. I am very grateful to José C. Martínez for sharing this corrido with me. The victims' graves can be found in Benavides, Texas.

4. Author's translation.

5. Paredes, *A Texas-Mexican Cancionero*, 81.

6. Ibid.

7. This version of "Los Tequileros" is adapted from Paredes, *A Texas-Mexican Cancionero*, 100–102. Paredes recorded it sometime in the late 1940s or early 1950s, some twenty years after the legendary ambush that inspired it. Note that the ballad-eer holds the date as February 2 rather than December 18, 1922, the actual date of the event. Other versions of the corrido place the date as November 15. Discrepancies regarding the date in various versions of the corrido are attributable to the song being recorded decades after the historical event and the likelihood that December 18 does not rhyme easily in Spanish. Differing dates extend to Leandro Villarreal's headstone, which holds November 3, 1922, as the date of his death. Carlos Gracia, the grand-nephew of the Silvano Gracia mentioned in the corrido, informed that the corrido was composed by a man named Raúl Benavides from Monterrey, Nuevo León. A still-unlocated version of the corrido unknown to outsiders is said to contain a final verse where locals bury the three tequileros. Finally, research has unearthed that Gerónimo García is the full name of the third tequilero referenced in the corrido. Díaz, "When the River Ran Red," 61.

8. Paredes, *A Texas-Mexican Cancionero*, 101–102.

9. Gilb, *Hecho en Tejas*, 38–41.

10. Ibid.

11. Paredes, *A Texas-Mexican Cancionero*, 87.

12. Ibid., 87–88.

13. Hernández, *Corridos Sin Fronteras*, 64.

14. Ibid.

Bibliography

ARCHIVAL AND MANUSCRIPT COLLECTIONS

Archivo General de la Nación (AGN), Mexico City

Hacienda Pública
Investigaciones Políticas y Sociales (IPS)
Justicia

Archivo Histórico de la Secretaría de Relaciones Exteriores de México (SRE), Mexico City

Benson Latin American Collection (BLAC), University of Texas, Austin, Texas

Collection Relating to the General Claims Commission (Mexico and United States) 1917–1926

Biblioteca de la Secretaría de Hacienda y Crédito Público "Miguel Lerdo de Tejada" (MLT), Mexico City

Comercio Internacional Aduanas, Contrabando, 1930–1949

Center for American History (CAH), University of Texas at Austin

Perez, Jesse, "The Memoirs of Jesse Perez," unpublished manuscript
Roy Wilkinson Aldrich Papers, 1858–1955
Walter Prescott Webb Papers

Centro de Estudios de Historia de México CARSO, Mexico City

Laredo Public Library, Laredo, Texas

Article Series Clipping File, Luciano Guajardo Historical Collection

National Archives and Records Administration (NARA), Fort Worth, Texas

Case Files on Investigations of Neutrality Violations, Laredo, Texas, Records of the U.S. Customs Service, Record Group 36
Case Files on the Investigations of Espionage and Sabotage, Laredo, Texas, 1942–1944, LR 4, A–32–48–4, Records of the U.S. Customs Service, Record Group 36
Criminal Case Files for Laredo, Texas, 48S078B, A–20–51–2, Records of the U.S. District Courts for the Southern District of Texas, Record Group 21
Impost Books for Laredo, Texas, 1851–1914, Vol. 1, E 1700, A–32–48–4, Records of the U.S. Customs Service, Record Group 36
Request for the Release of Seized Goods for the Port of Laredo, 1875–1894, LR 2, A–32–48–4, Records of the U.S. Customs Service, Record Group 36

Texas A&M International University Special Collections and Archives, Laredo, Texas

Civil and Criminal Cases, Case Files, Webb County Archival Records

Texas State Archives, Austin, Texas

Adjutant General Records

Webb County Heritage Foundation, Laredo, Texas

Maurolia De Los Santos, "Aspects of Prohibition" and "The Tequileros of Los Colorados de Abajo"
Pedro G. Vasquez, "Prohibition's Impact on Laredo"

NEWSPAPERS

Corpus Christi Weekly Caller	*Laredo Times*
Dallas Morning News	*Laredo Weekly*
Diario de Juárez	*Laredo Weekly Times*
El Correo de Laredo	*New York Times*
El Mundo de Tampico	*San Antonio Express*
Laredo Daily Times	*Zapata County News*

WORKS CITED

Acuña, Rodolfo F. *Occupied America: A History of Chicanos*. 7th ed. New York: Longman, 2011.

———. *Occupied America: The Chicano's Struggle Toward Liberation*. San Francisco: Canfield Press, 1972.

Adams, John A., Jr. *Conflict and Commerce on the Rio Grande: Laredo, 1755–1955*. College Station: Texas A&M University Press, 2008.

Adelman, Jeremy, and Stephen Aron. "From Borderlands to Borders: Empires, Nation-States, and the Peoples in Between in North American History." *American Historical Review* 104, no. 3 (June 1999): 814–841.

Aguilar Camín, Héctor, and Lorenzo Meyer. *In the Shadow of the Mexican Revolution: Contemporary Mexican History, 1910–1989*. Translated by Luis Alberto Fierro. Austin: University of Texas Press, 1993.

Alonso, Ana María. *Thread of Blood: Colonialism, Revolution, and Gender on Mexico's Northern Frontier*. Tucson: University of Arizona Press, 1995.

Anders, Evan. *Boss Rule in South Texas: The Progressive Era*. Austin: University of Texas Press, 1982.

Andreas, Peter. *Border Games: Policing the U.S.-Mexico Divide*. 2nd ed. Ithaca, N.Y.: Cornell University Press, 2009.

———. *Smuggler Nation: How Illicit Trade Made America*. New York: Oxford University Press, 2013.

Ankerson, Dudley. *Agrarian Warlord: Saturnino Cedillo and the Mexican Revolution in San Luis Potosí*. DeKalb: Northern Illinois University Press, 1984.

Aramoni, A. *Psicoanálisis de la dinámica de un pueblo*. Mexico City: B. Costa-Amic, 1965.

Bagley, Bruce M., and William O. Walker III., eds. *Drug Trafficking in the Americas*. Miami, F.L.: North-South Center Press, 1996.

Bailey, David. *¡Viva Cristo Rey! The Cristero Rebellion and the Church-State Conflict in Mexico*. Austin: University of Texas Press, 1974.

Bailey, John and Roy Godson, eds. *Organized Crime and Democratic Governability: Mexico and the U.S.-Mexican Borderlands*. Pittsburgh, P.A.: University of Pittsburgh Press, 2000.

Bakewell, Peter J. *Silver Mining and Society in Colonial Mexico: Zacatecas, 1546–1700*. Cambridge: Cambridge University Press, 1971.

Barker, Eugene C. *Mexico and Texas, 1821–1835*. Dallas, T.X.: P. L. Turner, 1928.

Beatty, Edward. "The Impact of Foreign Trade on the Mexican Economy: Terms of Trade and the Rise of Industry, 1880–1923." *Journal of Latin American Studies* 32, no. 2 (May 2000): 399–433.

Behr, Edward. *Prohibition: Thirteen Years that Changed America*. New York: Arcade, 1996.

Bell, Samuel E., and James M. Smallwood. *The Zona Libre, 1858–1905: A Problem in American Diplomacy*. El Paso: Texas Western Press, 1982.

Berbusse, Edward J. "Neutrality-Diplomacy of the United States and Mexico, 1910–1911." *Americas* 12, no. 3 (January 1956): 265–283.

Bernecker, Walther L. *Contrabando: Ilegalidad y corrupción en el México del siglo XIX.* Mexico City: Universidad Iberoamericana Departamento de Historia, 1994.

Biennial Report of the Adjutant General of Texas from January 1, 1917, to December 31, 1918. Austin, T.X.: Von Boeckmann—Jones, 1919.

Booth, Martin. *Cannabis: A History.* New York: Thomas Dunne Books, 2004.

Bravo, Nick. "Spinning the Bottle: Ethnic Mexicans and Alcohol in Prohibition Era Greater Los Angeles." Ph.D. diss., University of California, Irvine, 2011.

Brown, Norman. *Hood, Bonnet, and Little Brown Jug: Texas Politics, 1921–1928.* College Station: Texas A&M University Press, 1984.

Brown, Vera Lee. "Contraband Trade: A Factor in the Decline of Spain's Empire in America." *Hispanic American Historical Review* 8, no. 2 (May 1928), 178–189.

Brownlee, W. Elliott. *Federal Taxation in America: A Short History.* 2nd ed. Cambridge: Cambridge University Press, 2004.

Buffington, Robert F. "Prohibition in the Borderlands: National Government-Border Community Relations." *Pacific Historical Review* 63, no. 1. (February 1994): 19–38.

Bulmer-Thomas, Victor. *The Economic History of Latin America Since Independence.* 2nd ed. Cambridge, M.A.: Cambridge University Press, 2003.

Bunker, Steven. "Consumers of Good Taste: Marketing Modernity in Northern Mexico, 1890–1910." *Mexican Studies/Estudios Mexicanos* 13, no. 2 (Summer 1997): 227–269.

Calderón, Roberto R. "Mexican Politics in the American Era, 1846–1900: Laredo, Texas." Ph.D. diss., University of California, Los Angeles, 1993.

Callcott, Wilfrid H. *Church and State in Mexico, 1822–1857.* Durham: North Carolina University Press, 1926.

Campbell, Howard. *Drug War Zone: Frontline Dispatches from the Streets of El Paso and Juárez.* Austin: University of Texas Press, 2009.

Campbell, Randolph B. *Gone to Texas: A History of the Lone Star State.* New York: Oxford University Press, 2003.

Campos, Isaac. *Home Grown: Marijuana and the Origins of Mexico's War on Drugs.* Chapel Hill: University of North Carolina Press, 2012.

Carey, Elaine, "Women With Golden Arms: Narco-Trafficking in North America, 1910–1970." *History Compass* 6, no. 3 (May 2008): 774–795.

Carey, Elaine, and Andrae Marak, eds. *Smugglers, Brothels, and Twine: Historical Perspectives on Contraband and Vice in North America's Borderlands.* Tucson: University of Arizona Press, 2011.

Carman, Michael D. *United States Customs and the Madero Revolution.* El Paso: Texas Western Press, 1976.

Chance, Joseph E. *José María de Jesús Carvajal: The Life and Times of a Mexican Revolutionary.* San Antonio, T.X.: Trinity University Press, 2006.

Coatsworth, John H., and Alan M. Taylor, eds. *Latin America and the World Economy Since 1800.* Cambridge, M.A.: Harvard University Press, 1998.

Cohen, Andrew Wender. "Smuggling, Globalization, and America's Outward State, 1870-1909." *Journal of American History* 97, no. 2 (September 2010): 371-398.

Confidential U.S. State Department Central Files: Mexico, 1940-1944, Internal Affairs. Frederick, M.D.: University Publications of America, 1987. Microfilm.

Confidential U.S. State Department Central Files: Mexico, 1945-1949, Internal Affairs. Part I: Political, Governmental, and National Defense Affairs. Frederick, M.D.: University Publications of America, 1987. Microfilm.

Cook, Scott. *Handmade Brick for Texas: A Mexican Border Industry, Its Workers, and Its Business.* Lanham, M.D.: Lexington Books, 2011.

Courtwright, David T. *Dark Paradise: A History of Opiate Addiction in America.* Cambridge, M.A.: Harvard University Press, 2001.

Craig, Richard B. "La Campaña Permanente: Mexico's Antidrug Campaign." *Journal of Interamerican Studies and World Affairs* 20, no. 2 (May 1978): 107-131.

Cronon, David E. *Josephus Daniels in Mexico.* Madison: University of Wisconsin Press, 1960.

Cuéllar, Carlos E. "The House of Armengol: Doing Business on the Rio Grande Border, 1881-1939." Master's thesis, Texas A&M International University, 1990.

Daddysman, James W. *The Matamoros Trade: Confederate Commerce, Diplomacy, and Intrigue.* Newark: University of Delaware Press, 1984.

DeCamara, Kathleen. "The History of the City of Laredo." Master's thesis, Texas State College for Women, 1944.

"D. Guerrero VDA de Falcón v. United States." *American Journal of International Law* 21, no. 3 (July 1927): 566-568.

de la Garza, Beatriz. *A Law for the Lion: A Tale of Crime and Injustice in the Borderlands.* Austin: University of Texas Press, 2003.

Delaney, Robert W. "Matamoros, Port for Texas during the Civil War." *Southwestern Historical Quarterly* 58, no. 4 (April 1955): 473-487.

DeLay, Brian. *War of a Thousand Deserts: Indian Raids and the U.S.-Mexican War.* New Haven, C.T.: Yale University Press, 2008.

De León, Arnoldo. *The Tejano Community, 1836-1900.* Albuquerque: University of New Mexico Press, 1982.

———. *They Called Them Greasers: Anglo Attitudes toward Mexicans in Texas, 1821-1900.* Austin: University of Texas Press, 1983.

———, ed. *War Along the Border: The Mexican Revolution and Tejano Communities.* College Station: Texas A&M University Press, 2012.

Despatches from U.S. Consuls in Camargo, Mexico, 1870-1880. Washington, D.C.: National Archives Microfilm Publications, 1964. Microfilm, M288.

Despatches from U.S. Consuls in Guerrero, Mexico, 1871-1888. Washington, D.C.: National Archives Microfilm Publications, 1964. Microfilm, M292.

Despatches from U.S. Consuls in Nuevo Laredo, Mexico, 1871-1906. Washington, D.C.: National Archives Microfilm Publications, 1959. Microfilm, M280.

Dewey, Alicia M. *Pesos and Dollars: Entrepreneurs in the Texas-Mexico Borderlands, 1880-1940.* College Station: Texas A&M University Press, 2014.

Díaz, George T. "Twilight of the Tequileros: Prohibition-Era Smuggling in the South Texas Borderlands." In *Smugglers, Brothels, and Twine: Historical Perspectives on Contraband and Vice in North America's Borderlands*, edited by Elaine Carey and Andrae Marak. Tucson: University of Arizona Press, 2011.

———. "When the River Ran Red: Tequileros, Texas Rangers and Violence on the Central South Texas Border During Prohibition, 1919–1933." Master's thesis, Texas A&M International University, 2004.

Dobie, J. Frank. *The Longhorns.* Boston: Little, Brown, 1941.

Domenech, Emmanuel. *Missionary Adventures in Texas and Mexico: A Personal Narrative of Six Years' Sojourn in those Regions.* London: Longman, Brown, Green, and Roberts, 1858.

"Drug Enforcement Administration, 1970–1975." Accessed July 30, 2012. http://www.justice.gov/dea/about/history/1970-1975.pdf.

Dunn, Timothy J. *The Militarization of the U.S.-Mexico Border, 1978–1992: Low-Intensity Conflict Doctrine Comes Home.* Austin, T.X.: CMAS Books, 1996.

Eckes, Alfred E., Jr. *Opening America's Market: U.S. Foreign Trade Policy Since 1776.* Chapel Hill: University of North Carolina Press, 1995.

Edberg, Mark Cameron. *El Narcotraficante: Narcocorridos and the Construction of a Cultural Persona on the U.S.-Mexico Border.* Austin: University of Texas Press, 2004.

Emory, William H. *Report on the United States and Mexican Boundary Survey, Made under the Direction of the Secretary of the Interior.* 2 vols. Washington, D.C.: Cornelius Wendell, 1857.

Erlichman, Howard J. *Camino del Norte: How a Series of Watering Holes, Fords, and Dirt Trails Evolved into Interstate 35 in Texas.* College Station: Texas A&M University Press, 2006.

Essin, Emmett M., III. "Mules, Packs, and Packtrains." *Southwestern Historical Quarterly* 74, no. 1 (July 1970): 52–80.

Ettinger, Patrick. *Imaginary Lines: Border Enforcement and the Origins of Undocumented Immigration, 1882–1930.* Austin: University of Texas Press, 2009.

———. "'We Sometimes Wonder What They Will Spring on Us Next': Immigrants and Border Enforcement in the American West, 1882–1930." *Western Historical Quarterly* 37, no. 2 (Summer 2006): 159–181.

Fernandez Bravo, Vicente. *México y su desarrollo económico: Panorama económico el ingreso nacional intervencionismo de estado.* Mexico City: Costa-Amic, 1963.

Ficker, Sandra Kuntz. "Institutional Change and Foreign Trade in Mexico, 1870–1911." In *The Mexican Economy, 1870–1930: Essays on the Economic History of Institutions, Revolution, and Growth,* edited by Jeffrey L. Bortz and Stephen Haber. Stanford, C.A.: Stanford University Press, 2002.

Folmer, Henri. "Contraband Trade between Louisiana and New Mexico in the Eighteenth Century." *New Mexico Historical Review* 16, no. 3 (July 1941): 249–274.

Garza, James A. "On the Edge of a Storm: Laredo and the Mexican Revolution, 1910–1917." Master's thesis, Texas A&M International University, 1996.

The Garza Revolution, 1891–1893: Records of the U.S. Army Continental Commands, Department of Texas. Bethesda, M.D.: LexisNexis, 2008. Microfilm.

Geertz, Clifford. *Local Knowledge: Further Essays in Interpretive Anthropology*. New York: Basic Books, 1983.

Gilb, Dagoberto, ed. *Hecho en Tejas: An Anthology of Texas Mexican Literature*. Albuquerque: University of New Mexico Press, 2006.

Gilliland, Maude T. *Horsebackers of the Brush Country: A Story of the Texas Rangers and Mexican Liquor Smugglers*. Alpine, T.X.: Library of Sul Ross University, 1968.

Gonzales, Trinidad. "The Mexican Revolution, *Revolución de Tejas*, and *Matanza de 1915*." In *War Along the Border: The Mexican Revolution and Tejano Communities*, edited by Arnoldo De León, 107–133. College Station: Texas A&M University Press, 2012.

Goodwin, Michele. *Black Markets: The Supply and Demand of Body Parts*. New York: Cambridge University Press, 2006.

Gordon, Linda. *The Great Arizona Orphan Abduction*. Cambridge, M.A.: Harvard University Press, 1999.

Gould, Lewis L. *Progressives and Prohibitionists: Texas Democrats in the Wilson Era*. Austin: Texas State Historical Association, 1992.

Graf, LeRoy P. "The Economic History of the Lower Rio Grande Valley, 1820–1875." Ph.D. diss., Harvard University, 1942.

Graham, Don. *Kings of Texas: The 150-Year Saga of an American Ranching Empire*. Hoboken, N.J.: John Wiley, 2003.

Green, Stanley C. *A Changing of Flags: Mirabeau B. Lamar at Laredo 1846–1848*. Vol. 5 of *The Story of Laredo*. Laredo, T.X.: Border Studies, 1992.

———. *A History of the Washington Birthday Celebration*. Laredo, T.X.: Border Studies, 1999.

———. *Laredo, Antonio Zapata, and the Republic of the Rio Grande*. Vol. 8 of *The Story of Laredo*. Laredo, T.X.: Border Studies, 1992.

———. *The Story of Laredo*. 14 vols. Laredo, T.X.: Border Studies, 1991, 1992.

———. *Tilden's Voyage to Laredo in 1846*. Vol. 14 of *The Story of Laredo*. Laredo, T.X.: Border Studies, 1991.

Grigoriadis, Vanessa, and Mary Cuddehe. "An American Drug Lord in Acapulco." *Rolling Stone*, September 2011: 52–59, 74.

Guerra, Santiago. "From Vaqueros to Mafiosos: A Community History of Drug Trafficking in Rural South Texas." Ph.D. diss., University of Texas at Austin, 2011.

Haber, Stephen H. *Industry and Underdevelopment: The Industrialization of Mexico, 1890–1940*. Stanford, C.A.: Stanford University Press, 1989.

Haley, J. Evetts. *Jeff Milton: A Good Man with a Gun*. Norman: University of Oklahoma Press, 1948.

Hall, Linda B., and Don M. Coerver. *Revolution on the Border: The United States and Mexico, 1910–1920*. Albuquerque: University of New Mexico Press, 1988.

Hansen, Roger D. *The Politics of Mexican Development*. Baltimore, M.D.: Johns Hopkins University Press, 1971.

Harris, Charles H., III, and Louis R. Sadler. "The 1911 Reyes Conspiracy: The Texas Side." *Southwestern Historical Quarterly* 83, no. 4 (April 1980): 325–348.

———. *The Secret War in El Paso: Mexican Revolutionary Intrigue, 1906–1920*. Albuquerque: University of New Mexico Press, 2009.

———. *The Texas Rangers and the Mexican Revolution: The Bloodiest Decade, 1910–1920*. Albuquerque: University of New Mexico Press, 2004.

Hart, John M. *Empire and Revolution: The Americans in Mexico since the Civil War*. Los Angeles: University of California Press, 2002.

Hellman, Judith A. *Mexican Lives*. New York: New Press, 1994.

Hernández, Guillermo E., ed. *Corridos Sin Fronteras/Ballads Without Borders: Cancionero/Songbook*. Washington, D.C.: Smithsonian Institution, 2002.

Hernandez, Jorge A. "Merchants and Mercenaries: Anglo-Americans in Mexico's Northeast." *New Mexico Historical Review* 75, no. 1 (January 2000): 42–75.

———. "Trading Across the Border: National Customs Guards in Nuevo León." *Southwestern Historical Quarterly* 100, no. 4 (April 1997): 433–450.

Hernández, Kelly Lytle. *Migra! A History of the U.S. Border Patrol*. Los Angeles: University of California Press, 2010.

Hernández Sáenz, Luz María. "Smuggling for the Revolution: Illegal Traffic of Arms on the Arizona-Sonora Border, 1912–1914." *Arizona and the West* 28, no. 4 (Winter 1986): 357–377.

Herrera Pérez, Octavio. *La Zona Libre: Excepción fiscal y conformación histórica de la frontera norte de México*. Mexico City: Dirección General Del Acervo Histórico Diplomático, 2004.

Hickam, Homer H. "The Contrabandistas." *Air & Space Smithsonian* 11, no. 2 (June/July 1996): 62–67.

Hinojosa, Gilberto M. *A Borderlands Town in Transition: Laredo, 1755–1870*. College Station: Texas A&M University Press, 1983.

A History of Enforcement in the United States Customs Service, 1789–1875. Washington, D.C.: Department of the Treasury, 1986.

Hobsbawm, E. J. *Bandits*. London: Weidenfeld & Nicolson, 1969.

———. *Primitive Rebels: Studies in Archaic Forms of Social Movement in the 19th and 20th Centuries*. New York: W. W. Norton, 1959.

Hodson, C. E. "Saltillo." *Catholic World* 46 (January 1888): 438–450.

Investigative Case Files of the Bureau of Investigation, 1908–1922. Investigative Records Relating to Mexican Neutrality Violations ("Mexican Files"), 1909–1921. Washington, D.C.: National Archives Microfilm Publications, 1983. Records of the Federal Bureau of Investigation, Record Group 65.

Irigoyen, Ulises. *El Problema económico de las fronteras mexicanas*. 2 vols. Mexico City: n.p., 1935.

Isaac, Rhys. *The Transformation of Virginia, 1740–1790*. Chapel Hill: University of North Carolina Press, 1982.

Izquierdo, Rafael. "Protectionism in Mexico." In *Public Policy and Private Enterprise in*

Mexico, edited by Raymond Vernon. Cambridge, M.A.: Harvard University Press, 1964.

Jacoby, Karl. *Crimes Against Nature: Squatters, Poachers, Thieves, and the Hidden History of American Conservation*. Los Angeles: University of California Press, 2001.

Johnson, Benjamin H. *Bordertown: The Odyssey of an American Place*. New Haven, C.T.: Yale University Press, 2008.

———. *Revolution in Texas: How a Forgotten Rebellion and Its Bloody Suppression Turned Mexicans into Americans*. New Haven, C.T.: Yale University Press, 2003.

Kang, Deborah. "The Legal Construction of the Borderlands." Unpublished manuscript, 2006.

———. "Peripheries and Center: Immigration Law and Policy on the U.S.-Mexico Border, 1917–1924." In *Bridging National Borders in North America: Transnational and Comparative Histories*, edited by Andrew Graybill and Benjamin Johnson. Durham, N.C.: Duke University Press, 2010.

Karras, Alan L. *Smuggling: Contraband and Corruption in World History*. New York: Rowman & Littlefield, 2010.

Katz, Friedrich. *The Secret War in Mexico: Europe, the United States, and the Mexican Revolution*. Chicago: University of Chicago Press, 1981.

Kearney, Milo, and Anthony Knopp. *Boom and Bust: The Historical Cycles of Matamoros and Brownsville*. Austin, T.X.: Eakin Press, 1991.

———. *Border Cuates: A History of the U.S.-Mexican Twin Cities*. Austin, T.X.: Eakin Press, 1995.

Kennedy, David M. *Over Here: The First World War and American Society*. New York: Oxford University Press, 1980.

Kerig, Dorothy Pierson. *Luther T. Ellsworth: U.S. Consul on the Border During the Mexican Revolution*. El Paso: Texas Western Press, 1975.

Kerouac, Jack. *On the Road*. New York: Penguin, 1976. First published 1957.

Kinder, Clark, and William O. Walker III. "Stable Force in a Storm: Harry J. Anslinger and United States Narcotic Foreign Policy, 1930–1962." *Journal of American History* 72, no. 4 (March 1986): 908–927.

Klein, Alan M. *Baseball on the Border: A Tale of Two Laredos*. Princeton, N.J.: Princeton University Press, 1997.

Knight, Alan. *The Mexican Revolution*. 2 vols. Cambridge: Cambridge University Press, 1986.

Kopel, David B. "Mexico's Federal Law of Firearms and Explosives." University of Denver Sturm College of Law Legal Studies Research Paper No. 10-12, Denver, C.O., 2010. http://ssrn.com/abstract=1588296.

Kyvig, David E. *Prohibition: The 18th Amendment, the Volstead Act, the 21st Amendment*. Washington, D.C.: National Archives, 1986.

Lack, Paul D. "Slavery and the Texas Revolution." *Southwestern Historical Quarterly* 89, no. 2 (October 1985): 181–202.

Lamar, Mirabeau B. *The Papers of Mirabeau Buonaparte Lamar*. Edited by Charles A. Gulick Jr. and Winnie Allen. 6 vols. Austin, T.X.: Pemberton Press, 1968.

Letters Received by the Secretary of the Treasury from Collectors of Customs ("G," "H," *"I" Series), 1833–1869.* Washington, D.C.: National Archives Microfilm Publications, 1969. Microfilm, M174A.

Letters Sent by the Collector of Customs at Del Rio, Texas, to the Collector of Customs at Eagle Pass, 1909–1913. Washington, D.C.: National Archives Microfilm Publications, 2001. Microfilm, P2159.

Letters Sent by the Commissioner of Customs Relating to Smuggling, 1865–1869. Washington, D.C.: National Archives Microfilm Publications, 1963. Microfilm, M497.

Letters Sent by the Secretary of the Treasury to Collectors of Customs at All Ports, 1789–1847, and at Small Ports, 1847–1878. Washington, D.C.: National Archives Microfilm Publications, 1965. Microfilm, M175.

Levario, Miguel Antonio. *Militarizing the Border: When Mexicans Became the Enemy.* College Station: Texas A&M University Press, 2012.

Leventhal, Todd. "The Child Organ Trafficking Rumor: A Modern 'Urban Legend': A Report Submitted to The United Nations Special Rapporteur on the Sale of Children, Child Prostitution, and Child Pornography by the United States Information Agency." Washington, D.C.: United States Information Agency, 1994.

Limón, José E. "El Primer Congreso Mexicanista de 1911: A Precursor to Contemporary Chicanismo." *Aztlán* 5, nos. 1–2 (Spring/Fall 1974): 85–117.

Looney, Robert E. *Mexico's Economy: A Policy Analysis with Forecasts to 1990.* Boulder, C.O.: Westview Press, 1978.

Lorey, David E. *The U.S.-Mexican Border in the Twentieth Century: A History of Economic and Social Transformation.* Wilmington, D.E.: Scholarly Resources, 1999.

Lott, Virgil N., and Mercurio Martinez. *The Kingdom of Zapata.* San Antonio, T.X.: Naylor, 1953.

Machado, Manuel A. *The North Mexican Cattle Industry, 1910–1975: Ideology, Conflict, and Change.* College Station: Texas A&M University Press, 1981.

Magness, Phillip W. "From Tariffs to the Income Tax: Trade Protection and Revenue in the United States Tax System." Ph.D. diss., George Mason University, 2009.

Margolies, Daniel S. *Spaces of Law in American Foreign Relations: Extradition and Extraterritoriality in the Borderlands and Beyond, 1877–1898.* Athens: University of Georgia Press, 2011.

Márquez Colín, Graciela. "The Political Economy of Mexican Protectionism, 1886–1911." Ph.D. diss., Harvard University, 2002.

Martínez, Oscar J. *Border Boom Town: Ciudad Juárez since 1848.* Austin: University of Texas Press, 1978.

———. *Border People: Life and Society in the U.S.-Mexico Borderlands.* Tucson: University of Arizona Press, 1994.

———. *Troublesome Border.* Revised ed. Tucson: University of Arizona Press, 2006.

———, ed. *U.S.-Mexico Borderlands: Historical and Contemporary Perspectives.* Wilmington, D.E.: SR Books, 1996.

Martinez-Catsam, Ana Luisa. "'Los Precios Mas Baratos': The Role of Spanish-Language Newspaper Advertisements and the Biculturalization of Tejanos in San

Antonio and Laredo, Texas." *New Mexico Historical Review* 86, no. 1 (Winter 2011): 83–105.

Mayo, John. "Consuls and Silver Contraband on Mexico's West Coast in the Era of Santa Anna." *Journal of Latin American Studies* 19, no. 2 (November 1987): 389–411.

McClung, John B. "Texas Rangers Along the Rio Grande, 1910–1919." Ph.D. diss., Texas Christian University, 1981.

McCrossen, Alexis, ed. *Land of Necessity: Consumer Culture in the United States–Mexico Borderlands*. Durham, N.C.: Duke University Press, 2009.

McDonald, Roy. "Automobile Forfeitures and the Eighteenth Amendment." *Texas Law Review* 10 (February 1932): 140–162.

Mendoza, Alexander. "'For Our Own Best Interests': Nineteenth-Century Laredo Tejanos, Military Service, and the Development of American Nationalism." *Southwestern Historical Quarterly* 115, no. 2 (October 2011): 125–152.

Merz, Charles. *The Dry Decade*. 2nd ed. Seattle: University of Washington Press, 1970.

Meyer, Michael C., William Sherman, and Susan Deeds. *The Course of Mexican History*. 6th ed. New York: Oxford University Press, 1999.

Miller, Robert R. "Arms Across the Border: United States Aid to Juárez during the French Intervention in Mexico." *Transactions of the American Philosophical Society* 63, no. 6 (December 1973): 1–68.

Miller, Tom. *On the Border: Portraits of America's Southwestern Frontier*. New York: Harper & Row, 1981.

Molina, Juan. "Gold Stars and Ration Cards: A Social, Economic, and Diplomatic Study of Laredo, Texas, During World War II." Master's thesis, Texas A&M International University, 1996.

Montejano, David. *Anglos and Mexicans in the Making of Texas, 1836–1986*. Austin: University of Texas Press, 1987.

Moorhead, Max L. *New Mexico's Royal Road: Trade and Travel on the Chihuahua Trail*. Norman: University of Oklahoma Press, 1958.

Mora-Torres, Juan. *The Making of the Mexican Border: The State, Capitalism, and Society in Nuevo León, 1848–1910*. Austin: University of Texas Press, 2001.

Moreno-Bird, Juan Carlos, and Jaime Ros. *Development and Growth in the Mexican Economy: A Historical Perspective*. New York: Oxford University Press, 2009.

Mottier, Nicole. "Drug Gangs and Politics in Ciudad Juárez, 1928–1936." *Mexican Studies/Estudios Mexicanos* 25, no. 1 (Winter 2009): 19–46.

Musto, David F. *The American Disease: Origins of Narcotic Control*. 3rd ed. New York: Oxford University Press, 1999.

Myers, John Myers. *The Border Wardens*. Englewood Cliffs, N.J.: Prentice-Hall, 1971.

Nadelmann, Ethan A. *Cops Across Borders: The Internationalization of U.S. Criminal Law Enforcement*. University Park: Pennsylvania State University Press, 1993.

Naím, Moisés. *Illicit: How Smugglers, Traffickers, and Copycats are Hijacking the Global Economy*. New York: Anchor Books, 2005.

Nance, Joseph M. *Attack and Counterattack: The Texas-Mexican Frontier, 1842*. Austin: University of Texas Press, 1964.

Newcomb, W. W., Jr. *The Indians of Texas from Prehistoric to Modern Times*. Austin: University of Texas Press, 1961.

Niblo, Stephen R. *War, Diplomacy, and Development: The United States and Mexico, 1938–1954*. Wilmington, D.E.: SR Books, 1995.

Niemi, Albert W., Jr. *U.S. Economic History: A Survey of the Major Issues*. Chicago: Rand McNally, 1975.

Nugent, Paul. *Smugglers, Secessionists & Loyal Citizens on the Ghana-Togo Frontier*. Athens: Ohio University Press, 2002.

Ogden, Adele. *The California Sea Otter Trade, 1784–1848*. Berkeley: University of California Press, 1941.

Okrent, Daniel. *Last Call: The Rise and Fall of Prohibition*. New York: Scribner, 2010.

Paredes, Américo. *Folklore and Culture on the Texas-Mexican Border*. Edited by Richard Bauman. Austin, T.X.: CMAS Books, 1993.

———. *A Texas-Mexican Cancionero: Folksongs of the Lower Border*. Austin: University of Texas Press, 1995.

———. *With His Pistol in His Hand: A Border Ballad and Its Hero*. Austin: University of Texas Press, 1958.

Peavey, John R. *Echoes from the Rio Grande*. Brownsville, T.X.: Springman-King, 1963.

Perkins, Clifford Alan. *Border Patrol: With the U.S. Immigration Service on the Mexican Boundary, 1910–1954*. El Paso: Texas Western Press, 1978.

Piñon, Fernando. *Patron Democracy*. Mexico City: Contraste, 1985.

Pletcher, David. "Consul Warner P. Sutton and American-Mexican Border Trade during the Early Díaz Period." *Southwestern Historical Quarterly* 79, no. 4 (April 1976): 373–399.

Poppa, Terrence E. *Drug Lord: The Life and Death of a Mexican Kingpin*. Seattle, W.A.: Demand Publications, 1998.

Prince, Carl E., and Mollie Keller. *The U.S. Customs Service: A Bicentennial History*. Washington, D.C.: Department of the Treasury, U.S Customs Service, 1989.

Raat, W. Dirk. *Revoltosos: Mexico's Rebels in the United States, 1903–1923*. College Station: Texas A&M University Press, 1981.

Ramírez, José A. *To the Line of Fire! Mexican Texans and World War I*. College Station: Texas A&M University Press, 2009.

Ramos Aguirre, Francisco. *Historia del corrido en la frontera tamaulipeca, 1844–1994*. Victoria, Mexico: Prograf, 1994.

Recio, Gabriela. "Drugs and Alcohol: US Prohibition and the Origins of the Drug Trade in Mexico, 1910–1930." *Journal of Latin American Studies* 34, no. 1 (February 2002): 21–42.

Records of the Department of State Relating to Internal Affairs of Mexico, 1910–1929. Washington, D.C.: National Archives Microfilm Publications, 1961. Microfilm, M274.

Records of the Department of State Relating to Internal Affairs of Mexico, 1930–1939. Washington, D.C.: National Archives Microfilm Publications, n.d. Microfilm, M1370.

Records of the Department of State Relating to Political Relations Between the United States and Mexico, 1910–1929. Washington, D.C.: National Archives Microfilm Publications, 1961. Microfilm, M314.

Reglamento para el contra-resguardo de Nuevo León y Tamaulipas. Mexico City: Imprenta de las Escalerillas N. 7, 1850.

Reséndez, Andrés. *Changing National Identities at the Frontier: Texas and New Mexico, 1800–1850*. Cambridge: Cambridge University Press, 2005.

Reynolds, Clark W. *The Mexican Economy: Twentieth-Century Structure and Growth*. New Haven, C.T.: Yale University Press, 1970.

Rippy, J. Fred. "Border Troubles along the Rio Grande, 1848–1860." *Southwestern Historical Quarterly* 23 (July 1919–April 1920): 91–111.

———. *The United States and Mexico*. New York: Alfred A. Knopf, 1926.

Roark, Garland. *The Coin of Contraband: The True Story of United States Customs Investigator Al Scharff*. Garden City, N.Y.: Doubleday, 1964.

Robinson, Robert. "Vice and Tourism on the U.S.-Mexico Border: A Comparison of Three Communities in the Era of U.S. Prohibition." Ph.D. diss., Arizona State University, 2002.

Romero, Matías. "The Free Zone in Mexico." *North American Review* 154, no. 425 (April 1892): 459–471.

———. *Mexico and the United States: A Study of Subjects Affecting Their Political, Commercial, and Social Relations, Made with a View to Their Promotion*. 2 vols. New York: Putman, 1898.

Romero, Matías, and John Bigelow. *Railways in Mexico*. Washington, D.C.: W. H. Moore, 1882.

Romero, Robert Chao. *The Chinese in Mexico, 1882–1940*. Tucson: University of Arizona Press, 2010.

Romo, David Dorado. *Ringside Seat to a Revolution: An Underground Cultural History of El Paso and Juárez, 1893–1923*. El Paso, T.X.: Cinco Puntos Press, 2005.

Rosales, Arturo F. *¡Pobre Raza! Violence, Justice, and Mobilization among México Lindo Immigrants, 1900–1936*. Austin: University of Texas Press, 1999.

Rosenbaum, Robert J. *Mexicano Resistance in the Southwest: "The Sacred Right of Self-Preservation."* Austin: University of Texas Press, 1981.

Salvucci, Richard J. "The Origins and Progress of U.S.-Mexican Trade, 1825–1884: 'Hoc opus, hic labor est.'" *Hispanic American Historical Review* 71, no. 4 (November 1991): 697–735.

Sandos, James A. "Northern Separatism during the Mexican Revolution: An Inquiry into the Role of Drug Trafficking, 1919–1920." *Americas* 41, no. 2 (October 1984): 191–214.

———. "Prostitution and Drugs: The United States Army on the Mexican-American Border, 1916–1917." *Pacific Historical Review* 49, no. 4 (November 1980): 621–645.

———. *Rebellion in the Borderlands: Anarchism and the Plan of San Diego, 1904–1923*. Norman: University of Oklahoma Press, 1992.

Santleben, August. *A Texas Pioneer: Early Staging and Overland Freighting Days on the Frontiers of Texas and Mexico*. New York: Neale, 1910.

Saragoza, Alex M. *The Monterrey Elite and the Mexican State, 1880–1940*. Austin: University of Texas Press, 1988.

Schayegh, Cyrus. "The Many Worlds of Abud Yasin; or, What Narcotics Trafficking in the Interwar Middle East Can Tell Us about Territorialization." *American Historical Review* 116, no. 2 (April 2011): 273–306.

Schmeckebier, Laurence F. *The Bureau of Prohibition: Its History, Activities and Organization*. Baltimore, M.D.: Brookings Institution, 1929.

———. *The Customs Service: Its History, Activities and Organization*. Washington, D.C.: Johns Hopkins Press, 1924.

Schoonover, Thomas D., ed. *Mexican Lobby: Matías Romero in Washington, 1861–1867*. Lexington: University Press of Kentucky, 1986.

Schreiner, Charles, III. *A Pictorial History of the Texas Rangers: "That Special Breed of Men."* Mountain Home, T.X.: Y-O Press, 1969.

Scott, James C. *Seeing Like a State: How Certain Schemes to Improve the Human Condition Have Failed*. New Haven, C.T.: Yale University Press, 1998.

Settel, Arthur. *A Pictorial History of the United States Customs Service*. New York: Crown Publishers, 1975.

Shearer, Ernest C. "The Carvajal Disturbances." *Southwestern Historical Quarterly* 55, no. 2 (October 1951): 201–230.

Sierra, Carlos J., and Rogelio Martínez Vera. *El resguardo aduanal y la gendarmería fiscal, 1850–1925*. Mexico City: Secretaría de Hacienda y Crédito Público, 1971.

Smith, Ralph A. "Contrabando en la guerra con Estados Unidos." *Historia Mexicana* 11, no. 3 (January–March 1962): 361–381.

Smith, R. Elberton. *Customs Valuation in the United States: A Study in Tariff Administration*. Chicago: University of Chicago Press, 1948.

Smith, Thomas T. *The U.S. Army and the Texas Frontier Economy, 1845–1900*. College Station: Texas A&M University Press, 1999.

Sonnichsen, C. L., and M. G. McKinney. "El Paso—from War to Depression." *Southwestern Historical Quarterly* 74, no. 3 (January 1971): 357–371, 373–384.

Spener, David. *Clandestine Crossings: Migrants and Coyotes on the Texas-Mexico Border*. Ithaca, N.Y.: Cornell University Press, 2009.

Staudt, Kathleen A. *Free Trade? Informal Economies at the U.S.-Mexico Border*. Philadelphia, P.A.: Temple University Press, 1998.

Steakley, Dan L. "The Border Patrol of the San Antonio Collection District." Master's thesis, University of Texas, 1936.

Sterling, William Warren. *Trails and Trials of a Texas Ranger*. Norman: University of Oklahoma Press, 1979.

St. John, Rachel. *Line in the Sand: A History of the Western U.S.-Mexico Border*. Princeton, N.J.: Princeton University Press, 2011.

Tagliacozzo, Eric. *Secret Trades, Porous Borders: Smuggling and States Along a Southeast Asian Frontier, 1865–1915*. New Haven, C.T.: Yale University Press, 2005.

Taussig, F. W. *The Tariff History of the United States.* 7th ed. New York: G. P. Putnam's Sons, 1923.

Taylor, Arnold H. *American Diplomacy and the Narcotics Traffic, 1900–1939.* Durham, N.C.: Duke University Press, 1969.

Tenenbaum, Barbara A. *The Politics of Penury: Debts and Taxes in Mexico, 1821–1856.* Albuquerque: University of New Mexico Press, 1986.

"Teodoro García and M. A. Garza v. United States." *American Journal of International Law* 21, no. 3 (July 1927): 581–586.

Thompson, E. P. "The Moral Economy of the English Crowd in the Eighteenth Century." In *Customs in Common: Studies in Traditional Popular Culture.* New York: New Press, 1993.

Thompson, Jerry. *Cortina: Defending the Mexican Name in Texas.* College Station: Texas A&M University Press, 2007.

———. *Laredo: A Pictorial History.* Norfolk, V.A.: Donning, 1986.

———. *Vaqueros in Blue and Gray.* Austin, T.X.: State House Press, 2000.

———. *Warm Weather and Bad Whiskey: The 1886 Laredo Election Riot.* El Paso: Texas Western Press, 1991.

———. *A Wild and Vivid Land.* Austin: Texas State Historical Association, 1997.

Tijerina, Andrés. *Tejano Empire: Life on the South Texas Ranchos.* College Station: Texas A&M University Press, 1998.

Truett, Samuel. *Fugitive Landscapes: The Forgotten History of the U.S.-Mexico Borderlands.* New Haven, C.T.: Yale University Press, 2006.

Tyler, John W. *Smugglers and Patriots: Boston Merchants and the Advent of the American Revolution.* Boston, M.A.: Northeastern University Press, 1986.

Tyler, Ronnie C. "Cotton on the Border, 1861–1865." *Southwestern Historical Quarterly* 73, no. 4 (April 1970): 456–477.

———. *Santiago Vidaurri and the Southern Confederacy.* Austin: Texas State Historical Association, 1973.

U.S. Military Intelligence Reports: Mexico, 1919–1941. Frederick, M.D.: University Publications of America, 1984. Microfilm.

Valerio-Jiménez, Omar S. "Neglected Citizens and Willing Traders: The Villas del Norte (Tamaulipas) in Mexico's Northern Borderlands, 1749–1846." *Mexican Studies/Estudios Mexicanos* 18, no. 2 (Summer 2002): 251–296.

———. *River of Hope: Forging Identity and Nation in the Rio Grande Borderlands.* Durham, N.C.: Duke University Press, 2013.

Vanderwood, Paul J. *Disorder and Progress: Bandits, Police, and Mexican Development.* Lincoln: University of Nebraska Press, 1981.

van Schendel, Willem, and Itty Abraham, eds. *Illicit Flows and Criminal Things: States, Borders, and the Other Side of Globalization.* Bloomington: Indiana University Press, 2005.

Vera, Homero. "Los Tequileros." *El Mesteño* 3 (February 2000): 1–24.

Vernon, Raymond. *The Dilemma of Mexico's Development: The Roles of the Private and Public Sectors.* Cambridge, M.A.: Harvard University Press, 1963.

Wald, Elijah. *Narcocorrido: A Journey into the Music of Drugs, Guns, and Guerrillas.* New York: Rayo, 2001.

Walker, William O., III. "Control Across the Border: The United States, Mexico, and Narcotics Policy, 1936–1940." *Pacific Historical Review* 47, no. 1 (February 1978): 91–106.

———. *Drug Control in the Americas.* Revised ed. Albuquerque: University of New Mexico Press, 1989.

Ward, James Randolph. "The Texas Rangers, 1919–1935: A Study in Law Enforcement." Ph.D. diss., Texas Christian University, 1972.

Webb, Walter Prescott. *The Texas Rangers: A Century of Frontier Defense.* 2nd ed. Austin: University of Texas Press, 1965. First published 1935.

———. "Veteran Ranger Protects Border." *State Trooper* 6 (September 1924): 13–15.

Weber, David J. *The Mexican Frontier, 1821–1846: The American Southwest Under Mexico.* Albuquerque: University of New Mexico Press, 1982.

Weddle, Robert S. *San Juan Bautista: Gateway to Spanish Texas.* Austin: University of Texas Press, 1968.

Welter, Barbara. "The Cult of True Womanhood: 1820–1860." *American Quarterly* 18, no. 2, part 1 (summer 1966): 151–174.

White, James L. Personal letter to Manuel Guerra, May 19, 1994. Courtesy of Manuel Guerra.

Whitehead, Don. *Border Guard: The Story of the United States Customs Service.* New York: McGraw-Hill, 1963.

Wilcox, Seb. S. "Laredo During the Texas Republic." *Southwestern Historical Quarterly* 42, no. 2 (October 1938): 83–107.

Wilkinson, J. B. *Laredo and the Rio Grande Frontier.* Austin, T.X.: Jenkins, 1975.

Wood, Robert D. *Life in Laredo: A Documentary History of the Laredo Archives.* Denton: University of North Texas Press, 2004.

Worley, Alicia Consuelo. "The Life of John Anthony Valls." Master's thesis, Texas College of Arts and Industries, 1954.

Young, Elliott. *Catarino Garza's Revolution on the Texas-Mexico Border.* Durham, N.C.: Duke University Press, 2004.

———. "Deconstructing *La Raza:* Identifying the *Gente Decente* of Laredo, 1904–1911." *Southwestern Historical Quarterly* 98, no. 2 (October 1994): 226–259.

———. "Red Men, Princess Pocahontas, and George Washington: Harmonizing Race Relations in Laredo at the Turn of the Century." *Western Historical Quarterly* 29, no. 1 (Spring 1998): 48–85.

Zelden, Charles L. *Justice Lies in the District: The U.S. District Court, Southern District of Texas, 1902–1960.* College Station: Texas A&M University Press, 1993.

Index

Reséndez, Mariano, 38, 41, 45–48,
 50–52, 54, 57–58, 61, 84, 109
resistance, 27, 29, 45, 49, 97, 141
revenue, 8; changing sources of U.S.,
 65–66, 70–72, 82, 87, 133–134, 140;
 defrauding of, 40, 60; Mexican,
 23–28, 33, 35, 37, 45, 47, 115–118, 124;
 U.S., 20–23, 51, 130–131
Reyes, Bernardo, 72–73
Reyistas, 73
Reynosa, Tamaulipas, 29, 103, 115–116,
 122, 132, 136, 141
rifle(s), 21, 31, 41, 61, 71–75, 78, 87, 94,
 98, 101, 108, 118, 122, 126, 137. See also
 firearms
rinche(s), 73, 97, 100, 104, 106, 111
Rio Grande Valley, 42, 44, 78, 95
Río Rico, 124–125
Rodríguez, Jorge, 99
Rodríguez, Victoriana, 57. See also
 female smuggler(s)
Rojano, Antonio, 83–84
Roma, Texas, 22, 75
Romero, Matías, 31–32, 38–39, 45, 58,
 60–61
Ross, Lawrence "Sul," 58
Roubert, Joe, 107
rubber, 131
Ruiz, José Manuel, 138
rum, 95
rumrunner, 107
Rumsey, Robert S. Jr., 68–69, 71–73,
 83–84, 90, 94, 102–103, 105
ruses, 4, 34, 83
rustling, 22–23, 99. See also cattle

Salazar, Sister Dorothy, 138
Salinas Leal, Bonifacio, 124
Saltillo, 47, 58, 111, 126
Sánchez, Amador, 73–74, 80–81
Sánchez, Tomás, 14
San Luis Potosí, 67, 122
Santa Anna (Antonio López de), 19, 25

scarcity, 82–83, 131
Secretaría de Relaciones, 122
sedicioso(s), 78, 96–97, 100
seditionists, 65, 78, 115, 117, 119, 121,
 123, 125, 127, 129, 131, 133. See also
 sedicioso(s)
seditious, 120, 122, 125, 134
seizures: of alcohol, 68–69; of animals, 23; of arms, 73, 75; of arms for
 Juarezistas, 31; of drugs, 110–111, 113;
 of foodstuffs and consumer goods,
 35, 52; of luxury goods, 79; by Mexican Customs, 27; of military provisions, 21; of personal belongings, 13;
 of pistols, 137; and Prohibition violations, 98–99, 104, 107
shell(s), 75, 121, 125, 137. See also
 munitions
Sherman, Caleb, 21–22
shootout(s), 86, 94, 100, 104, 118
shoppers, 5, 71
shortages, 66, 82, 132
Sinaloa, Mexico, 92
Smith, Frank, 101–102
Smith, John, 86
Sonora, Mexico, 7, 92
sovereignty, 6, 18, 37, 65, 93
Spain, 31
Spaniards, 14
specie, 21, 27
Stagner, Inez, 91–92
Starr County, 95
Steiner, Max, 113
stereos, 139
Sterling, William Warren, 96, 100, 104
Stevens, Charles, 105–107. See also
 corrido(s), 106
Stille, Henry, 35
Stillman, Charles, 33
Stockdale, Douglas, 132–133
subterfuge, 40
surveillance, 57, 72, 112–113
Sutton, Warner P., 1–2

CPSIA information can be obtained
at www.ICGtesting.com
Printed in the USA
BVOW08s0336131216

470586BV00001B/5/P